Led into Mystery

*Faith seeking answers
in life and death*

John W. de Gruchy

scm press

© John W. de Gruchy 2013

Published in 2013 by SCM Press
Editorial office
3rd Floor
Invicta House
108–114 Golden Lane,
London EC1Y 0TG

SCM Press is an imprint of Hymns Ancient & Modern Ltd
(a registered charity)
13A Hellesdon Park Road
Norwich NR6 5DR, UK

www.scmpress.co.uk

All rights reserved. No part of this publication may be reproduced,
stored in a retrieval system, or transmitted,
in any form or by any means, electronic, mechanical,
photocopying or otherwise, without the prior permission of
the publisher, SCM Press.

The Authors have asserted their right under the Copyright,
Designs and Patents Act, 1988,
to be identified as the Authors of this Work

British Library Cataloguing in Publication data

A catalogue record for this book is available
from the British Library

978-0-334-05291-3

Typeset by Manila Typesetting Company
Printed and bound by
CPI Group (UK) Ltd, Croydon

IN MEMORY OF
Stephen Mark de Gruchy
16 November 1961–21 February 2010

Dedicated to all
who knew and loved Steve
who have supported us in our grief
who share our memories and our hopes

Contents

Acknowledgments

I am grateful to the members of my family and the many friends who have supported me during the writing of this book, especially those associated with the Volmoed Community in Hermanus of which Isobel and I have been members for the past decade. A number of friends and colleagues have also kindly read either sections or the whole of the manuscript, or discussed various issues along the way: Alex Boraine, Judy and Julian Cooke, George Ellis, William Everett, Timothy Gorringe, Lyn Holness, Wolfgang Huber, Bernard Lategan, Larry Rasmussen, Mark Solms, Robert Steiner, John Suggit, Wentzel van Huyssteen, Robert Vosloo, Graham Ward, and members of my 'Transforming Traditions' research group. I have benefitted greatly from their encouragement and comments. Isobel has, as always, been constant in her support, but even more in this instance; she has not only carefully read and commented on the text, but also contributed several of her poems. I am grateful to SCM Press in London for agreeing to publish, to Natalie Watson, the Academic Editor, who has ably piloted the project, and to my very helpful editor, Rebecca Goldsmith. I also thank the National Research Foundation of South Africa (NRF), the University of Cape Town, and the Stellenbosch Institute for Advanced Study (STIAS), for their ongoing support for my work.

John de Gruchy
Volmoed, Hermanus
Advent: Season of Hope
2012

Notes

1. Unless otherwise indicated, all biblical references and quotations are from the New Revised Standard Version of the Bible. JB refers to the Jerusalem Bible, AV to the Authorized or King James Version.
2. I have not used the prefix 'St' when referring to those commonly acknowledged as saints, thus 'Paul' refers to St Paul, etc.
3. References to God are, for stylistic purposes only, in the masculine, otherwise I have sought to be inclusive in my use of language.
4. Where I have not directly quoted a source but have been particularly dependent on one, I have provided a reference for readers who would like to follow up the discussion.

Prologue

The Day Steve Died

*The lack of mystery in our modern life means decay and
impoverishment for us. A human life is of worth to the extent that it
keeps its respect for mystery.*
Dietrich Bonhoeffer[1]
*The work of mourning is the cost of the work of remembering, but
the work of remembering is the benefit of the work of mourning.*
Paul Ricœur[2]
*Your favour had set me on a mountain fastness,
Then you hid your face and I was put to confusion.*
Psalm 29[3]
*Hope may be questionable but, if it is to remain hope, it can only
take the form of a question.*
Nicholas Lash[4]

Our eldest son, Steve, tragically died in a river accident on Sunday
21st February 2010. He was 48 years old and, at the time of his
death, a professor of theology at the University of Kwa-Zulu
Natal in Pietermaritzburg. I vividly recall that Sunday afternoon
when Marian his wife phoned to say that he was missing, feared
drowned, in the Mooi River at the foothills of the Drakensberg
while tubing with his son David. I was busy in my workshop putting the finishing touches to a Paschal candlestick for the chapel
at Volmoed, the community near Hermanus in the Western Cape,
where Isobel and I now live. Turned from pieces of a camphor

1 Dietrich Bonhoeffer, Sermon preached in London on Trinity Sunday
1934. Dietrich Bonhoeffer, *London: 1933–1935*, Dietrich Bonhoeffer Works,
vol. 13, Minneapolis: Fortress, 2007, p. 360.
2 Paul Ricœur, *Memory, History, Forgetting*, Chicago: University of
Chicago Press, 2004, p. 72.
3 Psalm 29, Grail translation of the Psalms. Psalm 30.7, NRSV.
4 Nicholas Lash, *A Matter of Hope: A Theologian's Reflections on the
Thought of Karl Marx*, Notre Dame, IN: University of Notre Dame Press,
1982, p. 270.

tree that had blown down on Volmoed during a storm, the candle-stick was in anticipation of the coming celebration of Easter, when Christians declare that 'Christ is risen', and listen to Paul's confident assertion that 'death has lost its sting'.

The next day Isobel and I flew to Durban, more than 1500 kilometres away and then travelled on to Pietermaritzburg to be with Marian and our grandchildren Thea, David and Kate. Early the next morning, together with Suellen Shay, a close friend of the family who had travelled with us, I was taken by another family friend, Dan Le Cordeur, on a further two-hour journey by car into the Natal Midlands to the remote area where the Mooi River winds its way through the grandeur of the surrounding hills and bushes. Tony Balcomb, a colleague of Steve's, who owned the property, met us, and soon we were descending to the place where Steve had last been seen by David. The sun was beating down on the austere beauty of the valley and the river, though subsiding, was still in full spate from the recent rains. I was taken to the spot, a rocky outcrop in the rapids, where it was feared Steve had been trapped under the fast-flowing water. The moment I arrived and sat beside the river I knew instinctively that Steve was lying in the water somewhere deep in front of me. I was inconsolable. I do not know how long I sat there and wept. Suellen and Tony, some distance away, wept with me but gave me the space and time I needed. I lost sense of the time, but it must have been more than an hour later that we returned up the hillside to the chalet from where Steve and David had set out that fateful Sunday. Along the way, I frequently stopped, crying out aloud in protest at his death.

Steve's body was recovered from the river the next day, when I returned to that tragic place, this time with Isobel, Jeanelle, Steve's sister, who had arrived from England the day before, Thea, his daughter, who was not with the family on the day he drowned, and James Anderson, Marian's cousin, who had led the search for Steve's body. It was now three days after the accident had occurred. But was that the end of Steve, I asked myself? I wanted so desperately to believe that in some way he was still present with us. But was I so traumatized by his sudden death that my sense of his presence and my inarticulate words addressed to him at the rapids were a delusion? Certainly, they were triggered off by the chemistry of my brain, programmed as it is to help us handle trauma. But was it all a delusion? Deep in the recesses of my mind, my confidence in the Easter acclamation came under attack. Such convictions, science and reason told me, are complex but illusory constructions of the brain to help us cope with tragedy.

Most Thursdays I lead the service of Holy Communion in the Volmoed chapel. The Paschal candlestick I was making the day Steve died now stands next to the altar with a small plaque in his memory, its large candle alight as a symbol of Easter hope. One of my tasks is to offer a short meditation on a biblical passage, usually related in some way to our life together in community or the wider society. These are then sent by email to a circle of friends who have requested them. They are also posted on the Volmoed website. When we returned to Volmoed from Steve's funeral in Pietermaritzburg and the memorial service, which followed shortly after in Cape Town, I was determined to give the meditation the following week as usual. I also decided to continue doing so each week, not just in fulfilment of my responsibility but also as a way of sharing something of the journey on which Isobel and I were now embarked. It was not easy, especially those first few weeks. After some months, several people suggested that I should start writing something more substantial. I was very reluctant to do so. The wounds were too raw.

Yet deep within me there was a need to find the words to express my faith and feelings, and a dogged unwillingness to surrender hope. I knew that the real enemy of faith is not doubt, but a faith unwilling to acknowledge doubt honestly. I had also learnt that hope is not wishful thinking or even optimism, but a question posed by faith in a world that gives us so much cause for despair and little for optimism.[5] As such, it requires people of faith to struggle with their doubts and give an account of the hope they affirm despite reasons to the contrary. What follows is my attempt to do that at this moment in my life that has become framed by tragedy, a time in which I am more than ever aware of the mystery of life and death.

---

5 Lash, *A Matter of Hope*, p. 270.

Karl Rahner, one of the great Catholic theologians of the twentieth century once remarked that theology is *reductio in mysterium* – literally being drawn back into mystery.[6] If that is the case, my being led into mystery began in a new way the day I sat beside the Mooi River right at the spot where Steve drowned and where his body still lay trapped. I cannot describe the desolation I felt or recall the inarticulate words I uttered, but I know that I was overwhelmed, as Rudolf Otto describes it, by the mysterious beyond my 'apprehension and comprehension'.[7] Yes, it is true, there are biological explanations for how I felt. Traumatic experiences trigger off chemicals in the brain that enable us to cope. But within the realm of faith, my brain chemistry was processing and interpreting my experience in a particular way. I had 'come upon something inherently "wholly other," whose kind and character are incommensurable with our own, and before which we therefore recoil in a wonder that strikes us chill and numb'.[8] That numbness has often recurred during the intervening months, but the sense of the mysterious has become less terrifying and incommensurable. The miracle of healing proceeds, but the scars remain and the questions keep nagging for answers.

Nagging questions

We received many letters of sympathy during the weeks and months that followed Steve's death. One was from the then Archbishop of Canterbury, Rowan Williams, who wrote: 'Stephen's death was an appalling blow to many friends and admirers, and a loss to a whole society. We at Lambeth join in giving thanks for his unfailing courage and intelligence, and send our love and deep sympathy to all who have gathered to commend him to the God of the

---

6 See *Karl Rahner: Theologian of the graced search for meaning*, in *The Making of Modern Theology* series, edited by Geffrey B. Kelly, Minneapolis: Fortress, 1992, p. 335.

7 Rudolf Otto, *The Idea of the Holy*, London: Oxford University Press, 1931, p. 28.

8 Otto, *The Idea of the Holy*, p. 28.

resurrection'.[9] Not being Anglicans, we especially appreciated this ecumenical expression of solidarity in our grief, as we did the many other gracious and caring words of sympathy and acknowledgment of what Steve had achieved in the course of his life. Among these was one from the South African Parliament which, on the day of his Memorial Service in Cape Town,[10] passed an unopposed motion honouring his contribution to the life of the country.[11] But why did this have to happen to him just as he was making such a contribution to the worldwide Church, academy and society?

Another letter we received was from an old friend, who had been a theological student with me at Rhodes University, Grahamstown, during the late 1950s. Our paths had not often crossed since then, so I was a little surprised to receive his lengthy hand-written and thoughtful letter. One passage in particular struck me forcefully.

Over the years you have spoken many words to people who have suffered the loss of a loved one, and even the loss of a child. You must have reminded them of the words of the gospel and its core conviction that Jesus has overcome death. Are you able to speak those words to yourself, today? Does not our ministry depend on this? Everything else is insignificant.

Such questions called for a response. They were an additional catalyst that got me started writing this book. But it was not a task I relished. Death, after all, is the bedrock of doubt, the great leveller as Northrop Frye reminds us, 'not because everybody dies, but because nobody understands what death means'.[12] At an empirical or rational level there are biological explanations but no easy answers, if there are answers at all, to the question of its meaning.

---

9   Tribute from the Archbishop of Canterbury read at Steve's Memorial Service at the Rondebosch United Church, Tuesday, 2 March 2010. Steve was an ordained minister of the United Congregational Church of Southern Africa.

10   Held at the Rondebosch United Church, Cape Town, on 28 February 2010.

11   This was proposed by Methodist Bishop Vumi Dandala, then a Member of Parliament, and read by him at Steve's Memorial Service in Cape Town.

12   Northrop Frye, *The Great Code: The Bible and Literature*, London: Routledge & Kegan Paul, 1982, p. 230.

But at the existential level at which faith, hope and love oper-
ate, the question is framed differently: 'What speaks to us across
our own death?' Frye asks. Is there a language that 'escapes from
argument and refutation'?[13]

Isobel mourned and remembered through writing poetry, which
is pre-eminently the language of mystery. The following poem,
reflecting her life-long journey with Julian of Norwich,[14] was written the week after Steve's death.

When the ordered tenor of our life
is shattered by the unimaginable;
when the phone-call that splinters
others' lives rings for us;
when a nightmare that horrifies
turns into reality;
how can we believe that
anything could be well again –
ever?
Anguish breaks over us in torrents,
like the torrents that overwhelmed you –
submerged you, extinguished your life:
but we surface again;
we go on living;
we face each day,
wounded and grieving.
We hold on to each other,
and take a halting step:
can we dare hope that
all shall be well,
and all shall be well,
and all manner of things shall be well again –
ever?[15]

---

13 Frye, *The Great Code*, pp. 230–1.
14 See Isobel de Gruchy, *Making all Things Well*, Norwich: Canterbury
Press, 2012.
15 Written for and read at the memorial service for Steve at Volmoed,
4 March, 2010.

Steve and I often discussed theological issues. This began in earnest in the classroom, when he was a student, and continued whether in person or by phone and email up until the week before he died. He once told me that one of the biggest problems he had in developing his own identity as a theologian was that we seldom disagreed on anything important, try as he might. But he often raised difficult and pertinent questions about things I had said or written. We sometimes found ourselves at the same conference listening to each other's papers. He would invariably challenge me on some point, as I would him, trying to outwit one another. But sometimes he would also acknowledge our agreement, a characteristic impish grin spreading across his face as he told those in the room: 'if you have known the son, you will also know the father'. Shortly before his death he asked me to peruse his CV before submitting it for some research grant. In doing so, I became aware of how much he had achieved already in the course of his life; I also recognized the extent to which his own thought had developed well beyond anything I could have taught him. Among my last words to him, on the phone the Thursday before he died, were: 'Steve, your CV is great! Well done!'

Steve has now posed his final question, that asked by my friend in his letter: how do I understand the mystery of life and death, the meaning of Christian hope, the 'God of the resurrection', the ultimate mystery of all things? As I write, I sense him looking over my shoulder, checking me out as it were, and prompting further questions. Where appropriate I will explicitly refer to Steve in my discussion, but even where not, he is my primary dialogue partner, as he often was over a cup of coffee or glass of wine. But my intention is to draw all readers into the conversation hoping that what I write will generate fresh thought and discussion. Along the way, I will refer to other interlocutors who have influenced the way I see things, even if I disagree with them. These include the many authors I refer to and from whose works I quote. Too many such references can interrupt the conversation. Yet, in an enquiry and exploration such as this, there is no easy way to avoid the danger without risking plagiarism.

When I first set out on this project, I was not sure where I was going or what conclusions I would reach. Steve, I knew, would also want me to take some risks, as he regularly did himself. So the answers we seek together will be found as the discussion proceeds, not by going round in circles but more in a spiral-like process, organically rather than in a linear manner, though there is a progression of thought that develops as the chapters unfold. I know Steve would push me for honest answers, however tentative, and no matter how ambiguous the issues and complex the subject. I know that he would not want me to trade on tragedy and come up with easy responses driven by emotion rather than critical thought. He knew as I do that answers, even when they become convictions, will always be tentative and open to further investigation. But the questions cannot be silenced, any more than the memories which evoke them can be ignored when they daily resurface to reinforce, yet strangely soften, sadness.

You have left us and gone on,
But gone on to where?
To heaven where you
join the saints gathered around God's throne
singing praises without end?
Have you walked from room to room
in the house of many mansions,
and found your forebears, old friends
and those you always wanted to meet?

Is it better than here –
even though here was good to you?
Is it tinged with sadness
by the absence and grieving
of those you left behind
or have you forgotten them in your rejoicing?

Where have you gone?
Gone to some place
where we will meet you again?

Or have you gone to some huge Waiting Room,
with a multitude of others,
milling around,
impatient with inactivity,
thinking that if this is heaven you want out?

Where have you gone?
Into nothingness?
A black hole?
Is this all there is in the afterwards –
Oblivion?
Is heaven just a big con?

Where have you gone?
Did Jesus meet you?
What are you doing?
Is it really heaven there?
One day, one day,
We will join you.
One day we will know:
Look out for us.[16]

Memory and mourning

Within weeks of Steve's death, Isobel began collecting stories
about his life. She wrote to friends who had known him request-
ing their help. She searched through boxes of photographs and
slides, and spent hours reading the few diaries she had kept with
a record of things Steve had said and done. Together we recounted
the memories that stretched back over almost 50 years. Some
brought tears to our eyes; others made us laugh, and they continue to come, as vivid as ever. Often they were prompted by
meeting people who had known Steve, by visiting places associated with his life, or reading what he had written, and above all

---

16 Isobel de Gruchy, 17 January 2011.

by being with other family members or celebrating anniversaries. In the early hours of the morning, during those first months after his death, I would often lie awake and recall episodes that we had shared together, the last being his visit to Volmoed with Marian and their children the month before he died. I recall the game of chess we played and which he won. The memory brings to mind that final chess scene in Ingmar Bergman's *The Seventh Seal*, in which we are brought face to face with our own finitude. Steve check-mated me with what now seems like terrible finality.

Even though I had difficulty in writing down my memories, remembering Steve was crucial in handling grief, especially at the beginning of the process. While we had to 'get on with life' – though nothing returns to earlier normalcy – we could only do so in a healing way by processing memories and telling stories. But the work of remembering is costly when coupled with mourning. Enigmatic as they are, Paul Ricœur's words placed at the beginning of this Prologue are apt. Mourning depends on the costly work of remembering, but in turn memory is quickened through mourning. Perhaps this is why those who mourn are blessed and find strength in the act of doing so.

As I struggled with grief in those early weeks, I remembered that an American friend, Nicholas Wolterstorff, professor of philosophy at Yale University in Boston, had written a book some years back entitled *Lament for a Son*. In it, he reflected on his own process of grieving following the death of his son Eric in a climbing accident in Austria in 1983. I had known Nick for many years. He once taught for a semester with me at the University of Cape Town not long after the death of Eric, visited us at Volmoed shortly after we moved here, and I had been with him and his wife Claire at the University of Virginia a few months prior to Steve's death. But I had been reluctant to read *Lament for a Son*, because I was not sure how I would cope with what he had to say—what if it happened to me? I was also reluctant because I did not want to pry into his pain. I wrote to Nick to tell him about Steve and my intention to read his *Lament*. He replied with a word of caution saying that I might not yet be ready for it; the grieving process is long and painful; it cannot be rushed. But ready or not, I had to read *Lament*. Sometimes I laid it aside for a few days, because it was too close to the bone. But it was an important resource in going forward and learning, as Nick put it in his Preface, to 'own my grief'.

Led into Mystery is not written as an aid to grieving. But it is an attempt to 'own my grief' by responding to the questions posed by Steve's death. Not everyone 'owns grief' in the same way; some do so more privately than others, as is the case even in our family and circle of friends. I respect that very much. Writing a book like this is a very public way to go about owning grief. As such, it carries with it the danger of abusing the process through lack of sensitivity to others who mourn differently and lack of prudence in exploring the issues to prevent sentimentality gaining the upper hand. But I cannot escape the risk of seeking answers to the questions posed. After all, is everything that I hold true and that has given purpose and direction to my life (and to Steve's) false, an illusion or what neuropsychologists call a confabulation, an explanation we construct which is a fantasy of the imagination?[17]

My response to such questions in what follows is, at one level, a conversation that I have had with myself for many years, but it has become more intense since Steve died, and it continues even as I commit my reflections to writing and therefore to wider scrutiny. I anticipate that there are readers who have trodden a similar path and may well have lost their faith in the process. I know that some friends wondered whether this was happening to me, and at times I have felt that they might be right. 'How are you doing?', they ask. My invariable response is 'OK'. It is often all I can manage, but I suspect that at times it sounds feeble and unconvincing. What follows is an attempt to offer a more considered response as I try to give reasons for my faith and hope as a Christian. In doing so, let me introduce another theme that is important for

17 See S. A. Graziano, *God, Soul, Mind, Brain: A Neuroscientist's Reflections on the Spirit World*, Teaticket, MA: Leapfrog Press, 2010, pp. 61–5; David J. Linden, *The Accidental Mind: How Brain Evolution Has Given Us Love, Memory, Dreams, and God*, Cambridge, MA: Belknap Press of Harvard University Press, 2007, p. 226; David Eagleman, *Incognito: The Secret Lives of the Brain*, New York, NY: Pantheon Books, 2011, pp. 101–50.

what follows in the book, namely my commitment to developing a contemporary form of Christian humanism about which I have previously written, and which led me to engage with others in a major interdisciplinary research project.

Being human

During 2009–10, I initiated the New Humanism Project based at the Stellenbosch Institute for Advanced Studies (STIAS). The project involved 39 fellow academics drawn from a range of disciplines and backgrounds, who shared a common concern for taking forward the humanist vision embodied in the Constitution of post-apartheid South Africa. Not all the participants were Christian or religious, some were Muslim, others atheist or agnostic; some were scientists, others lawyers, poets, philosophers and public activists, but all shared the same concern and were keen on the conversation. The project comprised two symposia, the first in July 2009; the second in February 2010. Steve died the weekend before the second symposium began. This meant that I could not attend. But his death had a decided impact on the symposium and will always be associated in my mind with the project, not just with respect to the coincidence of date, but also because the intellectual and existential dimensions of being human were brought together for me in a new way.

The New Humanism Project arose out of my interest in Christian humanism as an alternative to secularism and religious fundamentalism, an underlying theme of my book *Being Human: Confessions of a Christian Humanist*.[18] But while the initial conversation was around the theme of humanism, the focus soon became the question 'what does it mean to be human today?' Given the multi-disciplinary character of the project, and the range of perspectives brought to the conversation, it was not surprising that the complexity of the question and responses to it soon became evident. 'The acknowledgment of living in a complex world', one

---

18 John W. de Gruchy, *Being Human: Confessions of a Christian Humanist*, London: SCM, 2006.

participant commented, 'and the critical stance it implies does not simply confront us with a number of practical problems; it confronts us with questions about how our humanity is constituted'. It therefore requires a transformation of 'our understanding of what the central components of being human could be'.[19] This clearly has consequences for a Christian understanding of being human, as did the contributions of the scientists, secular humanists, and participants of other faith traditions now included in *The Humanist Imperative*, which documents the outcome of the project.

The contribution that challenged me most during the two symposia was that on the neurobiological evolutionary foundations of being human presented by Mark Solms, professor of Neuropsychology at the University of Cape Town. Solms concludes his essay in *The Humanist Imperative* with the comment:

> We do not know why we do what we do. Our actions are so far removed from the instincts that motivated them (and unconsciously guide them) that we no longer know what we are trying to achieve. If we could ask the remarkable human being who etched the first symbolic patterns into those pieces of ochre at Blombos cave,[20] some 75,000 years ago, why she did so and what the patterns mean, I am confident that she would not be able to answer the question. She would have to admit, in uniquely human fashion, that she has no idea why she does such things. (The whole 'meaning of life' is a mystery to her.) Or, perhaps more likely, and again in

19   Paul Cilliers, 'Imagining Better Futures: Complexity and Creativity', in *The Humanist Imperative in South Africa*, edited by John W. de Gruchy, Stellenbosch: SUN Press, 2011, pp. 39–40.

20   Findings at the Blombos Cave, an archaeological site along the southern Cape coast about 300 kilometres from where I live, have provided the earliest material evidence of the awakening of human symbolic sensibility, a major step in the development of language, and the birth of our ancestors' sense of self in relation to others and reality beyond. See Tattersall, 'Origin of the Human Sense of Self', in *In Search of Self: Interdisciplinary Perspectives on Personhood*, edited by J. Wentzel van Huyssteen and Erik P. Wiebe, Grand Rapids, MI: Eerdmans, 2011, pp. 44–7.

uniquely human fashion, she would deny the mystery and
make up a story about it. She would invent an explanation.
She would confabulate. And no doubt she would eventually
come to believe her own confabulations. The human capacity
for opaque motivation, self deception and hypocrisy is *truly*
unique.[21]

That Solms indicates a uniquely human capacity for self-reflection
in search of an explanation of the mysteries of life is critical to my
enquiry. He also highlights our unique capacity for self-deception
and hypocrisy. But this does not mean there is no truth, wisdom,
or genuine insight into the mystery of life and death in the vast
reservoir of human reflection over millennia, in the myths we construct and the beliefs we confess. In a personal note added to the
introduction to *The Humanist Imperative* I wrote:

> Despite all we know about the biological processes, birth
> remains a matter of wonder and hope just as death remains a
> tragic mystery. As a result of Steve's death my participation
> in the conversation of the symposium was reduced to reading
> the papers and the report some weeks after the event . . . But
> I did so with different ears and eyes, seeking to understand
> what it means to be human when faced with the extremities
> of life and death and the complex mélange and interplay of
> tragedy and sorrow, memory and hope.[22]

Of course, death understood as an inevitable part of the biological
cycle of life is not a 'tragic mystery'; the mystery lies, to return
to Frye's reminder previously mentioned, in the fact that nobody
understands what it means, if anything at all. But at the very least,
Steve's death has helped me to see things somewhat differently
from the way I did before and, equally, to respond to the challenges of complexity from a different perspective. Even so, I asked
myself when contemplating writing this book, how could I do so

---

21 Solms, 'Neurological Foundations', in *The Humanist Imperative*, p. 55.
22 de Gruchy, *The Humanist Imperative*, 'Introduction', pp. 16–17.

in a way that is both intellectually honest and existentially real? Was I prepared for the pain and perplexity that I knew I would experience in dealing with the issues? Could I possibly do so as both a grieving parent and an honest scholar, and contribute something of value to the ongoing discussion?

There is one further question that Steve would insist be part of my discussion. Questions about God and the meaning of life, and the way in which these are usually discussed in the West are neither the most urgent questions in an African context, nor are the ways in which Western scholars approach them always appropriate. Steve was well-trained in the scholarly debates that have attracted the attention and sapped the energy of the West since the European Enlightenment, but the focus of his own ministry, research and teaching was far more centred on questions relating to poverty, health, justice and the environment. He would want to press me on how my journey into mystery is relevant to what were his own passionate concerns.

With heart, soul and mind

Trying to weave together both personal biography and scholarly discussion has been the most challenging aspect of writing this book. I was vaguely aware that this might be the case when I began now more than two years ago. Already then, in mulling over how to proceed I gained insight from two disparate sources. One was Dietrich Bonhoeffer, the German theologian, pastor and martyr during the Third Reich, the other the celebrated eleventh-century Iranian mystic and intellectual al-Ghazālī.[23]

In the course of his life Ghazālī went through a major intellectual crisis during which the fundamental questions of life and death, Ebrahim Moosa tells us, brought him 'face to face with the limits

---

23 I am indebted to Ebrahim Moosa, a Muslim colleague and participant in the STIAS project, for introducing me afresh to the legacy of Ghazālī.

of the cognitive sciences'.[24] His writing 'was his therapy'.[25] Moosa identifies three stages in which Ghazālī's 'attitude toward memory and writing developed'.[26] The first was 'his obsessions with memory'; the next 'one of compulsive doxological writing' or 'a kind of memory-writing'; and finally 'heart writing', or what Moosa prefers to call 'dialogical writing' that went beyond where Ghazālī had been before. This is well expressed in Moosa's comment that Ghazālī began to 'think more creatively about the *act* of writing in relation to his being'.[27] Writing was not just borrowing or even stealing ideas from elsewhere, nor was it simply a retrieval of memories and images, but writing out of a different self, a self re-shaped by decisive experience. In Ghazālī's case this was mystical experience – in Moosa's words, 'he was *writing* his self', and in doing so he inevitably transgressed boundaries. The poetic imagination is not just working with image-laden memory, but an outworking of a soul in search of healing through writing from the heart. I am certainly not claiming that I have done this to the same degree and in the same depth, but Ghazālī's example has encouraged me to 'write my self' even as I enter into conversation with many others.

Readers of *Led into Mystery* must not expect, however, that what follows is about 'mystical experience' such as Ghazālī recounts. Being led into mystery certainly relates to Christian mysticism, apophatic theology, and contemplative spirituality, but mysticism is a subject open to a wide variety of interpretations.[28] So I have avoided the term. In any case, I would not (nor would anyone else) regard myself as a mystic, at least in the more popular sense of the word. But this does not mean that religious experience is unimportant, or that I lack appreciation for the mysticism of Romantic poets like William Wordsworth, or that of contemplatives like Evelyn Underhill or Thomas Merton. Nor does it

---

24 Ebrahim Moosa, *Ghazali and the Poetics of Imagination*, Chapel Hill, NC: University of North Carolina Press, 2005, p. 72.

25 Moosa, *Ghazali*, p. 110.

26 Moosa, *Ghazali*, p. 94.

27 Moosa, *Ghazali*, p. 104.

28 See the essays in *Mysticism and Philosophical Analysis*, edited by Steven T. Katz, London: Sheldon Press, 1978.

mean that I will not try to emulate Ghazālī' in writing with heart and soul, as well as mind. After all, that which gives theology its coherence and distinct character is precisely its exploration of the ultimate mystery we call God within our lived experience, and it is this which requires intellectual endeavour and engagement in the struggle for justice. Some would say that ultimately theology is about prayer, about contemplation as well as action and intellectual enquiry. Without commitment to this task, theology is a parody of its true nature.

Shortly before Steve's death, I completed the task of editing the new English edition of Bonhoeffer's *Letters and Papers from Prison*.[29] As I did so, reading yet again Bonhoeffer's last letter to his parents and their last letters to him that he never received, I was moved to tears. Fortunately, I finished the work before Steve died. I am not sure that I could have done so afterwards. Now, reflecting back, I am more than ever convinced that one of the reasons why Bonhoeffer's *Letters and Papers* has become a Christian theological *and* spiritual classic is because his searching theological explorations are embedded in his personal reflections and struggles in prison. Those familiar with Bonhoeffer's writings will know that mystery was a key element in his theology.[30]

Bonhoeffer's father, Karl, was a distinguished Professor of Psychiatry in Berlin and one of the foremost neurologists of his day; he was also an agnostic who was somewhat perplexed by his youngest son's interest in theology, though always impressed by his abilities, eventually supportive of his vocation and full of admiration for his opposition to Hitler. Also of note is the fact that Dietrich's eldest brother, Karl Friedrich, also an agnostic, became a distinguished scientist and physicist. This all too brief comment on the kind of intellectual family environment in which Dietrich was nurtured

---

29   Dietrich Bonhoeffer, *Letters and Papers from Prison*, Dietrich Bonhoeffer Works, edited by John W. de Gruchy, vol. 8, Minneapolis: Fortress Press, 2010.

30   See Andreas Pangritz, 'The Understanding of Mystery in the Theology of Dietrich Bonhoeffer', in *Mysteries in the Theology of Dietrich Bonhoeffer*, edited by Ulrik Nissen, Kirsten Busch Nielsen, Christiane Tietz, Göttingen: Vandenhoek & Ruprecht, 2007, pp. 9–26.

is significant, for from early on he was exposed to the kind of issues that later concerned him in prison and which are central to what follows in this book. But it was the blending of the intellectual and the existential in Bonhoeffer's prison writings that was of particular significance for me as I set out on this project.

Long before his imprisonment, Bonhoeffer had experienced death at first hand when his older and much admired brother, Walter, had been killed in the last days of the First World War. This was a shattering experience for him personally, as it was for the family as a whole. It certainly contributed to his early sense of calling to become a theologian and a pastor, something already evident when he and his twin sister Sabine as young children talked in the early hours of the night about death, heaven and life after death. But that was, as it later seemed to the prisoner in Tegel Military prison, so long ago. He had become much more acquainted with death, much more informed, mature and astute in his theological understanding, and he was facing his own possible execution if his role in the conspiracy against Hitler ever came to light. Separated from his family, his fiancée, and his confidant Eberhard Bethge to whom many of his letters were written, Bonhoeffer experienced intense loneliness and bouts of deep depression. This also led him into a new way of *seeing*, a 'reverent seeing' he called it,[31] that informed his theological quest and led to an outpouring of aesthetic creativity after the failure of the July 20th 1944 assassination attempt on Hitler. 'Who is Christ actually for us today?', the question that throbbed at the centre of his enquiry,[32] could not be considered in isolation from the question 'Who am I?', which he addressed in one of the ten poems he wrote in prison in a surprising new development.[33]

Bonhoeffer's provocative theological fragments on Christianity in a 'world come of age', which reflect the intellectual agility of his mind, went in tandem with this new venture into poetry which astonished both himself and Bethge. I think I now understand

31 Bonhoeffer, *Letters and Papers*, p. 507.
32 Bonhoeffer, *Letters and Papers*, p. 362.
33 Bonhoeffer, *Letters and Papers*, p. 459.

why the definitive study of his poetry is entitled 'the mystery of freedom'.[34] Consider these romantic lines written from the heart with his fiancée Maria von Wedemeyer in mind:

I want to inhale the fragrance of your bosom,[35]
absorb it, abide in it,
as heady[36] blossoms invite bees for a sip in summer's heat
and make them giddy;
as the privet makes the hawk-moth drunk at Night;
– but then a harsh gust comes and destroys fragrance and blossoms,
and I stand like a fool
before what has disappeared, is past and gone.
I feel as if red-hot tongs were tearing pieces out of my flesh,
as you, my past life, hurry away.
Frenzied defiance and rage beset me,
I sling wild, useless questions into the void.
Why, why, why? I keep asking . . .[37]

Such questions are not academic; they are intensely personal and theological, because they probe the mystery of life and death.

Apologia

A year before Steve died, the two of us had a long conversation about a book we thought we would write together. We conceived of the project as giving a more systematic account of what we believed and of its relevance for life in the world today. We did not get much further than agree on the approach we would take,

---

34 Jürgen Henkys, *Geheimnis der Freiheit: Die Gedichte Dietrich Bonhoeffers aus der Haft*, Gütersloh: Gütersloher Verlag, 2005.

35 As in the original manuscript. See Bonhoeffer, *Letters and Papers*, p. 419, n. 3.

36 I am following Isobel's translation here rather than using 'heavy' as in the new edition of *Letters and Papers from Prison*.

37 From the poem entitled 'The Past'. Bonhoeffer, *Letters and Papers*, p. 419.

namely to reflect on our respective experiences as theologians during the apartheid era and in the years that have followed its ending. That book obviously cannot be written now, nor is this an attempt to do what we had planned, something much broader in scope than what follows. Yet, in some respects, it is a continuation of the conversation we had and with a similar outcome in mind. For our main aim, we had decided, was to help those, whether Christian or not, who are hovering between faith and doubt, hope and despair, love and indifference, by giving an account of Christianity which they could espouse with integrity. Such an aim is normally described as an *apologia*, which does not mean apologizing for what one believes, but explaining why one believes it to be true and therefore commending it to others.

This aim is now inseparable from the questions posed by Steve's death, chief among them being whether I still believe in the resurrection and what this means for me today. In order to answer that question there are others that need to be considered, all of which are fundamental to historic Christianity as we know it. In addition, there are several themes that I have woven into the text that I regard as apposite for the task in hand for reasons already given. First is the challenge presented to Christian faith by science, especially neuroscience, that has to be faced head on in any contemporary Christian *apologia*; second is my conviction that the critical retrieval of Christian humanism provides an important perspective for developing such an *apologia* today; and third is my growing sense of theology as being led into mystery, which is the *cantus firmus* or that which holds everything together.

The word 'mystery' has multiple, layered meanings as will become evident in the book. Mystery is a word used to describe detective novels, the Christian sacraments, God and the universe, and anything that puzzles us and for which we are at a loss for words. It is also, as Rahner tells us, 'one of the most important key-words of Christianity and its theology'.[38] This might lead some to dismiss

---

38 Karl Rahner, 'Mystery', in *Encyclopedia of Theology: A Concise Sacramentum Mundi*, edited by Karl Rahner, London: Burns & Oates, 1975, p. 1000.

theology as the art of mystification or muddled thinking. I hope to show that the Christian experience and understanding of mystery is neither, nor is it other-worldly or a-historical, as some forms of piety and mysticism might be; it is being encountered by and engaging reality differently. It is not a question of solving problems, but of participating in something that transcends and ultimately overwhelms us as we struggle with matters of life and death, love and justice, faith and hope. In the end, this is what it means to be 'led into mystery', and in the process to become more fully human. For, to recall Bonhoeffer's words quoted at the beginning, our lives decay and are impoverished without mystery, hence the need to respect it.

The book is framed by this Prologue which sets the scene for what follows, and an Epilogue which rounds off the conversation, both of them more personal in character. The substance is contained in five chapters. In the first, I begin with comments on insight and the role of imagination in exploring mystery, and then reflect on some characteristics of mystery I unearthed in a diverse collection of stories and poems that I recalled or began reading after Steve's death. These 'echoes of mystery' which I heard in these readings are not specifically Christian, but they help uncover some of its layers of meaning and character. In the second, I focus on the way in which the Bible leads us into the mystery of God's reign or kingdom through the witness of prophets and sages and, above all, as disclosed in the life, death and resurrection of Jesus. In the third chapter, I explore the meaning of faith in God as ultimate mystery, mindful of the challenges presented above all by science to such faith claims. In the fourth, I turn my attention to our self-understanding as human beings, the mystery or enigma of who we are. Here I enter more fully into conversation with neuropsychology in order to answer the question whether we are unique within the animal kingdom, and if so, in what way. So the ground is prepared for Chapter 5 in which I finally come directly to the fundamental question raised by Steve's death, the resurrection conviction on which Christianity stands or falls, and argue that there is good reason for our hope in the coming of a 'new heaven and earth'.

I began to write *Led into Mystery* some 20 months after that awful day of parting beside the Mooi River, and anticipating the fiftieth anniversary of Steve's birth on November 16th 2011. I was by no means sure where this journey would take me. But this I now know, that as the months have passed and my writing both from the heart and the mind has gathered momentum, I have been led deeper into the mystery of faith, hope and love that has already been disclosed, and yet is always greater than we can grasp. So, step by step, and not without struggle, I have arrived at the point described by Karl-Josef Kuschel in the opening paragraph of his remarkable book *The Poet as Mirror*:

> A time comes when despite all seeking and further exploration, despite all questions and further questions, structures of thought have developed which one finds to be of greater firmness, more stable solidity. When such a time comes, it is a good thing to give an account and present things in order.[39]

---

39 Karl-Josef Kuschel, *The Poet as Mirror: Human Nature, God and Jesus in Twentieth Century Literature*, London: SCM, 1999, p. 1.

I

Echoes of Mystery

Since the Enlightenment, a "mystery" has been seen as something that needs to be cleared up. It is frequently associated with muddled thinking.
Karen Armstrong[1]

... if the writer believes that our life is and will remain essentially mysterious, if he looks upon us as beings existing in a created order to whose laws we freely respond, then what he sees on the surface will be of interest to him only as he can go through it into the experience of mystery itself.
Flannery O'Connor[2]

Mystery cannot be expressed in ordinary language. It is then misunderstood, reduced, desecrated.
Paul Tillich[3]

At the time of his death, Steve was reading Tolstoy's *War and Peace*, competing with his daughter Thea to see who could finish the lengthy tome first. Part 15 begins with an account of how Natasha and Princess Marya felt at the time of Prince Andrey's death.

Everything – the carriage driving along the street, the summons to dinner, the maid asking which dress to get out; words still of faint, feigned sympathy – set the wound smarting, seemed to insult it, and jarred on that needful silence in which both were trying to listen to the stern, terrible litany that had not yet died

---

1 Karen Armstrong, *A History of God*, London: Heinemann, 1994, p. 244.
2 Flannery O'Connor, *Mystery and Manners*, New York: Farrar, Strauss & Giroux, 1970, p. 41.
3 Paul Tillich, *Systematic Theology: Volume 1*, London: Nisbet & Co., 1953, p. 121.

away in their ears, and gaze into the mysterious, endless vistas that seemed for a moment to have unveiled before them.[4]

A few paragraphs later Tolstoy writes: 'It seemed to them that what they had felt and gone through could not be expressed in words. It seemed to them that every allusion in words to the details of his life was an outrage on the grandeur and holiness of the mystery that had been accomplished before their eyes.'[5]

Over the months following Steve's death, I struggled to find the words to express my feelings and thoughts and to recount the dreams that accompany traumatic experience. I then began to discover insights in a random set of texts that suggested ways into what was for me relatively unknown territory. Among them was another passage from Tolstoy, this time from *Anna Karenina*, sent to us by a friend soon after Steve's death. Kitty is about to give birth to her and Levin's first child, but all that Levin 'knew and felt' writes Tolstoy, 'was that what was happening was what had happened nearly a year before in the hotel of the country town at the deathbed of his brother Nikolay'. That, however, had been grief; this was joy.

Yet that grief and this joy were alike outside all the ordinary conditions of life; they were loop-holes, as it were, in that ordinary life through which there came glimpses of something sublime. And in the contemplation of this sublime something the soul was exalted to inconceivable heights of which it had before had no conception, while reason lagged behind, unable to keep up with it.[6]

Intense human experiences that transcend the ordinary conditions of life are loop-holes through which we glimpse mystery,

---

4   Leo Tolstoy, *War and Peace*, London: Reprint Society by arrangement with William Heinemann, 1960, p. 1021.

5   Tolstoy, *War and Peace*, p. 1021.

6   Leo Tolstoy, *Anna Karenina*, translated by Constance Garnett with an Introduction by Thomas Mann, New York: Random House, 1939, vol. 2, p. 847.

but always within those conditions. Not everyone discerns the mystery present in the ordinary; only those who, in the words of Flannery O'Connor, are willing to have their 'sense of mystery deepened by contact with reality' and their 'sense of reality deepened by contact with mystery'.[7] This involves an act of faith that precedes reasoned understanding, and the exercise of imagination without which it is impossible to express lived experience or gain insight. Being led into mystery is not irrational and undoubtedly requires more than an act of the imagination. But the journey is impossible without it, and reason, essential as it is, inevitably lags behind.

Imagination and insight

From earliest times, human beings have imaginatively expressed their self-conscious awareness of mystery in the reality around them through symbolic forms. These have evolved with their creators over the centuries as circumstances have changed, and as new insights have been garnered through experience and experiment. They might have begun as scratches on a rock but, laden with significance, they have led to the creation of great works of art. Or they began as tales told around a fire, and have since mutated into fables, legends, and myths that bring delight and suggest meaning; or discordant sounds and primitive rituals which have become the sources of majestic music, liturgy, poetry, drama, fiction and film. Such symbolic forms, as Rowan Williams tells us, 'are not just lying around, nor are they thought up as ordinary glosses on straight forward experience of the world, they are what we live through as humans'.[8]

We may share the human story shaped by common experiences of grieving and wonder, suffering and love, struggling and hope, of beauty, truth and goodness, as well as evil. But we each have our own personal lived experience that shapes our perceptions

---

7 O'Connor, *Mystery and Manners*, p. 79.
8 Rowan Williams, *On Christian Theology*, Oxford: Blackwell, 2000, p. 201.

of reality, the way in which we think and act, our awareness of the world around us, and the way in which you, the reader, respond to what I am writing. This is influenced greatly by the cultural matrix in which we are nurtured, whether religious or secular, regional or cosmopolitan, and by intellectual disciplines and training. The list of stated variables could continue almost indefinitely, and it would obviously include language diversity as fundamental to the way we perceive and describe reality. I work and think within the framework of the Christian tradition defined in terms of Christian humanism and as a male South African of English descent. Whatever else may contribute to my cultural matrix, these are dominant elements that shape my exploration of mystery. But *how* does that exploration take place? The answer lies in the capacity of our brains to remember and imagine.

Our brains hold a vast treasure store of memories that have built up over time enabling us to recognize what we daily encounter. Long before the advent of neuroscience, Augustine spoke of the 'fields and spacious halls of memory', a veritable 'storehouse' of memories on which his imagination drew.[9] Each day our brains also gather new information in their memory banks to help us negotiate the present and anticipate the future. Without this rich store of data we would not be able to probe questions about the mystery of the universe, or relate to our experiences of joy and grief, love and fear. This does not mean that there is no wisdom in learning to forget aspects of our past in order to cope with life, but the art of remembering is paramount. No one can live fully and meaningfully in the present unless their past is kept alive in their brain cells and expressed in words and images in appropriate ways. This requires the power of imagination.

Yet imagination has long been regarded as 'an inadequate and unreliable mode of knowledge, in contrast to reasonable, logical or empirical discourse'[10] and vain imagination, some biblical

---

9 Augustine, *Confessions and Enchiridion*, The Library of Christian Classics, vol. VII, London: SCM, 1955, x/viii/12, pp. 208–9.
10 Walter Brueggemann, *Theology of the Old Testament: Testimony, Dispute, Advocacy*, Minneapolis: Fortress Press, 1997, pp. 67–8.

texts tell us, leads to idolatry.[11] The fact that our memories are retrieved through our imagination, stimulated in various ways by our formation and experience, does not guarantee that everything we imagine is possible, good or true. We could be deluding ourselves and others, and often are. It is the same as assuming that the camera does not lie. The image stored on film or on disk can be manipulated in all kinds of ways whether in the dark room or on the computer screen. So imagination is often spurned as a dubious guide to seeking the truth precisely because of its ability to confabulate and deceive. Yet, there is another side to the story that has in more recent times been reinforced not just by the claims of artists, but also by neuroscientists. As Niels Gregersen tells us, imagination is not simply a 'faculty of free invention, bewildering in its content and arbitrary in its combinations' and as such somewhat isolated from our rational faculties. On the contrary, we 'cannot "imagine" human reasoning apart from imaginative activities such as envisaging, associating, conjecturing, or hypothesizing'. In fact, what we imagine is deeply rooted in our bodily experience.[12] This ties in well with Walter Brueggemann's insistence that imagination 'is a crucial ingredient' in the way in which reality is rendered in the Hebrew Scriptures,[13] as it is, for example, in Jesus' parables.

The truth is, without imagination we are unable to process memories whether in planning for the future, reflecting on the state of the nation, expressing love, doing theology and scientific research, or myth making. Imagination is not the fanciful creation of absent meaning, a thumb-sucking exercise as it were; it functions within the matrix of memories or traditions that have shaped our lives, both in common and personally. Imagination is 'the distinctively human capacity to envision multiple alternative

---

11   Ezekiel 13.2, 17; Acts 17.29.

12   Niels Gregersen, 'The Naturalness of Religious Imagination and the Idea of Revelation', *Ars Disputanti: The Online Journal for Philosophy of Religion* 3 (2003); www.arsdisputandi.org.

13   Brueggemann, *Theology of the Old Testament*, p. 67.

realities, scenarios, and outcomes'.[14] In doing so it 'frees us from the tyranny of the present, of the logical, of the "real," . . . from the constraints of the now; as it pictures what events were like in the historic past or what they might become in the future'.[15] Without imagination we would not be able to avoid danger, think about life, deal with depression, or consider the mystery of life and death. Without imagination we would not be able to see the world through the eyes of those who are suffering and therefore find ways to help them. Without imagination faith itself would be impossible, for in believing we internally constitute another world 'that expands our own being in the world'.[16] Imagination is, in sum, the capacity to organize memories of past and recent life experience into patterns of contemporary symbolic significance. As such it is an essential ingredient to our being human, the key to creative art, scientific endeavour and religious insight, and essential for the journey into mystery.

But how we use our imagination is crucial. Does our imagination lead us deeper into reality, preparing us for mystery's disclosure, or does it lead us away from reality and leave us self-satisfied in the shallows of life? Imagination requires a degree of discipline, for it functions within a tradition, cultural matrix, and bodily experience. But it refuses to be boxed in by their limitations and conventions. Great artists as well as scientists and theologians have always worked within a tradition, but they have become most creative when they have risked transgressing boundaries. Only then does imagination lead to genuine insight which, as Bernard Lonergan tells us, is not reached by learning rules, following precepts, or studying methodology, important as these are in

---

14 David A. Hogue, *Remembering the Future: Story, Ritual, and the Human Brain*, Cleveland, OH: The Pilgrim Press, 2003, p. 44.

15 Hogue, *Remembering the Future*, p. 45.

16 Graham Ward, 'Narrative Structures and Ethics: The Structures of Believing and the Practices of Hope', *Literature and Theology* 20: 4 (2006), p. 440.

preparing the way.[17] Genuine insight changes us and our perspective on life, supplementing or even subverting tradition.

Transforming tradition through insightful theological imagination is fundamental to the task of theology, as it is to this project.[18] Brueggemann speaks of the emancipatory role of imagination in giving birth to words and deeds that speak to the human and social condition of our time and to the cry for the flourishing of life.[19] Our imagination enables us to retrieve memory in order to re-describe and give fresh and meaningful form to human experiences of reality, to find the words and images necessary to express meaning that derives from seeing things differently. Such imagination enables us to respond to reality in ways that are creative, open and healing, and socially transformative rather than trapped in an unjust and ugly past. Insightful imagination makes it possible for us to be led into mystery.

The language we use to describe mystery may be ordinary language, the language of lived experience, but mystery cannot be adequately expressed in ordinary language. That is why mystery finds expression above all in art which imaginatively points to or even carries us beyond ourselves towards that which is ultimate. Any 'great work of art', Kuschel writes, 'is a world in itself, mysterious in the making, inexhaustible in significance, incalculable in effect. In this way the great work of art becomes an analogy to that reality which theologians denote with the unusable word "God"'.[20] For some, this is supremely true of music which not only has undoubted neurological and therapeutic value,[21] but also

---

17   J. F. Lonergan, *Insight: A Study of Human Understanding*, New York: Philosophical Library, 1973, p. 4.

18   John W. de Gruchy, 'Transforming Traditions: Doing Theology in South Africa Today', *Journal of Theology for Southern Africa* 139 (2011), pp. 7–17.

19   Walter Brueggemann, 'Prophetic Imagination Toward Social Flourishing', in *Theology and Human Flourishing: Essays in Honor of Timothy J. Gorringe*, edited by Jeremy Law, Mike Higton, and Christopher Rowland, Eugene, OR: Cascade Books, 2011, pp. 16–30.

20   Karl-Josef Kuschel, *The Poet as Mirror: Human Nature, God and Jesus in Twentieth Century Literature*, London: SCM, 1999, p. 11.

21   See Oliver Sacks, *Musicophilia: Tales of Music and the Brain*, New York: Picador, 2007.

draws us into the field of mystery. Quoting Claude Lévi Strauss to the effect that the 'invention of melody is the supreme mystery of man', George Steiner goes on to say that the 'truths, the necessities of ordered feeling in the musical experience are not irrational; but they are irreducible to reason or pragmatic reckoning'.[22] Likewise great literature and poetry leads us into the realm of mystery as it imaginatively probes the fundamental questions of being human in describing the ordinary events of life.

We can distinguish between different forms of imagination and it is helpful to keep these distinctions in mind as we proceed. *Historical* imagination describes the way in which historians re-construct the past in relation to the present, reading texts, including biblical texts, with fresh eyes and from different perspectives, as in feminist readings of Scripture.[23] *Theological* imagination describes the way in which we construct 'images of God' in relation to ourselves and the world in dialogue with the biblical text, the history of tradition, and the contemporary context.[24] *Prophetic* imagination describes the activity of prophets of social justice, their 'capacity to generate, evoke, and articulate alternative images of reality that counter what hegemonic power and knowledge have declared to be impossible'.[25] Likewise, *poetic* imagination is not just important for expressing personal experience, but also critical for the well-being of society, and is closely aligned to the theological exploration of mystery. There are mysteries, wrote Karl Barth, that can be grasped 'only by divinatory imagination' and these 'find expression only in the freer observation and speech

22 George Steiner, *Real Presences*, Chicago: Chicago University Press, 1991, p. 19.

23 See for example Elisabeth Schüssler Fiorenza, *In Memory of Her: A Feminist Theological Reconstruction of Christian Origins*, London: SCM, 1983, p. xx.

24 See Julian Hartt, *Theological Method and Imagination*, New York: Seabury, 1977; Gordon D. Kaufman, *The Theological Imagination: Constructing the Concept of God*, Philadelphia: Westminster Press, 1981, pp. 263–79; Sallie McFague, *Metaphorical Theology: Models of God in Religious Language*, Philadelphia: Fortress, 1982.

25 Brueggemann, *Theology of the Old Testament*, p. 68.

of poetry'.[26] Such poetry is an expression of faith struggling with experience before reason tries to analyse it.

All forms of imagination are processed by the brain in the same way but, for reasons that will emerge, I find it problematic and unsatisfying to reduce works of creative imagination to the chemistry of the brain, or to assume that it all ends in confabulation. Processes explain much, but not everything. They don't explain the awe or wonder that is evoked as art becomes the vehicle for transcendence, for the holy, for encountering and expressing mystery, or the inspiration that leaves the artist dumbstruck by her own creation. Creative imagination draws deeply from the sensual wellsprings that nourish the brain, but the truth of a story or the beauty of a work of art lies in the narrative and the image, not in brain processes. I rebel against the idea that everything can be explained simply by reference to myriads of busy molecules hard at work, amazing and breath-taking as that is. Such reductionism diminishes our humanity, our capacity for humaneness, compassion, altruism, protest and resistance. But let me desist from saying more about this until the appropriate time and share the first step I took in my journey into mystery as my imagination was stirred by that of others.

Searching for clues

My sense of being led into mystery was initially fed by a random set of texts – stories, poems, fairy tales – that I happened to recall or read during those awful days that followed Steve's death. They are eclectic in character and do not all belong to the canon of 'great literature' as do *War and Peace* or *Anna Karenina*. But each in some way has awakened memories and stirred my imagination, and in doing so has provided loop-holes in the 'ordinary conditions of life' through which I have glimpsed aspects or heard echoes of mystery. Such insights will accompany us as we proceed through each stage along the way ahead.

---

26 Karl Barth, *Church Dogmatics III/3: The Doctrine of Creation*, Edinburgh: T&T Clark, 1984, p. 374.

In *The Cunning Man*, the Canadian author Robertson Davies, a Renaissance man and unapologetic agnostic, weaves together an intriguing plot as he explores being human in a matter-of-fact ordinary kind of way. In a passage near the end of the novel, sitting in a restaurant in Toronto, the chief character, a doctor, the 'cunning man' (undoubtedly Davies himself), is asked by his niece Esme whether or not death is simply extinction. I did not recall this passage from an earlier reading, but on returning to the text with recent experience in mind, my interest was immediately aroused.

'I think extinction is coming it a bit too strong. It's said that energy is never lost, and there is a lot of energy in a human being, even an inferior one, and Gil certainly wasn't inferior.'

'So where is that energy now?'

'If I knew that I would indeed be a Cunning Man. But of course you realize that what we're saying is wildly unscientific?'

'About the energy being somewhere, you mean?'

'About any suggestion that there is a plan, or an order, or a scheme of any kind in the universe; no purposefulness in the evolutionary sequence whatever – not a particle. The scientific orthodoxy is that it all takes place by chance – even though it seems odd that chance phenomena can build up systems of vast complexity. It is wholly against the law of entropy–'

'You've lost me.'

'Don't worry. There is an alternative. And that's the notion of the Divine Drama. Don't worry, I'm not going to be heavy about it – not over dinner. But you know *The Mikado*? You remember Pooh-Bah who could trace his ancestry back to a protoplasmal primordial atomic globule? And here we are in this excellent restaurant, drinking this very good claret and eating cutlets, and not looking at all like people with a peculiar ancestry. That's the Divine Drama. The onward march of evolution. Astonishing, so far as it's gone, but we are probably only in Act Two of a five act tragicomedy.'

The conversation returns to the death of Gil and where he might be. The response is a poem written by Ovid, one of the great ancient Latin poets, which speaks of the immortality of the soul. There is an awkward pause; a reluctance to take the conversation further except in a light-hearted manner.

A night out at a restaurant is no place for such a conversation, or is it? After all some of the classic dialogues on serious subjects take place over a meal as the conversation partners engage each other. A symposium, in ancient Greece, was an after-dinner drinking party before it came to mean a philosophical discussion. Academics still often manage to combine both. But even so, our natural inclination on such occasions is to hold the mystery of death at arm's length, reluctant to probe too deeply. We skirt the borders of mystery, drawing back from the edge, not sure whether we really want to enter its domain. We turn to banter and humour to find an exit when we begin to cross the boundary line. But the mystery of death is real for all of us. So for a brief embarrassed moment our conversation flirts with death, even though we may have neither the resources nor the desire to pursue the matter very far. The conversation in *The Cunning Man* draws to a banal conclusion. Silence would have been more appropriate.

'Heavy stuff. Do you think Gil is hanging around, then?'
'I don't agree or disagree. Pythagoras thought so, and Pythagoras was no fool.'
'Do you think perhaps Gil hangs around his murderer?'
'That would be very disagreeable for the murderer, wouldn't?'
'And how!'[27]

If dialogues on death occur in novels reminding the reader that there is more to the mystery of life than that which convivial conversation allows, by contrast murder mysteries begin with someone's death that then becomes the preoccupation of the rest

---

27 Robertson Davies, *The Cunning Man*, London: Penguin, 1994, pp. 465–6.

of the story. 'Without a death, there is no mystery', Peter Erb reminds us.[28] Is this not a strange characteristic of being human: being repulsed and fascinated by death at the same time? If there is a reluctance to discuss death in *The Cunning Man*, there is a fascination with death in all its gory details in murder mysteries, and inevitably there will be more deaths that follow the initial one before the story comes to an end. Even great detectives seem impotent to prevent serial killings. Every page is seeped in death, in the bushes, in the bath tub, on the street corner or the Orient Express.

Watching war movies and violence on TV has made us all voyeurs of death as the substance of entertainment, like being mesmerized by a spitting cobra. This is one reason why I found it difficult to watch the movie *The Passion of the Christ* which so realistically portrayed the dying moments of Jesus on the cross. Was it not appropriate that in the original setting 'darkness covered the earth', as if to hide this awfulness from the gaze of the onlooker lest it became just another meaningless violent death? The Bible does not sanitize reality. There is no way round the fact that in the opening scenes of the narrative, Cain murders his brother in a ruthless killing that sets in motion a train of bloody events that leads inexorably to the murder of Jesus of Nazareth, an event that Martin Luther, long before Friedrich Nietzsche, dramatically described as the 'death of God'. The Christian mystery narrative begins with a murder scene and a victim. Only much later does it take us back to Bethlehem to recall the mystery of the victim's birth, but then, as the story immediately tells, there is the murder of the innocents – a stark reminder of the vulnerability of children in every age marked by the ravages of violence and war.

There are several reasons given for our fascination with detective and murder mysteries. Enjoyment and escapism are two, which is ironical when you come to think about the subject. I find good mystery novels gripping because of the surprising twists that await me as I turn the page. I search for clues to the eventual outcome,

---

28   Peter C. Erb, *Murder, Manners, Mystery: Reflections on Faith in Contemporary Detective Fiction*, London: SCM, 2007, p. 20.

yet am aware that a good mystery writer will lead me down blind alleys to outwit me before revealing the truth. I second-guess the author but am perplexed as one clue after another proves unreliable. Yet, I continue to read because I *know* for certain (not just *believe*) that in the end all will be disclosed. Nothing is ever fully disclosed until the end – that is the nature of mystery. In putting down the book we might well say: 'why didn't I think of that?' There is, of course, a qualitative difference between the disclosure of the mystery in a detective thriller and the cosmic revelation at the end of time as depicted in the biblical Apocalypse. That ending, if Jesus' parables about the Last Judgment are anything to go by, may be more surprising than the righteous too readily assume, and more unexpected than the mystery novel devotee could ever have imagined.

But what if there is no final revelation or apocalypse? What if I turned over the last page only to discover that I have been betrayed by lack of resolution, or that the conclusion is contrived, or that the author keeps the outcome a secret, laughing behind my back at my frustration? What if no Hercule Poirot, Sherlock Holmes, Miss Marple, Inspector Dalgleish or Morse arrives to point out to us how obvious and elementary it all is in retrospect? What if the apocalyptic vision of a 'new heaven and earth' is the all-time confabulation? What if, in the end, there is nothing, literally a dead end? The mere idea has tempted many a nihilist to commit suicide, and some have done so.

In the best-selling 'mystery novel', *The Girl with the Dragon Tattoo* (which I read as a way of escape from, but soon found myself confronted by, reality) Mikael Blomkvist tells his lover of the moment, Cecilia, about the murder he is trying to solve:

> It's actually a fascinating case. What I believe is known to the trade as a locked-room mystery, on an island. And nothing in the investigation seems to follow normal logic. Every question remains unanswered, every clue leads to a dead end.[29]

---

29   Stieg Larsson, *The Girl with the Dragon Tattoo: Millennium I*, London: Maclehose Press, 2008, p. 208.

I have sometimes felt like that when wrestling with the questions posed by Steve's death, confined to a locked-room mystery, where every clue that might lead to a satisfying answer takes me down another cul-de-sac.

Stieg Larsson could not allow his story to conclude in a dead end. The mystery had to be solved, even if, on finally putting the book down, we may feel that there are still questions begging answers, secrets kept and clues not honoured. But once the mystery has been solved, we are unlikely to read the story again, or with the same sense of suspense. There is no longer any mystery to draw us into itself as there is in the case of the death of a loved one or friend, nothing further to be discovered that might take us deeper into ultimacy. In fact, if, as in the case of a mystery story, all is revealed, there is no longer any mystery when we finally lay the book aside. The secret is out, the problem is solved. It is no different from the latest discovery in the university research laboratory, remarkable as it may be. Not so, when it comes to the death of someone we love or cherish.

While searching for some clues in speaking about mystery, I happened to watch a TV programme on the origins of the internet. The internet is a mystery I will probably never understand, no matter the language used or the power of my imagination; but it is not a mystery for computer scientists. They can explain it; they can also control it. On the same programme, I heard about a meeting between executives that took place behind closed doors to discuss a major deal between Google and another IT company. There was no positive outcome. 'What happened inside', the commentator said, 'will always remain a mystery'. That is, I thought to myself, unless someone goes public and tells the story. But is that really a mystery? Is it not more strictly-speaking a *secret,* something kept behind locked doors, which is something different?

Neurologists tell us that a secret reflects competing tendencies in the brain, between not being allowed to tell a story and eagerly desiring to do so.[30] Real mystery is about more than secrets

---

30 David Eagleman, *Incognito: The Secret Lives of the Brain*, New York, NY: Pantheon Books, 2011, p. 145.

waiting to be shared or problems waiting resolution. The fact that I have misplaced my pencil and cannot find it anywhere may be described by me as a 'bit of a mystery', but that is a shallow use of the word and, in any case, the pencil will probably reappear in my wife's studio. Mystery is encoded or hidden like a secret; but unlike a secret, mystery never ceases to invite enquiry and exploration, for there is always more to be discovered. Whereas an 'open secret' is a contradiction, the more a mystery is unveiled the more there is to be revealed. Mystery is not obscure but leads us beyond the boundaries of the ordinary into the deep things of life. As such, speaking about mystery requires a change of perception and the words to express things differently even if language is ultimately inadequate. That is why, as mentioned previously, Otto tells us that the 'truly "mysterious" object is beyond our apprehension and comprehension'. It is not a problem to be solved, but something that can strike us dumb.[31]

Life is not always like a satisfying mystery story. As we journey we detect clues that suggest some purpose and direction, and we live in the hope that eventually it will end in a way that, despite death, will not be haunted by shattered dreams, unfulfilled and meaningless; that the fragments might somehow be brought together in a satisfying way. But the story might suddenly end in midstream without reaching such a conclusion; or it may drag on seemingly without end. The doxological statement 'world without end' is, come to think of it, a rather terrifying notion which we Christians somewhat glibly utter as an appendage to Psalm singing. But believers take on faith (that's why we are believers) that there is more than endlessness to come and that outstanding issues will be resolved in a meaningful way. We discover clues that help us in our journey to that end, though they are often hidden, and we easily miss them. Even so, at the grave side we ponder the meaning of the life that has now ended, doubts gain strength, and we are bothered if we cannot see the purpose of it all. Life resembles Blomkvist's 'locked-room mystery' with no windows

---

31 Rudolf Otto, *The Idea of the Holy*, London: Oxford University Press, 1931, p. 28.

through which we can glimpse something that makes sense of it all, or doors that open into a new world. Is there an author of the script we are living, a transcendent hand that is somehow writing us into a fuller, more satisfying story? Is there a sequel perhaps, or is that hope merely wishful thinking?

The Girl with the Dragon Tattoo is the first volume in the *Millennium* trilogy. In the following two volumes some of the unanswered questions get resolved. Yet, we know that their Swedish author died tragically at a relatively young age.[32] Whether we are satisfied or not by the outcome, the story of Lisbeth Salander and Mikael Blomkvist has reached a dead end. Rumours of a sequel hidden in Larsson's desk, or on a hard drive waiting to be found, abound. But there is no certainty as to whether there is more to come. Maybe that is how all our stories end; maybe the mystery of life and death remains forever in a closed room; maybe what we thought were clues to guide us to a satisfying conclusion are only cruel illusions, confabulations.

Mystery stories are not just about reaching a satisfying conclusion, if that is ever possible. It is also the *journey* into the mystery that is important. In writing the *Millennium* trilogy, Larsson had more in mind than solving a crime. He raised important questions about the corruption of wealth and power, the abuse of women and children, the dangers of racist ideologies and bad religion, and the morality of hacking into other peoples' computers to lay bare their secrets. Good murder mysteries raise more questions than simply 'whodunit' ones. If we are only concerned to find out what happens in the end, perhaps even reading the final chapter in advance, we may miss the plot that relates the story to our lives in the real world, and to the real mysteries of life and death that are existentially perplexing the author. The disclaimer that all the

---

32 Stieg Larsson (1954–2004) died suddenly of a heart attack in November 2004. The trilogy was published posthumously. By 2010, more than 20 million copies had been sold in 41 countries. Larsson was the second bestselling author in the world in 2008. His books reflect something of his own life and the dangers he faced in opposing racism and right-wing extremism. See Dan Burstein et al. *Secrets of the Tattooed Girl*, London: Weidenfeld, 2011.

characters are fictional strengthens the sense that many a reader would be able to identify them in real life.

Mystery unfolds within the world we inhabit each day, not somewhere else. The mystery is in the telling about life as it is, in the raw, in the ordinary affairs of life. It may only be fully disclosed at the end, but it is the journey into mystery that challenges us and connects us to reality with its surprising twists and turns. In the *Millennium* trilogy the mystery of the particular crime waiting to be solved is only a fragment of something larger and more terrifying. Paul called it the 'mystery of iniquity'[33] that pervades the 'principalities and powers of this world'.[34] Stieg Larsson encountered it in his life and described it in his stories, which are now captured in movies set in the remote island inlets, and the dark forests and streets of an icy Nordic winter.

Seeing things differently

Barry Forshaw's *Death in a Cold Climate,* a study of Scandinavian crime fiction of which the *Millennium* trilogy is only one of numerous examples, traces the genre back to the ancient Icelandic sagas and folk tales.[35] Fairy stories likewise have mysterious origins, many of which can also be traced back to the dark and eerily silent forests of Northern Europe, where magic was supreme and enchantment was untouched by modern-day sophistication.

> . . . the silence of the forests hides things; it does not open them out but closes them off . . . Forests are full of surprises . . .The forests do not generate the huge god of the desert, nor the partisan, passionate, sexually active deities of the Greek mountains and islands. They produce little fragmented stories, of magic and human courage and dark plots, stories of secrets and silences. Over and over again in the old stories there is

---

33   2 Thessalonians 2.7 (AV).
34   Ephesians 6.12 (AV).
35   Barry Forshaw, *Death in a Cold Climate: A Guide to Scandinavian Fiction*, New York: Palgrave Macmillan, 2012.

a silence: mysteries; hidden names; concealed identities; things not told, withheld, cloaked by silence.[36]

Children need fairy stories, so wrote the distinguished clinical psychologist Bruno Bettelheim, in order to develop their personalities and the faculty for discovering meaning in their lives.[37] The tales can be misused, frightening children into submission to the adult world but, at the other end of the spectrum, they have also been seen as offering empowerment to women. You can, in fact, 'make of them what you will – they are shape shifters'.[38] They transmute as the hearer or reader enters their realm of fantasy, opening our eyes to see reality – and therefore also ourselves – differently. Such aesthetic sensibility is the heart beat of imagination.

My sister Rozelle took me as a small boy to see *The Wizard of Oz*, made the year I was born (1939). The movie, as John Updike wrote many years later, 'hit the jackpot . . . became a staple of postwar television' in the United States, and remains 'the main road into Oz'.[39] The original story, written by Lyman Frank Baum under the influence of the Brothers Grimm and Hans Christian Anderson, was first published as *The Wonderful Wizard of Oz* in 1900. The name 'OZ' probably derives from Percy Bysshe Shelley's sonnet Ozymandias, an ancient Egyptian 'king of kings', though more prosaic reasons have been given. But whatever its origin, Baum insisted that the story was sheer fantasy written for children – good, wholesome entertainment – which excluded all the horror bits in the original fairy story and, in the process 'lost its earthiness' and utopian vision.[40] Despite this, it has become the subject of critical scrutiny by Feminists, Marxists, Freudians, historians,

36   Sara Maitland, *A Book of Silence*, London: Granta Books, 2009, p. 179.
37   Bruno Bettelheim, *The Uses of Enchantment*, New York: Alfred A. Knopf, 1976.
38   Maitland, *A Book of Silence*, p. 179.
39   John Updike, '"Oz is Us"', a review of *The Annotated Wizard of Oz*, by L. Frank Baum, ed. Michael Patrick Hearn, New York: Norton, 2000 published in John Updike, *Due Considerations: Essays and Criticism*, London: Penguin Books, 2007, Kindle edition, location 4842.
40   Updike, 'Oz is Us', location 4906.

economists, political scientists, and literary critics whose discussions would have astounded Baum along with theologian Karl Barth for whom fairy stories were a 'degenerate form of myth' concerned about teaching the moral of the story and more 'interested in details than the whole'.[41] But fairy stories are not necessarily purveyors of generalized bourgeois morality – it all depends on how you read the text. One interpretation of *Oz* likens it to the Homeric myth of the heroic journey of self-discovery[42] and, like many other fairy tales, Baum set it within the context of a dream, for it is in that state that the unconscious often springs to life.

A 16 year-old orphaned farm girl from Kansas named Dorothy discovers who she is on returning home from her bizarre adventures. There are many life-threatening and affirming encounters along the way, not least when the 'wonderful wizard', whose presence and seeming omnipotence is shrouded in mystery, turns out to be a fraud, likable perhaps, but of no help whatsoever in defeating evil or in helping Dorothy find herself. Dorothy learns that she cannot depend on any *deus ex machina*, whether a magician or clinically-coated scientist; she has to learn to think for herself (finding a brain for the Scarecrow), feel for herself (finding a heart for the Tin Man) and find the courage (the Cowardly Lion) to defeat the wicked witch.

How are we to understand Dorothy's homecoming? That we find ourselves when we discover that the values of rural society give us meaning and security in an urban and industrial world gone awry, that there is no place like home on the farm? Is it when we discover that the real companions for our journey are those who love us but whom we take for granted? Is it when we reaffirm our earthly roots, come to terms with our sexuality, recognize our self-worth and need for self-reliance, rather than look for meaning and help in an unreal fantasy world over the rainbow where some 'wonderful wizard' is to be found? Or perhaps when, like the Prodigal Son, we return home from the far country to the waiting

---

41 Karl Barth, *Church Dogmatics* III.1: *The Doctrine of Creation*, Edinburgh: T.&T. Clark, 1958, p. 84.
42 See Updike, "Oz is Us," location 4800.

Father and Mother? It could be any or all of these, depending on who tells the story and how and when it is received. The story does not tell us. It invites us to look into a mirror and see who we are, stimulating our imagination and awakening our awareness of self and the world we inhabit. But, of course, a fairy tale can be given a fairy tale ending, as Baum gave his version, made saccharine to sooth away our uneasiness at confronting the real self, or to please the audience rather than portray the real world.

In one of his earliest sermons, preached on the Sunday after Easter in 1928 during his vicariate in Barcelona, Bonhoeffer began by speaking of fairytales and legends from the oldest times that 'tell of the days when God walked among human beings. Those were splendid times', he told his expatriate congregation, 'when one met a wanderer on the road who asked for lodging, then at home one recognized in this simple man the Lord God and was richly rewarded'. 'Those were wonderful times', he continued, 'when God and human beings were still so close that people could walk and talk with God'. Indeed, he went on,

> . . . those were the days recounted only by fairy tales and legends that spoke of all the slumbering, secret human hopes as if they had already become reality. The beginning of our own Bible also relates how the Lord God walked about in the garden of paradise in the evening and lived and conversed with human beings. Probably very few peoples do not have similar stories. How blessed were those people permitted to experience those times when God and human beings were still close.[43]

Years later, in August 1943, in a letter to his parents from Tegel Prison in Berlin, Bonhoeffer told them that he had been reading 'with great amusement' fairy tales in a book by Wilhelm Hauff, an early nineteenth-century writer of satire and poetry. After five months in prison, he was beginning to think he would never leave

---

43 Dietrich Bonhoeffer, *Barcelona, Berlin, America 1928–1931*, Dietrich Bonhoeffer Works, edited by Clifford J. Green, vol. 10, Minneapolis: Fortress Press, 2008, pp. 490–1.

alive. Most nights, he was awakened by the sound of Allied bombing, causing him to worry about the safety of family and friends. But fairytales, he wrote, 'transport a person into a completely different world, where the only fear remaining is that one might awake all too soberly from the realm of fantasy and dreams'.[44]

In some of his prison notes, Bonhoeffer jotted down his thoughts about the functioning of the brain, self-deception and illusion, the fading of memories, the emptiness but also healing of time, and the shock of waking up from a dream.[45] He also, so he tells us, dreamt virtually every night, often of his fiancée Maria and their future together,[46] and on waking he made the connection between his dreams and the world of fantasy and fairy tales.[47] Do such stories simply become for us a means of escape into another dream-world, or do they still have the capacity to help us see ourselves and reality in a new key, and so forge new paths for our life's journey?

Jack Zipes, a modern authority on the subject, tells us that fairy stories not only 'awaken the wonderment of the young' but 'project counterworlds to our present society' and in this way they 'serve a meaningful social function not just for compensation but for revelation'.[48] Revelation refers here to the disclosure of truth that is hidden from those who have lost the imagination of wonder and are trapped by what they presume is the 'real world'. Like the young boy who, in Hans Christian Andersen's tale about the vain emperor, cried out: 'But he isn't wearing anything at all!' The origins of this story can be traced back to a medieval folk tale that Andersen stumbled across in a later German version entitled 'This is the way of the world.' Andersen added the memorable ending based on an experience he had as a child. Standing in a crowd watching the Danish king pass by, and much to

---

44   Dietrich Bonhoeffer, *Letters and Papers from Prison*, Dietrich Bonhoeffer Works, edited by John W. de Gruchy, vol. 8, Minneapolis: Fortress Press, 2010, pp. 130–1.
45   Bonhoeffer, *Letters and Papers*, pp. 70–3.
46   Bonhoeffer, *Letters and Papers*, p. 63.
47   Bonhoeffer, *Letters and Papers*, pp. 106, 11, 109, 131.
48   Jack Zipes, 'Fairy Tales and Folk Tales', in *Oxford Encyclopedia of Children's Literature* vol. 2 edited by Jack Zipes, New York: Oxford, 2006, p. 53.

the embarrassment of his mother, he cried out 'Oh, he is nothing more than a human being!' The mystique of the king was uncovered. The tale became a telling critique of the hypocrisy of Danish aristocracy in the early nineteenth century. That is the way of the world; all is vanity. But only the childlike notice.

The capacity of children to see things as they are and intuitively grasp their significance was often noted by Jesus. His disciples were irritated by children who crowded around him, and had to be reprimanded for trying to keep them away.[49] Time and again Jesus called on his hearers to become like children in order to get the point of what he was telling them about the mystery of God's way in contrast to the 'way of the world'. We cannot literally become children again, nor is it possible to believe that God walked with Adam and Eve in the cool of the day (neither did the writer of that perceptive myth) any more than we believe in Father Christmas or the tooth fairy. But we can arrive at what Ricœur so helpfully calls a 'second naïveté',[50] that is a fresh, chastened ability to see and hear the truth in the tale, the fact in the fiction, the mystery beneath the real, and to recognize that a great deal else in which we place our confidence as sophisticated adults is ephemeral at best and dangerous at worst. The locked room needs to be opened from the outside if we are to walk through the door. We need loop-holes in ordinary life through which we can catch glimpses of something sublime amid the mundane. But our post-Enlightenment rationality often prevents our imagination from perceiving the mystery in the real, the awakening of aesthetic sensibility to grasp the actual. We need to be reminded that only those who are willing to face reality will discern mystery, and only those who are open to mystery will discover reality.

A mystery too deep for tears

The rediscovery of the works of the Greek philosopher Aristotle in the West in the Middle Ages, made possible by Muslim scholars,

---

49 Matthew 19.14.
50 Paul Ricœur, *The Mystery of Evil*, Boston: Beacon Press, 1969, p. 351.

had an enormous influence on the way in which Christianity was reformulated by Thomas Aquinas and, in turn, shaped Western European culture. Neo-Platonism, that had been such a potent influence in Christianity since earliest times, was now integrated into a more Aristotelian framework. Thomas insisted that all 'our knowledge starts in sense-perception',[51] not in mystical visions or dreams, let alone flights of the imagination divorced from reality. These, which had long been part of Christian experience, were now frowned on by the church establishment, as was anything that seriously challenged the authority of tradition and hierarchy. The Protestant Reformation in the sixteenth century did not change this mindset; it restructured it in new institutions and the restatement of dogma, not along the lines of Thomas' *Summa*, but in the form of systematic theology. In the controversies that ensued, the 'mysteries of faith' were clearly defined in order to distinguish Catholic and Protestant positions and to protect them from heresy.

Whereas in the Eastern Church, as in the Bible, God still communicated through dreams and visions, an important conviction also in African Christianity to this day, in mainstream Western Christianity God was known through Scripture and tradition, mediated through Word and Sacraments. Mystery certainly pervaded the Catholic sanctuary, liturgy, and piety, but it sometimes bordered on superstition and was carefully monitored and controlled where possible. The Reformers, bound by the teaching of Scripture, proclaimed the mystery of salvation and even predestination, but in doing so largely dispelled the mystery *as mystery*. In a rare, but not entirely uncharacteristic aside in John Calvin's writings, the Genevan reformer says in passing that, while he does not fully comprehend the Eucharist, he adores the mystery.[52] But on the whole, polemics required more logical precision. The mystery had to be explained in propositions rather than left to the vagaries of

---

51 Thomas Aquinas, *Summa Theologiae: A Concise Translation*, Timothy McDermott, Westminster, ML: Christian Classics, 1989, p. 3.

52 In a letter to the reformer Peter Martyr Vermigli, quoted in B. A. Gerrish, *Grace & Gratitude: The Eucharistic Theology of John Calvin*, Edinburgh: T&T Clark, 1993, p. 128.

experience, and biblical hermeneutics became a humanist exercise that sought clarity, eschewing allegory and mystical interpretation.

With the rise of Renaissance humanism and the development of empirical science, critical forces were let loose within Church and culture that began to undermine established religious authority on the basis of reason, just as it led to the disenchantment of nature and so of magic. By the seventeenth century, as the age of the European Enlightenment was dawning, the notion of mystery was increasingly considered dangerous to both science and religion.[53] Critical thinking replaced myth-making. Reason no longer lagged behind experience; it set the pace and determined the direction. The concept of God had to be reasonable and made as agreeable as possible so that it was beyond question. The recourse to mystery, instead of the logic and language of reason, was sure to lead to atheism or back to the Dark Ages with its superstitions, and dream worlds of fantasy and fairy tales.[54] The separation of body and soul as two distinct realms, most significantly propounded by the seventeenth-century French philosopher and mathematician René Descartes who, ironically, was brought to his conclusions in a dream, became fundamental to what would later be named 'modernity'.

In reaction to such rationalism and the dualism that separated mind and matter, soul and body, the Romantic Movement of the late eighteenth and early nineteenth century sought to recover the language of the imagination, of feeling and intuition, of personal experience and mysticism, of aesthetic sensibility. Poets and artists from Johann Wolfgang Goethe in Germany to John Keats, Samuel Taylor Coleridge and William Turner in England helped recover the sense of mystery within the real that had previously captivated the early Middle Ages. Nature was freshly imbued with divinity, a mysterious vital force or spirit that was active within it. Humanity and nature were organically connected as manifestations of a universal whole which was, in turn, experienced in its totality

---

53   See Peter Gay, *The Enlightenment: An Interpretation*, volume 1: *The Rise of Modern Paganism*, London: Wildwood House, 1973.

54   See Karen Armstrong, *The Case for God*, London: The Bodley Head, 2009, p. 201.

through aesthetic awareness and artistic expression. Skepticism about rationalism and science led to the affirmation of beauty as the touchstone of truth, and experience of life became the pathway to its discovery.

In his 'Ode on a Grecian Urn', Keats concluded that all we need to know on earth is that 'Beauty is truth, truth beauty'.[55] Contemplating the urn it is easy to grasp the beauty it depicts: sweet melody, love and ecstasy, fair maidens and youths in pursuit of embrace. A purely aesthetic reading of these words might end up denying truth at the expense of beauty. I am not sure whether Keats meant that to be the case, but the truth is surely conveyed in paradox. The beauty depicted on the urn's images, real as it is, does not endure. The inevitable sorrowful end is, in embryo, in the present lived experience, as it was for Keats himself, who died so young not long after he wrote the poem. But perhaps Keats sensed that the beauty depicted on his urn reflected something more lasting. Not the fading beauty of youth, but the lasting beauty of a relationship that endures heart-break and suffering; of human piety and devotion, which reflect a transcendent mystery. Keats awakens theological imagination and helps us to speak of the mystery of lasting beauty as never at odds with either truth or goodness, for only that which is true and good can be beautiful.

This move away from 'cold philosophy' as Keats put it, along with orthodox and more especially rationalist religion, to the primacy of the aesthetic, important as it was as a necessary reaction, nevertheless struggled to come to terms with the harsher realities of life to which its exponents were no strangers. Nowhere is this more evident than in Wordsworth's incomparable *Ode to Immortality*, where he engages the ravages of growing old and approaching death. Recalling his early years wandering in the hills above Grasmere in the English Lake District, he writes of a time when

---

55   John Keats, 'Ode on a Grecian Urn', in *The Norton Anthology of Poetry*, edited by Margaret Ferguson, Mary Jo Salter and Jon Stallworthy, fourth edition, New York; W. W. Norton, 1970, p. 849.

. . . meadow, grove, and stream,
The earth, and every common sight,
To me did seem
Apparelled in celestial light,
The glory and the freshness of a dream.

But, then, in his older years he wistfully continues:

It is not now as it has been of yore;
Turn wheresoe'er I may,
By night or day,
The things which I have seen I now can see no more.

The poem, too long to include here in full, continues as Wordsworth explores his journey through joy and sorrow, plotting
each stage along the way from childhood to old age, rejoicing in
the voices of children and the beauty of nature.

Of splendour in the grass, of glory in the flower;
We will grieve not, rather find
Strength in what remains behind,
In the primal sympathy
Which having been must ever be,
In the soothing thoughts that spring
Out of human suffering,
In the faith that looks through death,
In years that bring the philosophic mind.
. . . .
Another race hath been, and other palms are won.
Thanks to the human heart by which we live,
Thanks to its tenderness, its joys, and fears,
To me the meanest flower that blows can give
Thoughts that do often lie too deep for tears.[56]

---

56 William Wordsworth, 'Intimations of Immortality from Recollections
of Early Childhood', *Norton Anthology of Poetry*, pp. 728–32.

As we grow older, many of us can identify with Wordsworth's sense of loss, the passing of the freshness of childhood and youth, or falling in love. Looking back, everything now seems different from then, before time robbed us of our dreams, dampened our enthusiasm for life and made us a little cynical. Perhaps it wasn't quite as rosy as we think it was, and certainly wasn't for the vast majority of the poor and disinherited, and in all probability back then we would have expressed hopes for a brighter future. But we are now at a different point in our life's journey marked by achievements and memories, marred by disappointments, mistakes made, expectations unfulfilled and sudden tragedy. It is such thoughts, deeper than any tears, that haunted and perplexed me in the days and nights following Steve's death – the swift passing of time, the inevitability of death, the 'faith that looks through death' and the struggle to 'find strength in what remains behind'. This, too, is the language that perhaps unexpectedly led me into mystery, and continues to do so. Not the discursive language of reason as important as it is, but the language of the heart. Yet, suffering and death did lead this older and wiser Wordsworth to recognize the need for the 'philosophic mind' to ponder the thoughts that lay 'too deep for tears'. The heart cannot function adequately without the mind to guide and shape experience, nor can faith be reduced to intuitive feelings. Romanticism does not have the last word, but its protest and passion remain pertinent at each stage in our journey into mystery whether in life or in the ages that follow.

Flannery O'Connor tells us that the great novelist is engaged 'with all those concrete details of life that make actual the mystery of our position on earth'.[57] She goes on to say that 'such novelists find at its depths the image of its source, the image of ultimate reality'.[58] Two of the greatest to whom I frequently refer, are Fyodor Dostoevsky, to whom I will return in Chapter 3 in discussing Christian faith in God, and George Eliot to whom I now turn.

---

57 O'Connor, *Mystery and Manners*, p. 68.
58 O'Connor, *Mystery and Manners*, p. 157.

The mystery beneath the real

Born Mary Anne Evans in 1819, and living much of her life in Victorian England, when not travelling abroad in Europe, Eliot's contribution to English literature, women's emancipation, and theological translation was remarkable.[59] Like many others, I was hooked when I first read *Middlemarch* many years ago, arguably the greatest novel in English literature. But, as my starting point, let me go back to her first novel which was written on the cusp of Eliot's shift from her youthful evangelicalism to Romantic realism.

In *Adam Bede*, set in the heyday of Methodism in England, Eliot describes how 23 year-old Seth falls deeply in love with Dinah, an ardent itinerant preacher. After one of her heartfelt sermons, Seth, speaking about the 'mystery of marriage',[60] proposes to her but Dinah refuses his overture. Eliot comments:

> Love of this sort is hardly distinguishable from religious feeling. What deep and worthy love is so, whether of woman or child or art or music. Our caresses, our tender words, our still rapture under the influence of autumn sunsets, or pillared vistas, or calm majestic statues, or Beethoven symphonies all bring with them the consciousness that they are mere waves and ripples in an unfathomable ocean of love and beauty; our emotion in its keenest moment passes from expression into silence, our love at its highest flood rushes beyond its object and loses itself in the sense of divine mystery.[61]

This evocative passage, typical of the full-flowering of the Romantic Movement, expresses Eliot's response to the mystery of love and beauty in relation to the 'divine mystery' which, at this early

---

59 Apart from her own writings, see especially Peter C. Hodgson, *Theology in the Fiction of George Eliot*, London: SCM, 2001. The major biography I have consulted is Gordon Haight, *George Eliot: A Biography*, New York, NY: Penguin, 1985.

60 George Eliot, *Adam Bede*, New York, NY: New American Library, 1961, p. 44.

61 Eliot, *Adam Bede*, p. 47.

stage in her literary career was a daily reality in her experience. Eliot, as intimated, soon moved beyond her early evangelical piety and orthodox Christianity, but she never lost her religious sensibility, nor this sense of the mystery of love and beauty which she equated with the divine.[62]

Eliot's earlier Romanticism was soon chastened by experience, by a growing sense of social injustice, by an intense dislike of religious intolerance and hypocrisy, in short, by reality as she observed and experienced it. This is evident in *Daniel Deronda*, where her knowledge of Judaism and its mystical tradition comes to the fore along with her sense of injustice caused by anti-Semitism in England. It is equally apparent in her historical novel *Romola*, set in Savonarola's fifteenth-century Florence, which reflects both her striving for a genuine spirituality of love and compassion and her struggle against the abuses of religion and the intolerant bigotries of ideologically driven reformers. Towards the end of the novel, Savonarola insists: '"The cause of my party *is* the cause of God's kingdom." "I do not believe it" said Romola, her whole frame shaken with passionate repugnance.' Then she utters words which sum up her mature religious sentiment: 'God's kingdom is something wider – else, let me stand outside it with the beings that I love.'[63]

One of those beings to whom she was attracted was the German biblical scholar David Friedrich Strauss, whom she befriended on one of her many visits to Germany. This led to her becoming the translator of Strauss' eight-hundred-page study of the New Testament entitled *The Life of Jesus Critically Examined*.[64] The task took her two years. Strauss argued that the supernatural aspects of the gospel story were myth rather than history. This did not necessarily mean the end of faith in God or the significance of

---

62 There are different readings of Eliot's religious sensibility. See A. N. Wilson's essay 'George Eliot, the Word and the Lives of Jesus', in A. N. Wilson, *God's Funeral*, London: Abacus, 2000, pp. 160–94.

63 George Eliot, *Romola*, London: Penguin, 1996, p. 493.

64 Published in four editions between 1831–40. Eliot translated the fourth edition. David Friedrich Strauss, *The Life of Jesus Critically Examined*, Lives of Jesus Series, edited by Leander E. Keck, Philadelphia: Fortress, 1972.

Jesus, but it did require a radical deconstruction and then reconstruction of Christianity. Theologians and preachers who were
unwilling or unprepared to make this decisive shift could only do
so if they closed their minds to the truth, in which case they would
have to deal with their own hypocrisy. But the honest thing to
do, Strauss insisted, was either to recast their faith on an entirely
different basis, or to leave the church. Described as an 'alienated theologian', Strauss eventually embraced 'the flat bourgeois
materialism he earlier recognized as the deadly enemy of true religion'.[65] But his influence was immense, making him probably the
most 'famous theologian in Germany' in his time; certainly the
most infamous and the least likely to find a position 'in the church
or in the academic world'.[66] The reason for this was his claim that
much of the story of Jesus as told in the Gospels could not stand
the test of historical criticism, and so could not be taken literally
as 'fact'. The miracle stories and above all the resurrection narratives were myth, not historically true, and should be discarded. In
short, Strauss removed everything from the gospels which made
Jesus more than human, and so expunged the mystery of the
Incarnation from the centre of the Christian creed.

Eliot's translation of Strauss' *Life of Jesus* contributed greatly
to the spreading of his influence across the Anglo-Saxon world,
and his legacy remains even though the debate has moved on.[67]
Certainly, the question which prompted my own enquiry in this
book owes much to his detailed examination of the resurrection
narratives and the controversy this has generated over the past
century and a half. But despite the time and energy Eliot gave
to the translation project, she eventually became disillusioned by
Strauss' rationalism. For her, his treatment missed the point of
the gospel narrative. As she told friends, Strauss' book 'made her

---

65   Peter Hodgson, editor's Introduction, Strauss, *Life of Jesus*, p. xvi.
66   Karl Barth, *Protestant Theology in the Nineteenth Century*, London:
SCM, 1972, p. 541.
67   See Stephen Neill, *The Interpretation of the New Testament, 1891–
1961*, Oxford: Oxford University Press, 1964, pp. 16–19.

ill dissecting the beautiful story of the crucifixion',[68] and there were sections from which she recoiled.[69] She could only endure her mammoth task because she glanced, from time to time, at an engraving of Christ on her study wall and a small copy of Bertel Thorwaldsen's now famous sculpture of the *Risen Christ* standing nearby.[70] For her, the truth was in the story, not just illustrated by it as in the case of an allegory. She well knew, what modern literary studies teach, that the rationalist reduction of narrative eventually leads to meaninglessness. Meaning is not *illustrated* but *constituted*, Hans Frei tells us, 'through the mutual, specific determination of agents, speech, social context, and circumstances that form the indispensable narrative web'.[71] But I think Eliot also sensed something more profound, namely an assault on the aesthetic, not in the shallow sense of aestheticism, but in that of the infinite beauty that is true and good and gives meaning to life.[72]

The second German volume that Eliot translated was Ludwig Feuerbach's *The Essence of Christianity* first published in 1854.[73] The fact that Barth wrote an Introductory Essay to the republication of the book in 1957 indicates its stature even after a century. Barth applauds Feuerbach as a great philosopher who understood the issues and problems of theology better than most others of his day. But by insisting that God is a human projection, and reworking Christianity on that basis, Feuerbach negated all theology.[74] *'Man has his highest being, his God, in himself;'* Feuerbach wrote,

68   This was reported by one of her close friends, Mrs Charles Gray in writing to another, Sara Sopie Hennell, on 14 February 1846. *The George Eliot Letters*, vol. 1, edited by Gordon S. Haight, London: Oxford University Press, 1954, p. 206.

69   In a letter to Sara Hennell, 4 March 1846, *Letters*, p. 207.

70   Completed in 1821 for the Church of Our Lady, Copenhagen.

71   Hans Frei, *The Eclipse of Biblical Narrative: A Study in Eighteenth and Nineteenth Century Hermeneutics*, New Haven, CT: Yale University Press, 1974, p. 280.

72   See David Bentley Hart, *The Beauty of the Infinite*, Grand Rapids: Eerdmans, 2003, pp. 24ff.

73   Ludwig Feuerbach, *The Essence of Christianity*, New York, NY: Harper & Row, 1957.

74   Karl Barth, 'An Introductory Essay', in Feuerbach, *The Essence of Christianity*, pp. x–xi.

'not in himself as an individual, but in his essential nature, his species . . . The yearning of man for something above himself is nothing else than the longing after the perfect type of his nature'.[75] Thus anthropology becomes '*the mystery of Christian theology*' and the grand result of the history of Christianity is 'the unveiling of this mystery'.[76]

It must be said that Barth, who had so emphasized the transcendence of God in his early theology, eventually came to speak about the 'humanity of God' in a way that took seriously Feuerbach's challenge, but without turning theology into anthropology.[77] This contributed to my own interest in the Christian humanist tradition, which I suspect might well have attracted Eliot, if it had been an available option. In fact, in his preface to the same edition of *The Essence of Christianity*, another twentieth-century theologian, Reinhold Niebuhr, wrote that Eliot 'sought to retain the ethos of Christianity without its faith, its humanism without its theism, its hope for man without its hope for the sovereignty of God'.[78] This is problematic, for how can you retain the ethos of Christianity without its faith or hope in God? Yet, there is a kinship between Eliot and what is now described as theological humanism.[79] For the humanist vision makes a turn towards the theological when it becomes aware of transcendence within reality, not apart from its materiality but also not equated with it. I will develop this further in Chapter 3, when I discuss Christian humanism and mystery.

Eliot read Darwin's *Origin of the Species* when it first appeared and was well acquainted with the challenge it presented to religious convictions. She had little difficulty in embracing the empirical findings of natural science and would have relished the advances of neuroscience. But, commenting on Darwin's work,

---

75 Feuerbach, *The Essence of Christianity*, p. 281. Italics in the original.

76 Feuerbach, *The Essence of Christianity*, p. 336. Italics in the original.

77 Karl Barth, *The Humanity of God*, London: Collins, 1961, pp. 37–65.

78 Reinhold Niebuhr, 'Foreword', in Feuerbach, *The Essence of Christianity*, p. ix.

79 See William Schweiker, *Dust That Breathes: Christian Faith and the New Humanism*, Chichester: Wiley-Blackwell, 2010.

she wrote in a letter: 'To me the Development theory and other explanations of processes by which things came to be, produce a feeble impression compared with the mystery that lies under the processes.'[80] The outcomes of creative imagination cannot be equated with the process by which they come into being. Such comments lead Hodgson to maintain that Eliot remained a deeply religious thinker throughout her life, and to suggest that her religious vision is relevant to contemporary theological and religious reconstruction on 'whether and how it is possible to speak meaningfully of the presence and action of God (or of the Divine Mystery) in the world today'. Eliot's, says Hodgson, 'was an agonistic, apophatic faith, which kept the reality of God in suspense even as it affirmed the reality of duty and love'.[81] For her 'the idea of God or divinity is not an illusion arising out of psychological needs but a response to something awesome, mysterious, and overwhelming that presents itself in experience and demands reverence'.[82] Yet, this mystery is manifest in the world and is evident in the intellectual, sensuous and material realms of reality. What the novelist sees are the fragments of the mystery, tracking, as she does their 'patterns, connections, movements', and 'seeking therein traces of the whole, the mystery beneath the real'.[83]

But how do we know that it is truly the mystery of *God*? How do we know 'that the mystery beneath the real is not simply the sheer meaninglessness and absurdity of a purposeless universe'?[84] Is it not mere projection, as Feuerbach argued in his psychological interpretation of religion? Or is it, as others insist, a response to some transcendent reality 'that engenders a transformation from self-centredness to reality-centredness'?[85] For Eliot, it is, I suggest,

---

80   Letter to Barbara Bodichon, 5 December 1859 in *Letters* 3:227, quoted in Hodgson, *Theology in the Fiction of George Eliot*, p. 20.

81   Hodgson, *Theology in the Fiction of George Eliot*, p. 2. By 'apophatic' is meant the 'path of unknowing', that is, the negation of all our concepts of God in order to affirm that God is beyond all that exists, beyond all our concepts.

82   Hodgson, *Theology in the Fiction of George Eliot*, p. 8.

83   Hodgson, *Theology in the Fiction of George Eliot*, pp. 146–7.

84   Hodgson, *Theology in the Fiction of George Eliot*, p. 159.

85   Hodgson, *Theology in the Fiction of George Eliot*, p. 159.

the latter, demonstrated in the quality of her response to reality that goes well beyond self-centredness in its embrace of the other and its concern for justice. That is why the suffering of Jesus in solidarity with the 'other' (a central theme of Chapter 2) reveals the mystery we call God, the reason why Eliot took such exception to the way in which Strauss dealt with the crucifixion. The symbol 'God' might be the work of human imagination and best expressed in myth and poetry, but this does not reduce God as ultimate mystery to an illusion.[86]

I have been listening for echoes of mystery in an assortment of texts, seeking clues of its presence in lived experience and searching for a language to express the inexpressible. As yet, I have not turned to the Bible to do so, which may seem odd for a Christian theologian who, many might think with good reason, should start and possibly end there. But I am mindful of Steiner's remarkable claim that 'any coherent understanding of what language is and how language performs . . . any coherent account of the capacity of human speech to communicate meaning and feeling is, in the final analysis, underwritten by the assumption of God's presence'.[87] This is a remarkable statement which, if true as I believe it is, gives added reason for what I have attempted in this chapter. Rahner makes the same point differently in describing theology which, he tells us, is 'that human activity in which human beings, even at the level of conscious thought, relate the multiplicity of the realities, experiences, and ideas in their lives to that mystery, ineffable and obscure, which we call God'.[88] The reality to which language points is the substance of theology, and it is this that gives the Bible its distinctive character.

In Chapter 2, I will pursue this theme further, but in making the transition from literature in general to the Bible in particular I

86 See Hodgson, *Theology in the Fiction of George Eliot*, pp. 223–4, and fn. 23.

87 Steiner, *Real Presences*, p. 3.

88 'Reflections on Methodology in Theology', originally published in *Theological Investigations*, vol. 11, 1974. Reprinted in *Karl Rahner*, in *The Making of Modern Theology*, ed. Geffrey B. Kelly, Minneapolis: Fortress, 1992, p. 337.

am obviously changing gears. Nonetheless, the conversation that I have begun in this first chapter continues, because the Bible is itself a site of dialogue that has engaged many people over centuries around the same issues that I have been exploring to this point. Now, however, it continues specifically from the perspective of faith in the God who, it is claimed, is disclosed the biblical narrative. It is this perspective that gives this very complex book of many books its coherence, though let it be understood immediately that not all who read it understand and interpret it in the same way. My claim, as I turn the page from this chapter into the 'strange new world within the Bible',[89] is that its ongoing conversation is, in the end, all about the mystery we name God, and the way this God relates to the world of human experience in all its facets, including our hopes and fears about life and death.

---

89   Karl Barth, *The Word of God and the Word of Man*, New York: Harper & Brothers, pp. 28–50.

2

Walking Through the Door

Let us not mock God with metaphor,
Analogy, sidestepping, transcendence;
Making of the event a parable, a sign painted in the
Faded credulity of earlier ages:
Let us walk through the door.
John Updike[1]

When peaceful silence lay over all,
and night had run the half of her swift course,
down from the heavens, from the royal throne,
leapt your all powerful Word.
Wisdom 18.14 JB

The reality of God is disclosed only as it places me completely into
the reality of the world. But I find the reality of the world always
already borne, accepted, and reconciled in the reality of God. That
is the mystery of the revelation of God in the human being Jesus
Christ.
Dietrich Bonhoeffer[2]

I have set before you an open door,
which no one is able to shut.
Revelation 3.8

By happy coincidence, Isobel and I, together with our son Anton and his wife Esther, were in Santa Fe, New Mexico, on the day in November 2011 when Donald Jackson, the renowned British calligrapher and illuminator, was scheduled to give a public lecture on the *St. John's Bible*. Named after St. John's Abbey in Minnesota, where it was commissioned, it is the first handwritten illuminated Bible produced since the invention of the printing press, and

---

1 John Updike, 'Seven Stanzas at Easter', in *Telephone Poles and Other Poems*, New York: Alfred A. Knopf, 1964, p. 72.
2 Dietrich Bonhoeffer, *Ethics*, Dietrich Bonhoeffer Works, vol. 6, Minneapolis: Fortress, 2005, p. 55.

one of the most remarkable artistic, cultural and spiritual achievements of the New Millennium. A few days earlier, we had seen
two volumes of reproductions of the Bible, when visiting friends
in North Carolina, and viewed a DVD about its making. We were
also able to see an exhibition of some of the original manuscripts
in the Santa Fe Museum. But now we heard Jackson in person
telling how the biblical text had inspired him as an artist. He was
not a religious person, he told us, but working daily on the biblical text over many years had become a spiritual experience. He
described this as being 'encountered by the Word'.

I wondered then as now what the audience, largely drawn from
the world of the arts, made of Jackson's surprising testimony. He
did not elaborate, but his choice of words was clearly intentional.
So what did they mean for him and what sense can we make of
them for ourselves? Was his brain playing tricks, his imagination
running riot, or was his experience an encounter with the mystery we call God who, Jews, Christians and Muslims alike claim,
reveals himself through the Word? And if the latter, what is the
relationship between this Word and the Bible which, traditionally,
Christians label the Word of God? For many, the Bible is a closed-
room mystery, a somewhat strange, antiquated and mystifying
mélange of writings that make little sense in the modern world.
For me, the Bible is, at its core, precisely what Jackson discovered
it to be; a book in and through which we are led into mystery
or, as he put it, encountered by the Word. How this informs my
thinking about the questions raised by Steve's death is the substance
of what follows.

The Great Code

The distinguished literary critic Northrop Frye once described the
Bible as the 'great code'[3] that has provided the language – myths,
metaphors and typologies – that has indelibly shaped Western
culture and beyond, whether people believe its claims or not. In

---

3 Northrop Frye, *The Great Code: The Bible and Literature*, London:
Routledge & Kegan Paul, 1982.

similar fashion, Marilynn Robinson has observed that the 'Bible is the model for and subject of more art and thought than those of us who live within its influence consciously or unconsciously, will ever know'.[4] She refers in particular to the work of several great novelists of the past, Dostoyevsky, Melville and Faulkner among them, who drank deeply from the wells of the biblical narrative to probe the deepest human questions. They did not simply draw on biblical allegories, symbolism and metaphors by way of illustration, 'sidestepping transcendence', as Updike put it, but entered the world of the narratives as they told their own. This was part of the memory treasure trove that fed their imagination and feeds mine in turn.

The Word that encounters us in the Bible, so Christians believe, is not communicated through metaphysical discourse, but in a host of stories connecting 'the primordial quarrel of two brothers in a field to supper with a stranger at Emmaus'.[5] The irony in these somewhat disjointed and often disturbing biblical narratives, now inseparably bound between the same cover as one book, is that their witness to mystery is often veiled in insignificance. 'Moments of the highest import pass among people who are so marginal that conventional history would not have noticed them: aliens, the enslaved, people themselves utterly unaware that their lives could have consequence.'[6] Mystery is disclosed amid the ways of the world, not in the ideal one we hanker after. It is hidden in marginal events, ambiguous sayings and contradictions, in the lives of obscure and sometimes unkempt prophets, of aged sages, tragic and fallible heroes and heroines, and of heart-broken people talking with a stranger about the death of a friend that shattered hopes as they shared a meal. But this is the nature of mystery: its disclosure is always veiled within the ordinary.

Despite this irony, for multitudes over the centuries, whether learned or simple, the Bible has been far more than a religious book to be read in church or during private devotions, a book

---

4   Marilynne Robinson, 'The Book of Books', *New York Times* 25 December 2011. Book Review section, p. 10.
5   Robinson, 'The Book of Books'.
6   Robinson, 'The Book of Books'.

designed to be read as literature, prove some doctrinal point, provide liturgical guidance, or convey some moral truth. The Bible has been the code breaker that unlocks the door into the closed room of human existence enabling us to enter or, to change the metaphor, a window filtering light into a dark room even if the glass is sometimes opaque. This does not mean that there are no other windows through which the light may come, whether sacred texts, scientific discoveries, other people, or the natural world that surrounds us. Some contemporary cosmologists and quantum physicists describe their endeavours and experiences in ways that resonate with Jackson's testimony, as do people of other faith traditions.

The Word is, before anything else, a deed or action that can interpret itself as happens when we express love or compassion by what we do. That is why the Bible and the rest of us are sceptical about words that promise much but deliver little. So when the Bible or Christian faith speaks about the Word it is primarily referring to the Word as deed in disclosing mystery. Yet, for Christians, such experiences are seldom understood as something other than hearing the Word that speaks through or is confirmed by the words of Scripture. Neither scholarly exegesis nor faith is a precondition for such an encounter; faith often comes in the process of hearing or being 'encountered by the Word'. But the biblical text provides the language and symbolic form to express and communicate the experience. In the process, ordinary words and images are given new significance. They convey the truth and substance of what is believed. In reading the Bible, we become part of an ongoing conversation with those who originally wrote it. We hear the same Word they experienced as deed and communicated through words, though sometimes differently. And we engage in dialogue with them as we try to understand our own experience, and seek answers to the questions we now ask. My conversation with Steve cannot by-pass the biblical text if for no other reasons than the fact that it has shaped our shared perceptions of reality.

But is it really still possible, as Christians do, to speak of the Bible as inspired by the Spirit and as witness to 'the Word of God', or like Jackson, claim that one has been encountered by the

Word in and through its pages? Amid the cacophony of words that invade our lives, within the confusing texts of our secular and sacred books, or the apparent certainties of scientific essays, is there a Word that speaks to our condition through the biblical text? Even the question itself has become rare, especially in secularized Western culture, despite the historic role of 'the great code'. Certainly there are prophets and sages among us, as there are inspired artists of every genre, but their voice is no longer heard as the 'Word of God' except in the conventicles of believers where prophecy has, in any case, taken on a different 'spiritualized' meaning or speaks only about coming apocalyptic end times. There is no lack of words about God, no lack of sermons and general religious rhetoric, but too little listening for the Word or expectation that the Word will break the silence and encounter us in a life- and world-transforming way. We live in an historical and cultural period that Steiner describes as the 'After-Word' or the Epilogue.[7]

But why is this so? Why is it that today for many people whose roots are in the Christian tradition the Bible has become a closed book? Why has ignorance of the biblical text and its narratives become a cause for jest or boasting within segments of post-Christian society rather than a sign of woeful lack of cultural knowledge if not spiritual wisdom? One major reason has undoubtedly been the disenchantment of the world that has occurred through the endeavours of modern science and, concomitantly, the burial of the Bible beneath the weight of biblical criticism. We live, so we are often told, in a world where for many, though not all, rationality has replaced creative imagination and science has silenced the Word. There is no need to listen for the Spirit-inspired Word which now carries, so it is assumed, no more authority than the Wizard of Oz. So it comes as something of a surprise that someone avowedly secular claims to have been encountered by the Word within the pages of the Bible. What are we to make of this?

---

7 George Steiner, *Real Presences*, Chicago: Chicago University Press, 1991, p. 94.

The Word becomes Deed

In the Genesis creation myth God breaks the silence that envelops the galaxies by fashioning planet Earth through his Word, and breathes life through his Spirit into all creatures made of the dust. In this act the Word becomes creative Deed: 'And God said', is the constant refrain that describes how day and night, along with all forms of life, come into being. Yet, throughout the biblical narrative that follows there is a perplexing sense of God's silence when humans try to discern who God is, what God is doing, or intends to do. 'Truly, you are a God who hides himself', exclaims the prophet (Isa. 45.15) as he ponders the events of history in search of meaning and purpose. Jeremiah, who experienced God's absence most intensely of all the prophets, spoke and acted out of his own painful experience to a nation in danger: 'while you look for light, God turns it into gloom and makes it deep darkness' (13.16). This sense of cosmic darkness and divine absence is poignantly expressed in the book of Job as it is on virtually every page of the Psalms, reaching its nadir in the soul-wrenching lament: 'why do you hide your face from me? . . . now darkness is my one companion left' (Psalm 88.14, 18 JB). The Psalms were on Jesus' lips as he died on the cross and uttered his cry of dereliction as darkness covered the earth (Psalm 22; Matthew 27.45–6).

The questions posed by suffering and death are precisely those that raise doubts in the minds of all believers, and those who would be in their company. If there is a God, why is God silent, why does God not do something, when we desperately need some word of guidance and affirmation, some intimation of divine presence? Such questions abound in the pages of the Bible. Is there any Word from the Lord? Why does God not break his silence, rend the heavens and disclose himself in our world of experience as at creation's dawn, when the Spirit breathed on the waters and God said 'Let there be light', and there *was* light? Yet woven into the biblical narrative is the recurring 'nevertheless' of faith, hope and love, sometimes expressed haltingly, but often with the conviction that the Word of God's grace does break into human consciousness whether through our own experience or the words of prophet and sage alike, inviting us to enter through an open door into the mystery it seeks to unveil.

When the ancient Hebrew prophets were called to proclaim 'the Word of the Lord' they often complained that they did not have the words, they were too inexperienced, ill-equipped or sinful, and the task laid on them was an unbearable burden. Yet, they could not keep silent or refrain from acting. Jeremiah's cry says it all: 'If I say, "I will not mention him, or speak any more in his name," then within me there is something like a burning fire shut up in my bones; I am weary with holding it in, and I cannot.' (20.9). Not all the prophets experienced the same intensity of anguish, or troubled uncertainty as Jeremiah. But they knew that to claim to speak the 'Word of God' was generally regarded as a sign that you were mad, deluded, vain, or all three, and an invitation to persecution. After all, the Word was invariably one of judgment and demand before it became that of redemption and hope. Through the Spirit, God called prophets to speak truth to the powerful, as well as liberation and comfort to the oppressed. Deeply burdened by injustice, greed and human cruelty, their prophecy became the voice God gave to the silenced poor and oppressed. And in this way, too, the Word became embodied in action.

The words of the prophets are not the outcome of genius, but the imaginative demonstration and construction of faith discerning the Word that comes from beyond themselves in addressing the present moment. They speak out of a faith tradition in which the mystery of this Word has previously been disclosed but too often forgotten, challenging the way in which it has become acculturated and rendered impotent. No one has put it better to my mind than the author and poet Kathleen Norris. 'A prophet's task', she writes, 'is to reveal the fault lines hidden beneath the comfortable surface of the worlds we invent for ourselves, the national myths as well as the little lies and delusions of control and security that get us through the day'.[8] Prophets are, we might say, the enemies of all our self-deluding confabulations, whether

---

8 Kathleen Norris, *The Cloister Walk*, New York, NY: Riverhead Books, 1996, p. 34.

social and political, religious or personal. Artists of every generation and genre can be counted among them, perceiving reality differently from the way of the world, and expressing what they discern driven by an inner compulsion.

There are other mediators of the Word in the biblical tradition who function differently from the prophets but are equally considered inspired by the Spirit. In his lecture that evening in Santa Fe, Jackson told us how he had been particularly struck by the Word that found expression in the Wisdom literature: Psalms, Ecclesiastes, Proverbs and Job. Their forte is practical wisdom as distinct from prophetic proclamation or theoretical knowledge. Much of this wisdom is homely stuff, and much reinforced traditional cultural and religious values. But frequently a pearl of truth is discovered that speaks directly to the human condition, as in the opening words of the book of Ecclesiastes which speaks to the vanity and futility of life, or as in Job's wrestling with the problem of innocent suffering. Whether in riddles or parables, allegories or proverbs, these ancient sages addressed the human condition more obliquely than the prophets and, as if with a surgeon's scalpel, opened heart and mind to discern the mystery beneath the real. Jesus later described them as having the ability to bring out of the treasures of the tradition both 'what is new and what is old' (Matt. 13.52). Jesus, a master-craftsman of this art, often turned conventional wisdom on its head in disclosing the mystery of God's character and way.

The Wisdom literature is complementary to the prophetic, a distinct other voice within the biblical text, another witness to the mystery of the Spirit-filled Word. Its focus is not so much on the pursuit of justice, mercy and peace in anticipation of the coming of God's reign of righteousness, but on the transformation of the self in relation to others amid the daily tasks of life. It reflects what the sages of ancient Israel learned through lived experience and 'discloses to serious discernment something of the hidden character and underpinnings of all reality'.[9] This, no less than the words and

---

9 Walter Brueggemann, *Theology of the Old Testament: Testimony, Dispute, Advocacy*, Minneapolis: Fortress Press, 1997, p. 681.

actions of the prophets, mediates the mystery of God's Word. But instead of the Word breaking into our world from beyond in judgment and promise, it is the revelation of that mysterious One who is 'the generous, demanding guarantor of a viable life-order that can be trusted and counted on, but which cannot be lightly violated'.[10] Both of these Old Testament trajectories, the wisdom and the prophetic, are important for us in seeking to understand the Word of faith to which the Spirit bears testimony in the biblical narrative. Christian faith takes one further dramatic and audacious step, and on this it stands or falls. Nowhere is this more clearly stated than in the majestic prologue to the Fourth Gospel. The Word that was in the beginning, the Word that was with God, the Word that was God, became flesh 'and lived among us full of grace and truth'. This truly human and historical disclosure of the divine mystery is at the same time hidden and revealed, veiled and seen – 'he was in the world' but the world did not know him, his own did not accept him, 'but we have seen his glory' (John 1.1–14). Or as in the opening verses of the first letter of John: 'We declare to you what was from the beginning, what we have heard, what we have seen with our eyes, what we have looked at and touched with our hands, concerning the word of life – this life was revealed, and we have seen it and testify to it . . .' (1–2). Nowhere is the Word as Deed more clearly evident than in the drama of the Word becoming a human being.

The mystery of God embodied in Jesus of Nazareth, the carpenter, is veiled in insignificance and self-emptying (*kenosis*).[11] He is not some timeless truth about God or a new concept of God, but the disclosure of God's redemptive, compassionate love and grace *for* humanity. He is the living Word, who brings life to the world. As such, he is the primary image of Christian imagination, the more remarkable because it is inseparable from an unspeakable crime against humanity honed to cruciform perfection in ancient Rome. But it is in this grotesque event that the supreme revelation

---

10 Brueggemann, *Theology of the Old Testament*, p. 681.
11 See Philippians 2.5–11.

of God is disclosed. This is the mystery of the Incarnation that Denise Levertov probes:

It's when we face for a moment
the worst our kind can do, and shudder to know
the taint in our own selves, that awe
cracks the mind's shell and enters the heart:
not to a flower, not to a dolphin,
to no innocent form
but to this creature vainly sure
it and no other is god-like, God
out of compassion for our ugly
failure to evolve entrusts, as guest, as brother,
the Word.[12]

Faith, history and hermeneutics

In *Being Human*, I shared something of my journey away from a youthful biblical fundamentalism, which briefly claimed my loyalty. The chief prompt was my introduction to the critical study of the Bible, something that often undermines the faith of aspiring and well-seasoned ministers and priests alike, as did Strauss' *The Life of Jesus* for George Eliot's generation, and Rudolf Bultmann's programme of demythologizing the New Testament did for mine.[13] The problems are real and not to be underestimated. They have to do chiefly with the relation between faith and history, and the way in which we interpret the biblical narrative in our own historical context, which scholars refer to as the task of hermeneutics.

Many people reject the Bible as a book of fables, myths and improbable events relating little to historical fact, and they do so because this happens to be true in some measure. Its spiritual

---

12   Denise Levertov, *The Stream & the Sapphire*, New York: New Directions Books, 1997, p. 19.

13   Rudolf Bultmann, *Kerygma and Myth*, New York, NY: Harper & Row, 1961.

value, they insist, also with some justification, is submerged in unsavoury realities, imprecatory Psalms and superstition, and its commands to butcher enemies or stone adulterers (it's in the Bible and not just the Quran) undermines much of what is profoundly true, good and majestic. But biblical revelation occurs in the midst of reality as it is, in the ordinary painful and often unsavoury facts of life, not in some idealized spiritual world that we romantically construct. So while it may be true that biblical criticism has led some away from the testimony of Scripture, in company with many others, I have often been led deeper into the mystery to which it points as a result of these endeavours. This has not come about without a struggle to retain faith, for the challenges to the integrity of the Bible are real, not imagined. The great pioneers of biblical criticism were invariably men (it was a patriarchal club) of piety who, in pursuing their research with painstaking honesty often found themselves unwittingly out on a limb, if not out of a job.

The biblical authors and editors were not scribal puppets of an Almighty and Omniscient being capturing and decoding infallible truths inerrantly off a divine website. They were human beings like the rest of us who drew on a variety of sources in recording the events and telling their stories from the perspective of faith in God. In the process oral tradition became written text, an imaginative mix of myth, saga, history, legend and poetry. This, in turn, was compiled and edited at various stages, its books subjected to a process of canonization or selection, until the Bible as Christians know it in two testaments finally emerged. None of the first disciples of Jesus ever had a copy of the Bible in their hands, and none of the authors or editors involved in the process had the slightest idea that one day their work would be part of the 'Word of God', a 'book' within the 'Book of books' conveniently subdivided into chapter and verse. In time, a multitude of different versions emerged reflecting differences in ancient manuscripts, theological understanding and cultural transmission. Anyone familiar with the history of the translation of the King James or Authorized Version of the Bible, to take but one classic example, will know that whatever its undoubted value, it was the outcome of considerable political manoeuvring and theological debate.[14] Fundamentalists usually ignore this history, whether of the original biblical text or of its many translations, and compound the problem by insisting that we must accept the infallibility and inerrancy of the Bible because the Bible tells us to do so!

One of the first biblical critics was Hermann Reimarus whose *Wolfenbüttel Fragments* on the origins of Christianity and the life of Jesus, published posthumously in 1774–78, created as much stir at the time as did Strauss' *Life of Jesus* 70 years later.[15] Reimarus was deeply influenced by the Enlightenment and its Deist philosophy, which rejected the mysterious elements in Christianity in favour of a natural religion within the limits of reason alone. John Tolland's book *Christianity not Mysterious*, published in 1696, a standard and influential text of the time, played an important role in the process. A devout man, Reimarus ended up living a bifurcated life: publicly, he maintained that natural religion prepared the way for Christianity; privately, he believed that it replaced Christianity. So concerned was he that his views on the New Testament would upset people of his day, undermining their faith, that he kept the manuscript of *Fragments* locked in a drawer in his desk. Only after his death did the philosopher, essayist and playwright Gotthold Ephraim Lessing pluck up the courage to publish it, and, at the same time, provide an alternative point of view to which we will shortly come.

Reimarus' attempt to keep silent for the sake of not offending the faithful is something which many theologians and pastors have sought to do ever since rationalist biblical criticism first challenged faith in the mystery of the Word. To this day, there are attempts within conservative Christian colleges and seminaries to prevent students from studying books critical of the Bible, and those who graduate often seem oblivious of the issues. There are also those ministers and priests who apparently do not struggle with such challenges or, mindful of the dangers, hang on for dear

---

14   Adam Nicolson, *God's Secretaries: the Making of the King James Bible*, New York: Harper Collins, 2003.

15   See the Introduction to Samuel Reimarus, *Fragments*, translated by Ralph S. Fraser, edited by Charles H. Talbert, London: SCM, 1971.

life to their faith, refusing to entertain any ideas that might drive a wedge between their apparent confidence and their insecurity. I don't think in all honesty that there is any alternative but to face up to the challenges, and this book, as the reader already knows, is an attempt to do so at the end of my career as a theologian and pastor confronted by personal tragedy and prompted by Steve's careful watch over my shoulder. Claims of biblical inerrancy and infallibility are of no help to me any more than the few cliché-filled letters were at the time of his death, however well intentioned.

Biblical scholarship has moved a great distance since the days of Reimarus and Strauss. All the criticisms they and their followers have raised have been examined, some accepted, others rejected, amended or honed; and problems remain unsolved as new issues come on the table. But none of the contributions of succeeding generations of scholars would have been possible without the advances made by the pioneers of biblical criticism. As I enter into dialogue with them through the biblical text, I find myself in a world that, while strange in many respects, is as real as my own, and in conversation with people who, like many of us, live in hope often against the odds. But as I have said more than once, the mystery that is revealed in the Bible is hidden in ambiguity and paradox, veiled in insignificance in marginal events, obscure people and the longings of heart-broken people. Just as the self-disclosure of God's mystery is embodied for Christians in the 'Word become a human being', so, too, is the Bible as witness to that Word a truly human and worldly book. To grasp for infallibility, when the key to its witness lies precisely in its humanity through which we discern the mystery of the divine Word, is to miss the point.

But I have jumped the gun. In turning to the Bible as worldly witness to the mystery of the Word, I still have to ask myself in what sense is its testimony credible, and in what way does it help me and others to respond to the questions raised by Steve's death. When all is said and done, I am still left with more questions that derive from my original query which I know Steve would want me to address: is Christian hope not perhaps a confabulation concocted by the first disciples of Jesus to counter their disappointment that he had failed to bring in God's kingdom of justice and peace? Is the resurrection story not a legend constructed within their traumatized brains to handle their despair at Jesus' untimely and tragic death? Were the two on the road to Emmaus not right in believing that their hopes were dashed; was the stranger who met them along the way not a figment of their imagination, and the story itself a myth and therefore false, as popular opinion would have it? In short, if the biblical narrative which tells of God's revelation is not historically true, can it be trustworthy?

This latter question, tinged with anxiety, was put to me by a group of theological students from Stellenbosch University at the time I was writing this section. They knew the history of biblical criticism and had no difficulty in accepting that Moses did not write the Pentateuch or that Jonah was not swallowed by a big fish. But they were less comfortable when biblical criticism raised questions about the veracity of the life and deeds of Jesus, claims that the miracles can be explained without reference to the supernatural and that the Easter narratives are historically suspect. If Christianity were only a philosophy of religion that could exist independently of history, this would not be a problem. But history does matter, if Christians claim that the Bible is a witness to and interpretation of a particular set of events, happenings and deeds and that the gospel narratives are in some sense historical. Christianity not only has a history, nor is it only founded in specific historical events, places and people, but certain historical events, the life and death of Jesus for example, are intrinsic to the Christian faith.[16]

In *What is History*, the historian E. H. Carr makes three observations about history that are pertinent and that Steve, a history major, knew so well. The first is that 'the facts of history never come to us pure, since they do not and cannot exist in a pure form: they are always refracted through the mind of the recorder'. For this reason, we should study the historian before we begin to study what he or she has written.[17] History is not bare facts, but

---

16 Herbert Butterfield, *Christianity and History*, London: Collins Fontana, 1957, p. 156.

17 E. H. Carr, *What is History?*, London: Penguin Books, 1964, pp. 22–3.

an interpretation of the facts. This leads to Carr's second observation, namely that historians need imagination to get into the mind and context of those they write about.[18] Carr's third observation is that 'we can view the past, and achieve our understanding of the past, only through the eyes of the present'.[19] Historians do not write simply to recount what they have found out or imagined happened, but to understand its significance for today. This means that of necessity they have to be selective, and write from a particular perspective as well as for a particular purpose. There is no way that all the events that occurred at a given time can be recalled and recounted, even on one day of the chosen period or one place of the chosen location, any more than the role of every person involved could be described and examined. One of my ancestors, Marshall de Grouchy, was a general in Napoleon's army. Some historians claim he was inadvertently responsible for the defeat of the French at the Battle of Waterloo, others argue differently. Probably the truth will never be known other than that he and his troops arrived too late to make any contribution to the battle. We simply cannot recover the whole story of what happened that fateful day.

The upshot of all this is that just as historical and literary texts cannot be fully and finally validated by historical methods, neither can the Bible.[20] We cannot know the 'verdict of history' on the literary luminaries of the past let alone those of today, because the jury is still out and will be for as long as critics are interested in the subject. Let us not forget how John's Gospel ends: 'There are also many other things that Jesus did; if every one of them were written down, I suppose that the world itself could not contain the books that would be written.' (21.15). John, like the other three evangelists, had to be selective, and he constructed his gospel in a remarkably imaginative way for the sake of those for whom he was writing. The four Gospels are neither biographies nor chiefly historical chronicles; they are the outcome of historical construction

---

18   Carr, *What is History?*, p. 24.
19   Carr, *What is History?*, p. 24.
20   W. G. Kümmel, *The New Testament: The History of the Investigation of its Problems*, London: SCM, 1973, p. 405.

and theological imagination combined. This does not necessarily mean that they are not historical in important respects, for even saga and legend, to say nothing of the traditions with which the evangelists worked, may tell us about real events even if we cannot access them through historical methods. Nor does it mean that revelation cannot occur through their imaginative weaving together of faith, history and tradition, at least not if we believe that imagination is open to the Spirit's creative prompting.

Hermeneutics, the attempt to read texts in a way that speaks to us today, is not a denial of the historicity of the events to which they refer, but neither is it dependent on the total historical verifiability of its testimony. Hermeneutics, we might say, is the theological imagination at work as it engages both the biblical text and the historical context in which we now live in order to discern the Word for us today. We are seeking something beyond what Richard Palmer calls the 'bogus objectivity of the theoretical and scientific' that requires no self-engagement or self-understanding to grasp their significance. 'We are searching', he says, 'for the historical in the plea for "personal knowledge," in the impatience with science's frantic search for origins, causal grounds, neurological antecedents, and in the plea for a return to the richness and complexity of concrete awareness in interpreting literature'.[21] We are also seeking ways whereby the truth of the Word can again become deeds in our own time, for hermeneutics is not about translation but transformation.

Broadly speaking there are three possibilities in relating faith and history. The first is that faith is contingent on historical fact as both Reimarus and Strauss argued, and as do more conservative scholars on the other side of the equation. If this is the case, then the moment historians demonstrate with cogency that some of the events in the Bible are historically implausible, faith comes under threat. Then the claims we make about Jesus cannot be true either, or are at the least shaky. His teaching may be practical

21   Richard E. Palmer, *Hermeneutics: Interpretation Theory in Schleiermacher, Dilthey, Heidegger, and Gadamer*, Evanston, IL: Northwestern University Press, 1980, p. 253.

and profound, evoking deep religious feeling and insight, but the stories, even if they have some historical basis, are largely later constructions of the evangelists. It is for this reason that some fundamentalist Christians spend a fortune trying to discover the location and remains of Noah's Ark and similar endeavours.

The second possibility is a riposte to the first. The truth of Christianity is not dependent on historical verifiability, but is one of several expressions of the religious consciousness to be found in all human beings. Lessing, who was responsible for publishing Reimarus' *Fragments*, was among the first to offer an alternative not based on historical fact. Arguing that if 'no historical truth can be demonstrated, then nothing can be demonstrated by means of historical truths'. This meant, he continued, that 'accidental truths of history can never become the proof of necessary truths of reason'.[22] Christianity for Lessing was a version of natural religion rather than one based on historical revelation, and its verification could only be tested at the end of time.

There is a third possibility. While the origins of Christianity occur in history, and while history is important for understanding Christian faith and helping to substantiate its truth claims, historical research cannot get at *all* the facts of the past as they actually happened. This does not make them less historical because this is true of all history, not just that recorded in the Bible. The biblical text like all great literature is not 'the clean, clear world of scientific concepts' but that 'of conflict, ambiguity, and suffering in which we live our daily lives'.[23] Such lived experience is historical in its structure and can certainly be examined historically, but it cannot be reduced to historical verification. At some point a reasonable judgment of faith is required.

It was this necessity that led Ludwig Wittgenstein, the Viennese and Cambridge philosopher, to insist that 'Christianity is not based on a historical truth; rather, it offers us a (historical) narrative and says: now believe!' In the end, when the historians have

---

22 *Lessing's Theological Writings*, edited by Henry Chadwick, London: A & C Black, 1957, p. 18.
23 Palmer, *Hermeneutics*, p. 253.

completed (if ever) their work, it is a matter of faith. This faith, Wittgenstein went on to say, is not 'the belief appropriate to a historical narrative' but believing 'through thick and thin, which you can only do as the result of a life'.[24] In other words, faith is a trusting and hopeful commitment, and while reasonable, it is beyond rational proof. Faith, as Paul insisted, comes from hearing the Word, not through argument (Rom. 10.17), though good arguments certainly help to clarify what is believed.

Having said this, it can nevertheless be argued that the biblical interpretation of history correlates in significant ways with the data of history as described by the historian. There is a 'compatibility or correlation of history as experienced and comprehended with history as interpreted in Scripture'.[25] The Bible may not always be historically accurate, but it is historically realistic. This is the way the world is; this is human nature. Mystery is hidden in the ordinary; the divine is incarnate in the human. The Bible's reference to the transcendent does not alter the fact that its diagnosis of ills and its prognosis of the way forward is reality-centred, albeit embodied in stories or myths, legends and sagas. But whereas for early Christian writers and, indeed, for Christians through the centuries up until more recent times, history and myth, legend or saga were placed on the same time line, we can no longer do this.[26] We must, as Barth insisted, abandon the idea 'that the Bible declares the Word of God only when it speaks historically'.[27] If we discard saga we not only lose a subsidiary theme but the main point: the biblical witness.

---

24 Ludwig Wittgenstein, *Culture and Value*, translated by Peter Winch, edited by G. H. von Wright, Oxford: Basil Blackwell, 1980, p. 32c.

25 Langdon Gilkey, 'Scripture, History and the Quest for Meaning', in *History and Historical Understanding*, edited by C. T. McIntire and Ronald A. Wells, Grand Rapids, MI: Eerdmans, 1984, p. 4.

26 Oscar Cullmann, *Christ and Time*, London: SCM, 1962, p. 95.

27 Karl Barth, *Church Dogmatics* III.1: *The Doctrine of Creation*, Edinburgh: T & T Clark, 1958, p. 82.

The Christian mythos

In *The Great Code*, Northrop Frye discusses Edward Gibbon's well-known *History of the Decline and Fall of the Roman Empire*. He makes the point that the title is a good example of historical imagination at work, for it 'indicates the narrative principle on which Gibbon selected and arranged his material: that is his *mythos*, and without such a *mythos* the book could have no shape'. Frye goes on to say:

> The extent to which the Bible is historical in the same way is a more complicated matter, but not many would disagree with the statement that it tells a story; and for me the two statements "The Bible tells a story" and "The Bible is a myth" are essentially the same statement.[28]

In this sense myth does not mean something untrue, but that these stories are 'charged with a special seriousness and importance'.[29] They disclose mystery. In other words, instead of 'myth' meaning something inferior and less trustworthy than 'history', it carries more weight, because it has revelatory significance. But, of course, I am fully aware that this is not the common sense understanding of the 'myth', or even that of some scholars.

The well-known nineteenth-century philologist Max Müller was one scholar who had a pejorative view of myth, calling it a 'disease of language', and Strauss had an equally jaundiced view. This did not satisfy George Eliot as we have seen, neither did it satisfy the later literary critic C. S. Lewis who said that myth is not misunderstood history, diabolical illusion, priestly lying, 'but at its best, a real though unfocused gleam of divine truth falling on human imagination'.[30] A late convert to Christianity, Lewis also had this to say:

---

28 Frye, *The Great Code*, p. 32.
29 Frye, *The Great Code*, p. 33.
30 C. S. Lewis, *Miracles*, London: Geoffrey Bles, 1947, p. 161, fn. 1.

The heart of Christianity is a myth which is also a fact. The old myth of the Dying God, without ceasing to be myth, comes down from the heaven of legend and imagination to the earth of history . . . By becoming fact it does not cease to be myth: that is the miracle.[31]

Some readers will know of Lewis' friendship and collaboration with J. R. R. Tolkien, a devout Catholic, an authority on fairy stories, mythology and Icelandic saga and celebrated author of *The Lord of the Rings*. But what is often not appreciated is that Lewis' conversion to Christianity was in significant measure the result of a conversation with Tolkien one evening in the grounds of Magdalen College, Oxford, on the significance of myth for understanding Christianity.

At one point in the discussion, Tolkien insisted that 'pagan myths are . . . never just "lies": there is always something of the truth in them'.[32] After further discussion, Lewis turned to Tolkien and asked: 'Do you mean . . . that the death and resurrection of Christ is the old "dying god" story all over again?' To which Tolkien replied: 'Yes . . . except that here is the *real* Dying God, with a precise location and definite historical consequences. The old myth has become a fact. But it still retains the character of myth.' And, he concluded, 'if God is mythopoeic, man must become mytho*pathic*'.[33] Myth thereafter became Lewis' 'master key to life as well as to literature; with it, he opened many different doors'.[34] 'God', he wrote, 'is none the less God by being Man, so the Myth remains Myth even when it becomes Fact'. And again, the gospel story is 'not only a religious and historical but also an imaginative

31 C. S. Lewis, 'Myth became Fact', in *God in the Dock*, edited by Walter Hooper, Grand Rapids: Eerdmans, 1970, p. 67.
32 Humphrey Carpenter, *The Inklings: C. S. Lewis, J. R. R. Tolkien, Charles Williams and Their Friends*, London: Unwin Paperbacks, 1981, p. 43. See also A. N. Wilson, *C. S. Lewis: A Biography*, London: Collins, 1990, pp. 114–32.
33 Carpenter , *The Inklings*, p. 45.
34 Dabney Adams Hart, *Through the Open Door: a New Look at C. S. Lewis*, Tuscaloosa, AL: University of Alabama Press, 1984, p. 29.

response . . . directed to the child, the poet, and the savage in us as well as to the conscience and to the intellect'.[35]

Tolkien and Lewis' understanding of the 'Christian myth' as *both* connected to pagan mythology *and* rooted in history is not only fundamentally different from the way in which myth was understood by Strauss and is by many of our own contemporaries, but its relevance for the restatement of Christian faith and life can be demonstrated in reading the Bible through Lewis' eyes.[36] To speak about the 'myth of God incarnate' was, for Lewis, an affirmation not a rejection of that central claim of Christian faith, as the phrase has generally come to be understood. While I am a little wary of Lewis' apologetics, because he often fails to acknowledge that the claims made in the New Testament are post-resurrection interpretations of Jesus, not claims necessarily made by Jesus himself, he is right about the relationship of myth and historical fact, and his position is corroborated by Wolfhart Pannenberg, one of the major twentieth-century theologians. Already in the writings of Paul, says Pannenberg, the 'non-mythical story of the man Jesus of Nazareth' is 'turned into the characteristic "mythologization" of his person'.[37] But it is a new use of the Hellenistic myth of the incarnate redeemer, because it is now associated with a historical character, namely Jesus.[38] What we see already evident in the New Testament but more especially in the post-apostolic period, is 'a reflective consideration of Christian faith' in relation to the Hellenistic mythological tradition.[39]

In the light of Pannenberg's detailed discussion of the issues, we can speak about the 'new myth' that emerges in Christian thinking about the life, death and resurrection of Jesus. 'New' precisely because the categories of myth are used to interpret the realities of

35 Lewis, *Miracles*, p. 161, fn. 1.
36 See Roger J. Newell, *The Feeling Intellect: Reading the Bible with C. S. Lewis*, Eugene, OR: Wipf & Stock, 2010.
37 Wolfhart Pannenberg, 'The Later Dimensions of Myth in Biblical and Christian Tradition', in *Basic Questions in Theology, Vol. 3*, London: SCM, 1973, p. 68.
38 Pannenberg, 'Dimensions of Myth', p. 72.
39 Pannenberg, 'Dimensions of Myth', p. 79.

history which lie beyond historical verification. So, for example, it is beyond reasonable historical doubt that Jesus of Nazareth was born and lived in Palestine, but it is mythical to speak of his virginal conception. Likewise the truth of his resurrection, however reasonable the arguments for claiming its basis in historical fact as I shall argue later, is ultimately a faith-claim rather than an historical fact that can be empirically proved beyond shadow of doubt. Walter Wink suggests that this confusion of myth and history is built into the foundations of Christianity, because without the myth of the crucified and risen Christ the story of Jesus does not touch our lives or the world in any deep or redemptive way.[40] Bonhoeffer would have concurred.

In prison, Bonhoeffer tells us, he eagerly devoured an 'outstanding book' on the gods of ancient Greece,[41] and also reflected on Bultmann's programme of 'demythologizing' the biblical message.[42] While he opposed ecclesiastical attempts to silence Bultmann, he disagreed with his proposal which fell 'into typical liberal reductionism' by trying to take out the 'mythological' elements in Christianity. 'My view', Bonhoeffer declared,

> is that the full content, including the "mythological" concepts, must remain – the New Testament is not a mythological dressing up of a universal truth, but this mythology (resurrection and so forth) is the thing itself! . . . these concepts must now be interpreted in a way that does not make religion the condition for faith . . .[43]

This meant not interpreting them either in a metaphysical or individualistic way, for neither 'is appropriate, either for the Biblical message or for people today'. Nor interpreting them, Bonhoeffer

40 Walter Wink, *The Human Being: Jesus and the Enigma of the Son of the Man*, Minneapolis: Fortress, 2002, p. 141.

41 W. F. Otto, *Homeric Gods: The Spiritual Significance of Greek Religion*, New York: Octagon Books, 1978.

42 See Rudolf Bultmann, *Kerygma and Myth*; Bonhoeffer, *Letters and Papers*, pp. 436–40.

43 Bonhoeffer, *Letters and Papers*, p. 430. See Mircea Eliade, *The Myth of the Eternal Return, or Cosmos and History*, Princeton, NJ: Princeton University Press, 1973, pp. 34–48.

continued, 'in the anthropocentric sense of liberal, mystical, pietistic, ethical theology, but in the biblical sense of the creation and the incarnation, crucifixion and resurrection of Jesus Christ'.[44] It was with this in mind that Bonhoeffer speaks about hermeneutics not simply as the interpretation of Scripture, but sharing in God's suffering in the world whereby we become drawn into Christ's action in solidarity with all who suffer.[45]

Bonhoeffer's concern, then, was the significance of this 'Christian mythos' for our lives here and now, rather than for some world beyond this one. Unlike the ancient Egyptian and Babylonian myths of redemption, which 'look for eternity outside of history beyond death',[46] the

> Christian hope of resurrection . . . refers people to their life on earth in a wholly new way . . . Unlike believers in the redemption myths, Christians do not have an ultimate escape route out of their earthly tasks and difficulties into eternity.[47]

The 'new myth' concerning the Incarnate, Crucified and Risen Christ is therefore not only rooted in history, but its significance is as Pannenberg says, 'eschatological'. That is, it has to do with the mystery of God's reign in this world heralded in the coming of Jesus as the Messiah in anticipation of the fulfilment of all things at the end of time.

There is another critique of Bultmann's demythologizing project, which comes from the perspective of Eastern Orthodox theology, but reaches a similar conclusion and takes us back to Eliot's reaction to Strauss' treatment of the crucifixion of Jesus.[48] Bultmann notoriously excluded the aesthetic and the concept of beauty from playing any role in the Christian life here and now. This was related to his rejection of all myth as untrue because it cannot fit into

---

44 Bonhoeffer, *Letters and Papers*, pp. 372–3.
45 Bonhoeffer, *Letters and Papers*, p. 480.
46 Bonhoeffer, *Letters and Papers*, p. 447.
47 Bonhoeffer, *Letters and Papers*, p. 448.
48 David Bentley Hart, *The Beauty of the Infinite*, Grand Rapids: Eerdmans, 2003, pp. 22–5.

history understood as a closed causal system. Nothing, Bultmann argued, can break into either nature or history from beyond; there can be no transcendence except in terms of the self understood in self-conscious existential terms. As a result, 'the Christian story of salvation no longer really interacts with the world, but is partitioned off into the hidden depths of the self'.[49] The 'salvation of the soul' in a better more beautiful world becomes the ultimate purpose of the gospel, rather than the redemption of the world itself. To wrench history and myth apart like that shifts theology away from the concrete particularity of life in the real world, and reduces the Word to a disembodied metaphysical idea rather than a historical deed. Acknowledging that this is so is a fundamental building block in seeking an answer to the original question posed by Steve's death. I know he would agree.

Who is Jesus for us today?

The New Testament was written out of the conviction that Jesus of Nazareth, crucified 'under Pontius Pilate', was raised from the dead 'on the third day'. The gospels which tell the story in the New Testament were written many years later. They are not biographies but confessions of faith in Jesus as the risen Lord of life. This does not mean that the Gospel narratives are prefabrications without historical basis, but that they were written from this faith perspective. The 'search for the historical Jesus', which began with Reimarus, was an attempt to get behind this perspective to find out who Jesus was before his followers came to believe in him as the risen Lord. This question is fundamental for Christians because it determines how we understand life, ourselves, the world and the mystery we call God. But the Christological question is not only about who Jesus *was*, but about who that Jesus *is* for us here and now. This is a hermeneutical question. As such, it requires more than a theoretical answer about what Christians have traditionally believed; it asks for an existential commitment

---

49   Hart, *The Beauty of the Infinite*, p. 23.

which Bonhoeffer described as 'being pulled into walking the path that Jesus walks'.[50]

For Christians, the questions who Jesus *was*, and who he *is for us today*, are two sides of the same coin.[51] This is already evident in the four canonical gospels, as it is also implicit in the apocryphal Gospels, like that of Thomas, or the many movies that have been produced about Jesus. You only have to compare *The King of Kings*, *The Greatest Story Ever Told*, *The Last Temptation of Christ*, *The Gospel according to St. Matthew*, *Jesus of Montreal*, *Godspell*, *Jesus Christ Superstar*, and the *Passion of the Christ*, to discover that every attempt to tell the story of Jesus of Nazareth becomes an interpretation of who he is for those who tell it.[52] But, even so, it remains important for Christians, and not just Christians, that the interpretation of Jesus' significance today is anchored in who he was.

Anyone familiar with the 'search for the historical Jesus', which continues to our own day, will agree that it is one of the most intense and detailed of all critical literary endeavours. Just to browse through the 800 pages of Strauss' *Life of Jesus*, to say nothing of the many other volumes that eventually led to Albert Schweitzer's comprehensive analysis *The Quest for the Historical Jesus*,[53] or the outcomes of the more recent *Jesus Seminar*, will dispel any notion that this was superficial scholarship pursued with the aim of undermining Christian faith or simply bolstering its claims. Those involved have been 'passionately convinced that they' are 'contending for high stakes'.[54] That is why the quest persists. It has to do with the conviction that Christian faith is inseparable from Jesus of Nazareth. This has 'been debated, narrowed and nuanced,

50 Bonhoeffer, *Letters and Papers*, p. 480.
51 See the fine essay by Steve entitled 'Jesus the Christ', in *Doing Theology in Context: South African perspectives*, edited by John de Gruchy and Charles Villa-Vicencio, Cape Town: David Philip; Maryknoll, NY: Orbis, 1994, pp. 55–67.
52 Adele Reinhartz, *Jesus of Hollywood*, Oxford: Oxford University Press, 2007.
53 Albert Schweitzer, *The Quest for the Historical Jesus*, New York, NY: Macmillan, 1968, first published in 1906.
54 Ben F. Meyer, *The Aims of Jesus*, London: SCM, 1979, p. 95.

weighed and found wanting, elaborately denied; but the conviction endures, massive, solid, stubborn, taking its stand on creeds that have ridden out the ages'.[55]

Although some questions remain contentious, considerable consensus has been reached on who Jesus was, and what he did and said. Jesus was a first-century Jewish Spirit-filled prophet, teacher, healer, and, some would say, mystic.[56] This portrait of Jesus has become much clearer in our time than ever before, but scholars rightly stress that we must always keep in mind the distinction between the pre-Easter Jesus and the post-Easter Christ within the gospel narrative. This corresponds to Paul's distinction between knowing Christ 'according to the flesh' and knowing him as the risen Lord 'according to the Spirit'.[57]

A good introduction to the contemporary debate that brings together what we know about the historical Jesus, and how that knowledge contributes to our faith in Jesus as the Christ today, is *The Meaning of Jesus* jointly authored by Marcus Borg and N. T. Wright.[58] Respecting each other's Christian commitment but disagreeing at significant points, Borg and Wright address the key claims of Christian faith in dialogue with one another. The point on which they mostly diverge takes us to the centre of the debate, namely the historical credibility for New Testament claims about the resurrection. This is a critical issue, for the gospels, as C. H. Dodd aptly wrote, 'record remembered facts' but understand them 'on the farther side of resurrection'. Yet there 'is no reason',

55 Meyer, *The Aims of Jesus*, p. 95.
56 Among the seminal books are Günther Bornkamm, *Jesus of Nazareth*, London: Hodder & Stoughton, 1960; C. H. Dodd, *The Founder of Christianity*, London: Collins, 1971; John Howard Yoder, *The Politics of Jesus*, Grand Rapids: Eerdmans, 1972; Geza Vermes, *Jesus the Jew*, London: Fontana, 1973; James D. G. Dunn., *Jesus and the Spirit*, London: SCM, 1975; Albert Nolan, *Jesus Before Christianity*, Cape Town: David Philip, 1976; Richard Horsley, *Jesus and the Spiral of Violence*, San Francisco: Harper & Row, 1987; Dominic Crossan, *The Historical Jesus*, San Francisco: Harper, 1991; Walter Wink, *The Human Being: Jesus and the Enigma of the Son of the Man*, Minneapolis: Fortress, 2002; J. Marcus Borg, *Jesus*, London: SPCK, 2011.
57 Cf. Paul's comments in Romans 1.3–4 and 2 Corinthians 5.16
58 J. Marcus Borg & N. T. Wright, *The Meaning of Jesus: Two Visions*, San Francisco: HarperCollins, 2000.

he added, 'why this should be supposed to falsify or distort the record, unless, of course, it be assumed at the outset that such a belief cannot be true'.[59] I will discuss the historicity and significance of the resurrection of Jesus in Chapter 5. For now we note with Dodd that

> [i]f the resurrection is the true dénouement of the whole story and not a "happy ending" tacked on to a tragedy, then there is an element in the story itself which brings us to the frontiers of normal human experience, where experience runs out into mystery.[60]

But the fact remains, how we understand Jesus as the risen Christ depends on how we understand who Jesus actually was, otherwise he becomes a purely mythical figure in the ancient Greek sense with no historical substance. For Christians, the Christ of faith *is* the Jesus of history. That is why the Gospels, though written from the perspective of the resurrection, set out to tell the story of Jesus so that those who were being instructed in the faith would know who he was, what he said and did, and what led to his death.[61]

The pre-Easter Jesus, then, was fully human – he developed as any other boy, got tired, hungry, thirsty, and when necessary, got angry as well. He did not know about the theory of relativity, the functioning of the brain, or most other technological advances we take for granted. His knowledge was that of a first-century Palestinian Jew, not a twenty-first century computer genius. He knew a great deal about people, he was schooled in the Torah and the Hebrew Scriptures, and all who heard him and saw him in action marvelled at his Spirit-filled teaching, his healing power, and his compassion for all people, irrespective of who they were. But he had a special concern for women who were despised and abused, for social outcasts, the poor or those in need. His compassion made him passionate about justice, and he was for the duration

---

59 Dodd, *The Founder*, p. 29.
60 Dodd, *The Founder*, p. 29.
61 See Luke 1.1–4.

of his short ministry (one year according to the synoptic Gospels; three according to John) a forthright critic of the political and religious power elites who oppressed the peasant class of which he himself was a member. Undergirding all else was his awareness of and relationship to God as *Abba* (father) which found expression in a prayerful life of ministry nurtured by the Psalms.

Invariably wherever he went people had strong opinions about him and wanted to know his secret. Who was he really? Sometimes even his family thought he was mad or deluded; his followers thought he might be the promised Messiah who would deliver Israel from Roman domination and usher in God's kingdom of righteous peace; religious leaders challenged his way of life and his teaching as contrary to the Torah and even blasphemous, and the political and Temple authorities in Jerusalem regarded him as a threat to society and their own power, and eventually had him crucified. But almost everyone wanted to know who he really was. There was undoubtedly something of a mystery about him, not least to his closest followers, and even his mother Mary was puzzled. Jesus often referred to the mysterious 'Son of Man', an enigmatic figure in the book of Daniel, in a way that seemed to refer to himself, though not all scholars agree that this was so. But even if he did, Jesus refused to tell in a way that left no one in some doubt. Many Christians assume he thought he was the Son of God in the sense that we now think of him, but as a devout Jew he probably would have regarded that as blasphemous. But he did believe that God had called him to proclaim the mystery of God's reign in word and deed. This was his mission.

Mystery disclosed

The reality of mystery in the Bible is qualitatively different from the words used to describe it. There are many experiences of the mystery of God, for example, where the Greek word *musterion* or its Hebrew and Aramaic equivalents do not occur. The story of Moses going up into the clouds on Mount Sinai to receive the Ten Commandments is shot through with mystery, as are the experiences described in many of the Psalms, in the visions of Isaiah in the Temple and Ezekiel in exile in Babylon, or the story of the Transfiguration of Jesus. Likewise Paul's experience of being taken up into Paradise 'where he heard things that are not to be told, that no mortal is permitted to repeat' (2 Cor. 12.4) is, to say the least, mysterious. But there is neither reference to *musterion* in the text nor any reason why there should be. The experience exceeds our terms and descriptions. But an examination of the use of the word *musterion* in the New Testament provides helpful insight into early Christian understanding of its meaning.

Musterion was a word already loaded with meaning within the Hellenistic world before it was used in the New Testament.[62] Most probably derived from *müein*, it literally means 'to shut up', be silent or mute. In this sense it becomes the term used in the Greek mystery cults, and then in Gnosticism, for those secrets into which initiates were instructed and about which they were sworn to silence. The New Testament was written within this religious milieu, but its authors were concerned to distance themselves from the notion that Christianity was another mystery religion, or that Gnosticism could be reconciled with the gospel of the Incarnation. John's Gospel and the Johannine letters actually avoid the word *musterion*, probably for this reason. But when it is employed within the canon, especially in the writings of Paul, it locates the Christian mystery at a qualitative distance from its Hellenistic competitors.

In the Septuagint (LXX), the Greek version of the Old Testament used by the writers of the New Testament, *musterion* was used to translate the original Hebrew in two distinct ways. The first was to assert that God does not speak in secret (Isa. 45.19; 48.16, Amos 3.7f), for God's words and actions are always public, even if not always heard or understood. The second usage was in the profane sense of political and military secrets or those

---

62 The standard resource is the multi-volume *Theological Dictionary of the New Testament (TDNT)*, edited by Gerhard Kittel, trans. by Geoffrey Bromily, Grand Rapids: Eerdmans, 1967. The entry on μυστήριον is by Günther Bornkamm, IV, pp. 802–28.

shared by friends. It is only in the book of Daniel that mystery refers to that which is hidden or only known to God, but which will be disclosed in future events,[63] the sense in which it is also used in the book of Revelation. Yet, throughout a distinction is made between those things which are known to God alone and those which have been or will be revealed to mortals. 'The secret things belong to the Lord our God, but the revealed things belong to us and to our children forever, to observe all the words of this law.' (Deut. 29.29). In other words, the ultimate mystery we refer to as God is always beyond human grasp, but what we *need* to know God reveals to us. It is in this sense that *musterion* is used in the New Testament, not as knowledge that is kept secret except among spiritual elites, but as reference to the reality of God in relation to humanity and the world.

Musterion understood in this latter sense is used in various ways in the New Testament, each relating to different textual locations. First, according to the synoptic Gospels, there is the mystery of God's rule revealed in the life and ministry of Jesus. This is made explicit in the parables:

> When he was alone, those who were around him along with the twelve asked him about the parables. And he said to them, "To you has been given the *musterion* of the kingdom of God, but for those outside, everything comes in parables . . ." (Mark 4.10–11)

The parables of Jesus, Günther Bornkamm tells us, point to 'the incursion of the divine rule in the word and work of Jesus'. The *musterion* of God's reign is 'veiled in the parables, not because they are obscure or complicated, but precisely because of their simplicity'.[64] The parables almost tease us into the truth about God's reign, just as they made Jesus' hearers laugh at themselves and the self-righteous among them, as Jesus turned their conventions of piety and caricatures of God's will upside down. But like

---

63 *TDNT* IV, p. 815.
64 *TDNT* IV, p. 819.

in the tale of the 'emperor's new clothes', the parables require a second naiveté without which we cannot begin to grasp the *mysterion* revealed. The fact that not everyone sees or understands is not because God's reign is purposefully obscure, but because hearts and minds are closed rather than open to its incursion into their experience. Even the disciples seldom understood what Jesus was saying. It was only by following him in the light of the Easter event that their eyes were finally opened.

Christianity gestated in a time of apocalyptic rumour and expectation, and like a mystery story whose plot always anticipates the final scene, much of the New Testament was written in anticipation of the 'end of history'. We are not trapped in an endless cycle of birth and return, but on a journey towards a goal or *telos* which keeps hope alive.[65] The kingdom or reign of God is thus understood as an eschatological (*eschatos* meaning 'last') reality. By this is meant the presence of God's reign in the life and ministry of Jesus is an anticipation of the coming of God's reign on earth 'as it is in heaven' at the end of time. This eschatological expectation is sometimes expressed within an apocalyptic framework, as in the book of Revelation which, with its dramatic symbolic descriptions of the war between God and Satan, is shot through with mystery. Not just the mystery of God's purpose, but also 'the mystery of iniquity' that stands against it and is personified in the 'Great Whore', namely Imperial Rome. 'The mystery', writes Frye, 'turns into a revelation of how things really are, and the obvious power of Nero rolls into the darkness of the mystery of the corrupted human will from which it emerged'.[66]

Paul's understanding of the mystery revealed is in continuity with the synoptic Gospels' teaching on the reign of God, but at a deeper level than is at first apparent. Both have to do with the revelation of God's will and purpose in the present in anticipation of the 'end of the age', that is, they are both eschatological in character. For Paul, the mystery that we are now led into in the

---

65   See Jürgen Moltmann, *Theology of Hope*, London: SCM, 1967; and Trevor Hart Bauckham, *Hope Against Hope: Christian Eschatology at the Turn of the Millennium*, Grand Rapids: Eerdmans, 1999.

66   Frye, *The Great Code*, p. 136.

risen Christ through the Spirit is in anticipation of the mystery yet to be revealed when all things are finally brought to completion in him (Col. 1.15–20). However, in Paul's writings, we are not invited to consider the *musterion* revealed in Jesus' life and teaching, but rather to reflect on the significance of the *musterion* of God's saving grace disclosed in the death and resurrection of Jesus as the Christ.

Typical is Paul's reference to his proclamation of the gospel 'according to the revelation of the *musterion* that was kept secret for long ages but is now disclosed' (Rom. 16.25–26; cf. Col. 1.24–30). Remarkably, *musterion* is usually found in the singular, 'as though the most important "mystery" of the Christian gospel is the way in which by the grace of God all people (and not only Jews) are invited to share in the privileges originally reserved for Jews. (Rom. 11.25;16.25; Eph. 1.9; 3.3; 4.9; Col. 1.26, 27; 2.2: 3.3)'.[67] At the centre of the mystery unveiled is Paul's conviction that 'in Christ God was reconciling the world to himself' (2 Cor. 5.17), which, in Paul's thought, is inseparable from the restoration of justice for the poor and oppressed.[68] This is in anticipation of the final disclosure of the 'mystery of God's will', which is, in 'the fullness of time, to gather up all things in Christ, things in heaven and things on earth' (Eph. 1.9–10). That, according to the letter to the Ephesians, 'is the plan of the mystery hidden for ages in God' that has now become known (3.9). It is nothing less than the transformation of reality as we know it, perhaps best captured in the vision of *shalom* as depicted in the Old Testament prophets.

The disclosure of God's mysterious purpose is, then, the substance of Christian hope, as can be seen in passages where Paul speaks about the glory that is still to be revealed, and for which the whole creation 'waits with eager longing' (Rom. 8.19). Likewise to the Colossians, Paul writes about the 'riches of the glory of this mystery' revealed in the gospel, 'which is Christ in you,

---

67 John Suggit, emeritus professor of New Testament at Rhodes University, in private correspondence.
68 See Christopher D. Marshall, *Beyond Retribution: A New Testament Vision for Justice, Crime and Punishment*, Grand Rapids: Eerdmans, 2001, pp. 35–69.

the hope of glory' (1.27). He also writes about our waiting in hope for the 'redemption of our bodies', which we do not yet see, and concludes with the rhetorical question: 'For who hopes for that which is seen?' What believers know is that what is not yet seen has already been disclosed in the gospel. But even then, it remains unfathomable mystery: 'For who knows the mind of the Lord?', asks Paul (Rom. 11.34). His judgments are unsearchable and his ways inscrutable. There are things not revealed, things that remain hidden until the end. Yet the end has already been anticipated. This is the critical point: *the mystery still to be revealed will not be contrary to that already disclosed in Christ; it will be the unveiling of that mystery in its entirety.*

In light of the mystery revealed in Christ, Paul encourages the Colossians to be united in love so that they 'may have the full riches of complete understanding, in order that they may know the *musterion* of God, namely, Christ, in whom are hidden all the treasures of wisdom and knowledge' (2.2–3). This wisdom (*sophia*) is not that of the world, that is, of the sophists or Gnostics, but 'God's secret wisdom, a *musterion* that has been hidden and that God destined for our glory before time began' (1 Cor. 2.6–10). But there is a vital caveat in Paul's teaching. Those who claim to 'understand all mysteries' but do not love have failed to understand the mystery revealed (1 Cor. 13.2).

Even though the word *musterion* does not occur in the Johannine literature in the New Testament, the mystery of the Incarnation is all-pervasive. This mystery is described in many ways in John's Gospel, where Jesus of Nazareth and the Incarnate 'Word made flesh' are indistinguishable. John provides no account of the Transfiguration. The reason may well be that his whole Gospel was intended to convey the mystery of the revelation of God's glory in 'the face of Jesus Christ'. This is certainly the point of the Johannine signs or Messianic deeds, as in the turning of water into wine at the wedding feast in Cana (John 2.1–11), and in the raising of Lazarus from the dead (John 11). Such signs, John is saying, enable us to recognize the significance of Jesus, to see through the veil that shrouds the mystery.

With the sign of the raising of Lazarus we are introduced to the mystery of the resurrection, and are thereby brought directly to the central question of this book as raised by my friend at the time of Steve's death. In approaching the story, we are therefore on the threshold of *the* Christian mystery – 'Christ is risen!' – but we are not quite there. According to John, it is actually this event that results directly in the plot to kill Jesus (11.45–53). Nonetheless, the raising of Lazarus is an anticipatory sign of what is coming. So in concluding this chapter with this story, I am preparing the way for Chapter five in which the resurrection of both Christ and the dead is my central focus. I invite you to read it with that anticipation in mind as I believe John intended.

Through an open door

The metaphor of Jesus as 'the door' in John's Gospel (10.7–10), is introduced just prior to story of Lazarus being raised from the dead. In ancient Middle Eastern and Greek as well as later Gnostic literature, human beings entered heaven through a door, and it was through the same door that the redeemer figure descended from heaven to earth.[69] The idea of a 'heavenly doorway' is also found in the Old Testament, notably in apocalyptic literature as also in the book of Revelation. Knowledge and salvation are conveyed to human beings through the 'doors of heaven', something symbolized in Eastern Orthodox worship where the doors in the iconostasis, the screen which symbolically separates earth and heaven, are the portals through which the gospels and the sacramental bread are brought to the congregation. The metaphor of the door also relates to sayings in the synoptic gospels that refer to entry into the *musterion* of the kingdom of God. This is not a metaphor for some heavenly realm unrelated to this world, but one that brings together much that we have been thinking about in this chapter which began with Jackson's experience of the Word as he worked on *The St. John's Bible*.

---

69 C. K. Barrett, *The Gospel According to St. John*, London: SPCK, 1978, pp. 372–3.

We have shown the DVD of Jackson's account of the making of illuminated manuscript many times. On one occasion, a visiting Catholic friend, Brother John, was entranced by the splendid illustration of the raising of Lazarus. The picture did not depict Jesus going into the tomb but a shadowy Lazarus slowly coming out of the darkness into the light. How are we to understand the story? Both Raymond Brown and C. K. Barrett, two of the leading Johannine scholars of the twentieth century, affirm that it has some historical basis.[70] There was in all probability a man named Lazarus who lived in Bethany with his sisters Mary and Martha, all of whom knew Jesus. Something dramatic must have happened to give rise to the story, even if the question whether Jesus literally raised Lazarus from the dead is a matter for debate. If you do not believe in miracles, then the miraculous is ruled out, but even if you do, this one stretches credulity to breaking point. Was Lazarus actually dead for four days, or was he only in a deep coma that was not recognized as such? John is at pains to tell us that he was dead. So what is he trying to tell the reader, not least the sceptical one, with this sign?

According to John, when Jesus tells Martha that her brother will be raised to life again, she assumes Jesus is speaking about the final resurrection of the dead as believed by devout Jews. Jesus makes it clear that he does not mean his words to be taken in that sense, but as a present reality of risen life. 'Those who believe in me', he says, 'even though they die will live, and everyone who lives and believes in me will *never* die'. A literal reading would conclude that Lazarus, far from never dying, actually died twice! The first time when he was entombed he died like all of us must die and was dead for four days. If he was literally brought back to life, he would have had to die a second time, which doesn't tally with what Jesus is saying if taken literally. Martha wanted Jesus to save Lazarus from death, not try to bring him back to life after four days – 'consider the stench', she says! In any case, why did

70 Raymond Brown, *The Gospel According to John I–XII*, Garden City, NY: Doubleday, 1966, pp. 419–37; Barrett, *Gospel According to St. John*, pp. 387–403.

he delay his coming to Bethany, especially if he loved Lazarus so deeply and wept on account of his death?

The point is clear in Jesus' response to his disciples who were puzzled by his tardiness to go to Bethany. The story is a sign which reveals God's glory. This sounds rather crass if it means that Jesus allowed Lazarus to die in order that God's glory should be revealed through what he did. But that is surely the point of the story *as John tells it*. Like Lazarus, John is saying, those who believe in Jesus enter into 'eternal life' now, prior to death, that is, the life of the new age over which death does not have the last word. This is a central theme of the Fourth Gospel. The words of the risen Christ: 'I am the resurrection and the life' is a metaphor like all the other 'I am' sayings, but it is more than a metaphor. The significance of the resurrection of Jesus is not that we shall live for ever as human beings *in the same way* as we live now, if only we believe, but that through him we are brought out of the tombs that enclose us into the fullness of life over which death does not have the last word. Eternal life begins now; the final resurrection, as Jesus tells Martha and us, is still to come. The tombs that bind us and the rest of humanity may be many, and Jesus might come early, or he might arrive late on the scene of our lives. But when he does come to us he becomes the door into the mystery of God's reign. He *is* the resurrection and the life.

What actually happened to Lazarus that day in Bethany is now impossible to say. To rationalize it renders it impotent as a sign; to take it literally poses more questions than the story answers. But what if we become, as Denise Levertov describes herself, 'literalists of the imagination', those who follow Updike's counsel and leave metaphors aside in order to walk with Lazarus through the open door from darkness to light?[71] After all, as Jesus told us, any child can grasp the secret of the open door, just as Lucy did in the first chapter of Lewis' *The Lion, the Witch and the Wardrobe*. Exploring the big house that had become their war-time home, Peter, Susan, Edmund, and Lucy

---

71   Levertov, *The Stream & the Sapphire*, p. 79.

looked into a room that was quite empty except for one big wardrobe: the sort that has a looking-glass in the door . . . "Nothing there!" said Peter, and they all trooped out again – all except Lucy. She stayed behind because she thought it would be worth while trying the door of the wardrobe, even though she felt almost sure it would be locked. To her surprise it opened quite easily . . . she immediately stepped in . . .[72]

Then Lucy went in further, and further again, until she discovered herself in a new world, a different space with surprises around every corner.

The mystery of the kingdom of God disclosed in Jesus is a new world that is already present in the old. The way is by no means without suffering and struggle, but the door is always open inviting us to enter and explore further. Sometimes I find myself, like Lucy, still trying to find a way through the coats hanging in the cupboard in order to take the next step on the journey. But it can only begin as we enter and are led deeper into the ultimate mystery we call God and so discover the fullness of life and freedom which is God's gift to us, both hidden and revealed in the manger as on the cross. To do that we must heed Updike's urging to us as we began this chapter, to leave metaphors, parables and signs behind, and enter the door. The door is always open, for no one is able to shut it, so anyone who chooses to do so can walk through.

Our holiest act is to enter into mystery,
just as God's holiest act was to enter
into mortal flesh, into death—
the only mystery available to Him.[73]

72   C. S. Lewis, *The Lion, The Witch and the Wardrobe*, London: Fontana-Lions, 1980, pp. 11–12.
73   Luke Hankins, *Weak Devotions*, Eugene, OR: Wipf and Stock, 2011, p. 45. Used by permission.

3

The God Question

The most beautiful thing we can experience is the mysterious. It is the source of all true art and all science. He to whom this emotion is a stranger, who can no longer pause to wonder and stand rapt in awe, is as good as dead: his eyes are closed.

Albert Einstein[1]

Science is an unending quest: as its frontiers advance, new mysteries come into focus just beyond those frontiers. Most of the questions now being addressed simply couldn't have been posed fifty years ago (or even twenty); we can't conceive what problems will engage our successors.

Martin Rees[2]

Faith knows God as the ultimate and authentic mystery of the world. Yet at the same time, faith understands God as that which is most self-evident.

Eberhard Jüngel[3]

. . . all the data that God's creation gives us . . . God has given us the curiosity, the intelligence and the consciousness to explore. Lots of it, to encourage you, is, unsurprisingly but delightfully, very, very beautiful.

Sara Maitland[4]

My soul thirsts for God, For the living God.

Psalm 42.2

1   Albert Einstein, back cover of *Inside the Mind of God*, edited by Michael Reagan, Philadelphia: Templeton Foundation, 2002.

2   Martin Rees, 'Conclusion: Looking Fifty Years Ahead', in *Seeing Further: The Story of Science & the Royal Society*, edited by Bill Bryson, London: Harper, 2010, p. 469.

3   Eberhard Jüngel, *God as the Mystery of the World*, Grand Rapids: Eerdmans, 1983, p. 246.

4   Sara Maitland, *A Big-Enough God: Artful Theology*, London: Mowbray, 1995, p. 15.

John Updike's novel *In the Beauty of the Lilies* begins with a sadly moving scene in which Clarence Wilmot, a Presbyterian minister in New Jersey at the turn of the twentieth century, suddenly declares to himself 'there is no God'. 'It was', writes Updike, 'a ghastly moment, a silent sounding of bottomlessness'.[5] His previous 'believer's mental contortions' were now relaxed for he no longer had to fight the persistent battering of biblical criticism on the citadel of his mind. At the same time 'the depths of vacancy revealed were appalling'.[6] If there was no God, as Clarence had come to believe, ironically, then the future looked as bleak as the encroaching wintry darkness beyond his study window. His atheism had been a long time coming, gestating in the chemistry of his brain. Many of the books surrounding him were signposts of that painful journey from youthful ministerial faith and spiritual conviction to this delayed mid-life crisis that threatened to destroy all that he had lived for, with diminishing conviction, over many years. The consequences appalled him. But the findings of science and the 'higher criticism' of the Bible, about which he had first learnt at Princeton Theological Seminary, had finally taken its toll, the erudite apologetics of devout scholars no longer retaining their previous plausibility and the counsel of his superiors equally unconvincing. The mystery had dissipated in the cold night air of biblical criticism and scientific investigation. There was no God and therefore no Word to obey or proclaim, no Word of comfort and hope, only a precarious future selling encyclopaedias door to door to indifferent clients. Life had been emptied of meaning, bereft of mystery. A slow death in obscurity awaited him as he stood on the edge of the abyss. The world had become cold and grey, emptied of beauty to transfigure life and awaken hope.

Atheism has become a more popular creed in our time than it was in Clarence Wilmot's day. The writings of the media-acclaimed 'new atheists', have struck a responsive cord in the consciousness of many people disenchanted with religion. At the same time there has been a resurgence of religion that challenges the thesis that global

---

5 John Updike, *In the Beauty of the Lilies*, London: Penguin 1996, p. 6.
6 Updike, *In the Beauty*, p. 7.

secularization signals its end. Dubbed the 'revenge of God',[7] this resurgence, not all of it good, is one of the noteworthy contradictions of contemporary culture. The spread of secularism and the resurgence of religion feed off each other. As A.N. Wilson noted in *God's Funeral*: 'No sooner have the intelligentsia of one generation confined the Almighty to the history books than popular opinion rises against them.'[8] The God-question simply does not go away.

The reason seems obvious to me. In the end, whether of the day, our lives, or the world, there is either nothing, or something that gives it all meaning, a *telos*. If it all ends in nothingness, so that even memories are no more, then nihilism must *ultimately* be our creed despite the fact that many non-believers live their lives with purpose and compassion. Those who believe in God resist this conclusion. Instead of putting our trust in some *thing*, we believe that in the end God is the ultimate mystery that gives everything coherence and significance. But faith in God remains a questioning faith; a journey into a mystery that embraces us, yet remains greater than we can fully grasp.

A questioning faith

Some years before his death, Steve gave a lecture on Richard Dawkins' widely read book, *The God Delusion*.[9] Steve was subsequently invited to come to Hermanus to repeat the lecture. The Volmoed chapel was full to capacity for the occasion, indicating a widespread interest in the subject among the audience, which included a good number of retired academics and professionals of various hues. Steve spent much of the time explaining Dawkins' argument before raising some critical questions. Dawkins' scientific achievements were acknowledged, and his judgment on the evils of bad religion was affirmed. Discussing the lecture with Steve afterwards, we both agreed that if we ever wrote our *apologia* this would be our approach. Those of us who believe in God

---

7   Gilles Kepel, *The Revenge of God: The Resurgence of Islam, Christianity and Judaism in the Modern World*, Cambridge: Polity Press, 1994.

8   A.N. Wilson, *God's Funeral*, London: Abacus, 2000, p. ix.

9   Richard Dawkins, *The God Delusion*, London: Black Swan, 2007.

need to listen carefully to those who do not. Only then could we fairly and honestly respond.

The core of Dawkins' critique is not on the failures of religion; it is on their perceived cause, namely the infantile belief in a God who does not exist. And that is where our response must focus. To his credit, Dawkins acknowledges that there are various understandings of divinity, insisting that his target of attack is the supernatural deity associated with the Abrahamic traditions rather than the deistic views of Einstein and the drafters of the American Constitution (the enlightened Thomas Jefferson and John Adams). He also gives a positive nod in the direction of God as understood by the likes of Tillich or Bonhoeffer, though it is not clear how much Dawkins has read of either. Nonetheless, near the beginning of *The God Delusion* Dawkins does say that 'if only such subtle, nuanced religion predominated, the world would surely be a better place', and he 'would have written a different book'.[10] But the fact that according to him this is not the kind of religion that predominates, leads him to discredit *all* religion and *every* version of Christian faith. So the possibility that promotion of a better religion would make the world a better place is ruled out by default. Maybe Dawkins will write that 'different book' someday and, like John Adams, come to understand that a sense of ultimate mystery is essential to life,[11] even if, unlike Adams, he does not have an 'irresistible impulse to fall on' his knees 'in adoration of the power that moves, the wisdom that directs, and the benevolence that sanctifies this wonderful whole'.[12] In the meantime, I echo Friedrich Schleiermacher's words to the 'cultured despisers of religion' of his day to those who may be inclined to swallow Dawkins' arguments whole: 'I would ask you . . . just to be well informed and thorough-going in' your contempt.[13]

---

10 Dawkins, *The God Delusion*, p. 15.

11 David McCullough, *John Adams*, New York, NY: Simon and Schuster, 2001, pp. 629–30.

12 McCullough, *John Adams*, p. 630.

13 Friedrich Schleiermacher, *On Religion: Speeches to Its Cultured Despisers*, New York, NY: Harper & Row, 1958, p. 12.

The 'new atheist' arguments have now been dissected by theologians,[14] as well as a few scientists,[15] though none have been more dismissive than social critics Terry Eagleton and Simon Critchley, despite, their avowed atheism.[16] In his *The Faith of the Faithless*, Critchley, it seems to me, does attempt to write that other book that Dawkins said he might have written instead of arrogantly claiming, according to Critchley, that God and religion are 'some sort of historical error that has happily been corrected and refuted by scientific progress'.[17] By contrast, Critchley's atheism begins out of 'religious disappointment', a genuine sense of the 'death of God', which does not lead him to disparage religious faith, but to seek other ways to express it. 'When I talk about faith', he writes, 'it is not at all a matter of belief in the existence of some metaphysical reality like God'. It is 'a fidelity to the infinite demand', which, Critchley asserts, has to do with the powerful way the Judeo-Christian tradition articulates 'questions of the ultimate meaning and value of human life in ways irreducible to naturalism'.[18] Even though Critchley cannot accept the answers provided by Christian faith, he acknowledges the gravity of the questions raised and the inability of reason alone to answer them.

Critchley's 'idea of the faith of the faithless' speaks to those who can neither believe in traditional theism, nor live without fidelity to 'the infinite demand' that theism traditionally represents. This leads him to take seriously Bonhoeffer's notion of a 'religionless Christianity'. But his quest becomes the opposite of Bonhoeffer's. For Critchley, it 'is not a matter of how we speak of God without religion, but rather how we speak of religion – as that force which

---

14   David Bentley Hart, *Atheist Delusions: The Christian Revolution and Its Fashionable Enemies*, New Haven, CT: Yale University Press, 2009; Alister E. McGrath, *Why God Won't Go Away: Engaging with the New Atheism*, London: SPCK, 2011.

15   Francis S. Collins, *The Language of God: A Scientist Presents Evidence for Belief*, London: Pocket Books, 2007.

16   Terry Eagleton, *Reason, Faith & Revolution: Reflections on the God Debate*, New Haven, CT: Yale University Press, 2009; Simon Critchley, *The Faith of the Faithless: Experiments in Political Theology*, London: Verso, 2012.

17   Critchley, *Faith of the Faithless*, p. 19.

18   Critchley, *Faith of the Faithless*, p. 19.

can bind human beings together in association without God'.[19] Yet, Critchley's understanding of religion is not that which Bonhoeffer rejected, nor is the God he rejects the God Bonhoeffer affirms. But whether we warm to his 'faith of the faithless' or seek to be true to the faith of the faithful, this much is certain, faith in *God* cannot be other than *faith* in God.

Christian theologians have generally sought to give a reasoned account of why they believe in God, and it is important to do so. But how to relate faith and reason has long been debated among them. Some insist that reason prepares the way for faith; others, that faith is the presupposition for understanding that which is believed. There is no hard and fast rule on their relationship other than they work hand-in-glove. But any attempt to confine the quest within the limits of reason alone, as attempted by Enlightenment philosophers, is bound to fail precisely because of those limits. We can be just as deluded by the claims and outcomes of reason as we can by faith claims.

Romanticism, in its passionate response to the Enlightenment, was not a protest against reason but against its unwarranted claims and the sidelining of aesthetic sensibility. For Keats, reason had become cold, incapable of handling mystery except through imposing control.

> Do not all charms fly
> At the mere touch of cold philosophy?
> There was an awful rainbow once in heaven:
> We know her woof, her texture; she is given
> In the dull catalogue of common things.
> Philosophy will clip an Angel's wings,
> Conquer all mysteries by rule and line . . .[20]

But this protest, appropriate as it may be, is no excuse for shoddy thinking or eschewing reason and scientific enquiry. For these

---

19   Critchley, *Faith of the Faithless*, pp. 19–20.
20   The poem, entitled 'Lamia', was written in 1819. *Keats: Poetry with an Introduction and notes* by Henry Ellershaw, Oxford: Oxford University Press, 1931, p. 72.

also enable us to explore the beauty of the world and understand it better.[21] Bonhoeffer was suspicious of those who too quickly criticized rationalism because he feared that in doing so they were also impugning the importance of reason. The liberation of reason during the Enlightenment, he wrote,

> created an atmosphere of truthfulness, light and clarity. A fresh wind of bright intelligence cleared up prejudices, social conceits, hypocritical proprieties, and stifling sentimentality. Intellectual honesty in all things, including questions of faith, was the great good of liberated *ratio*.[22]

Nonetheless, our knowledge of God is not the outcome of reason however important that is for understanding; it is a knowledge that derives from faith questioning itself in response to that which we believe prompted the search in the first place.

Faith is not blind; it is always open to scrutiny, but it is not a mental exercise objectively pursued and scientifically verified. It is a life lived in commitment, not to a vague, nebulous idea, or a system of religion and philosophy, but to the claims made by the mystery we call God within a particular mythos or narrative, a transcendent Word that gives meaning to life. It is, as Critchley rightly states, 'fidelity to an infinite demand'. The chief exemplar of biblical faith is Abraham stepping out in trust without knowing precisely where he was headed, though he knew what he was leaving behind.[23] It is a questioning of God from the inside, as it was for Job in his despair; not looking in objectively from the outside. Elie Wiesel, the Jewish author and Auschwitz survivor, describes it well:

> I went through many stages. At times I felt that God was cruel, that God was absent. The main thing I felt was that God was

---

21 See Richard Dawkins, *Unweavng the Rainbow*, Boston: Houghton Mifflin, 1998; David Rothenberg, *Survival of the Beautiful: Art, Science, and Evolution*, London: Bloomsbury, 2012.
22 Dietrich Bonhoeffer, *Ethics*, Dietrich Bonhoeffer Works, vol. 6, edited by Clifford J. Green, Minneapolis: Fortress, 2005, p. 115.
23 Genesis 12.1 as interpreted in Hebrews 11.8.

silent. But it's still a question: Was he indifferent? Was he cruel? Was he trying to punish for love? My questioning of God goes on. But even in the beginning I believed in questioning God from inside faith. It is because I believe that I am all the time questioning.[24]

But who is this God in whom we questioningly believe from 'inside faith'?

Imaging God

When we say we believe in 'God' or that we no longer do so; or when we say 'God bless you' or 'God bless our nation', what do we actually mean? Are these more than clichés, however well meant? To whom or what are we referring, and what blessing are we invoking? Does it amount to more than wishing someone good luck? Or are we using the word 'God' to justify our prejudices and identities, our national ambitions and ethnic assumptions? A moment's reflection suggests that the word 'God' has become virtually unusable without serious qualification or far-reaching reconstruction. All images of God, no matter how lofty, are inevitably human constructions by virtue of the language we use. It is the task of theology to analyse, criticize, and reconstruct them as part of its questioning faith.

The *concept* 'God' has a history,[25] or, we might say, it has evolved. This is not the same as saying that 'any creative intelligence, of sufficient complexity to design anything . . . comes into existence only as the end product of an extended process of evolution'.[26] It is our *understanding* of God which evolves, not God, just as our understanding may also regress. This was

---

24 Elie Wiesel, from an interview with *Bostonia*, quoted in *Inside the Mind of God*, p. 129.

25 Karen Armstrong, *A History of God*, London: William Heinemann, 1993, and her much more positive statement, *The Case for God*, London: The Bodley Head, 2009.

26 Dawkins, *The God Delusion*, p. 52.

in Nietzsche's mind when he castigated the *Christian* God as the 'God of all the dark corners and places, of all unhealthy quarters throughout the world', and went on to declare that 'it even represents the low-water mark of the descending development of the God type' because it came to represent the *'contradiction of life, instead of being its transfiguration and eternal Yes!'*[27]

An equally negative portrait of the Judeo-Christian God is André Brink's 'LordGod' depicted in *Philida*, a historical novel based on the life of a slave girl of that name.[28] Philida lived on the wine farm Zandvliet between Franschhoek and Stellenbosch in the Western Cape, just prior to the Emancipation of the Slaves in the Cape Colony in December 1834. The biblical quotations Brink uses to depict the 'LordGod' are as terrifying as they are extensive, and well-known to anyone who has read the Old Testament. This is the god of the bigoted, guilt-ridden, chauvinistic and despotic farmer Cornelis Brink (possibly a distant relation of the author) who cruelly rules his farm and its slave labourers, convinced that he is upholding Christian values and civilization. Philida, anticipating emancipation, is a young woman struggling against all odds, not least sexual abuse, to find her true self by asserting her freedom as a human being and woman despite her slave status. Towards the end of the story the 'LordGod' is contrasted unfavourably with Allah, the compassionate God who stands in solidarity with the slaves, many of them Muslims who originally came from the East Indies. Philida eventually converts to Islam, though Brink himself becomes less positive in his understanding of Allah.

Brink's autobiography, *A Fork in the Road*,[29] provides insight into his rejection of the 'LordGod'. He grew up in an ultra-Calvinist social environment in which an infallible Bible and its 'LordGod' justified racism, repressed sexuality and brooked no critical questions. Though toying for a while with the idea of studying theology, Brink cast it aside to affirm his humanity,

27 See theses 17–18 of 'The Anti-Christ'. Friedrich Nietzsche, *Twilight of the Idols: The Anti-Christ*, Penguin: London, 1968, p. 128.
28 André Brink, *Philida*, London: Harvill Secker, 2012.
29 André Brink, *A Fork in the Road: A Memoir*, London: Harvill Secker, 2009.

freedom, abhorrence of apartheid and his aesthetic interests. His revolt is paradigmatic; but his iconoclasm, spurred on by bad experiences of religion, whatever his personal motives, is also necessary to clear the decks in our own quest of the God who is worthy of consideration and commitment. Whoever that God is, he, she or it is not Brink's 'LordGod', so it is appropriate that he should have elided 'Lord' and 'God' to make his point.

It is no wonder, then, that my orthodox Jewish students insisted on writing 'G-d' in their essays in religious studies in protest against the abuse of the word, and in obedience to the commandment not to take God's name in vain. This had particular reference to the Name revealed to Moses at the 'burning bush', a story told in Exodus 3 that is foundational for the biblical narrative. God is disclosed beyond human control or imagining. God is who God is, 'I am who I am', – YHWH. Image making, as the First Commandment insists, is idolatrous. Yet, despite this injunction, the Old Testament describes YHWH in a wealth of metaphors which enable us to imaginatively grasp who God might be in relation to ourselves and the world in which we live. It cannot be otherwise if we are to speak of God.[30]

The God of much traditional African religion shares a family resemblance with YHWH. Klaus Nürnberger has remarked that the 'Supreme Being in Africa is no "ancestor" whom one knows and with whom one can strike bargains, let alone a "pal" with whom one can spend quality time'. He goes on to say that 'the God of modern Christianity may exist only in our pious fantasy and fail to touch the seriousness that is linked with the concept of Yahweh in the Bible or the Supreme Being in Africa'.[31] How to speak of God as holy, incomprehensible mystery and yet at the same time as 'father' and 'friend', is one of the challenges facing theology. In speaking of God we cannot avoid paradox, but how we speak of the character of God is clearly as important as whether we believe in God in the first place.

---

30 See Sallie McFague, *Metaphorical Theology: Models of God in Religious Language*, Philadelphia: Fortress, 1982.

31 Klaus Nürnberger, *The Living Dead and the Living God: Christ and the Ancestors in a Changing Africa*, Pietermaritzburg: Cluster Publications, 2007, p. 30.

That the character of God is a burning issue today is no more apparent than in the relationship between the three Abrahamic religions, Judaism, Christianity and Islam within the framework of the so-called 'clash of civilizations'. To put it starkly: is the Christian God the same God as Allah? Many Christians and Muslims would categorically answer in the negative. But this response is based on misunderstanding and ignorance, and it is dangerous.[32] According to the Abrahamic traditions there is only one God, and while there are different understandings of this God within the Abrahamic family, these have more in common than the differences that distinguish them. What is more important than whether the God of Jew, Christian and Muslim is the same God, is whether or not the God who is *actually* acknowledged, worshipped and obeyed is true or false. The God who is used to justify terrorism or crusades is an idol; the God who is merciful, compassionate, just, beautiful and loving is, according to the core convictions of the Abrahamic traditions, the true God. But can we 'prove' the existence of such a God, or is God only a figment of our imagination?

The arguments for and against the existence of God traditionally understood are much the same today as they have been over the centuries. The argument *against* is that there is no empirical evidence for the existence of God, and all claims to the contrary can be falsified by reasoned argument. God is a figment of the imagination. That was enough to drive Clarence Wilmot to atheism, as it is has done many others. The argument *for* begins with the insistence that while the existence of God cannot be empirically verified, neither can it be disproved, and that the God who is disposed of in this way cannot possibly be God. Even Dawkins agrees, though for him the existence of God is 'highly, highly improbable'.[33] But in any case, what does it mean to say 'God *exists*', if God is greater than can be imagined, as the much-debated ontological argument has it? How do we conceive of God if all our images

---

32 Miroslav Volf, *Allah: A Christian Response*, New York, NY: Harper One, 2011.
33 Dawkins, *The God Delusion*, p. 136.

are ultimately inadequate, starting most obviously with that of a big Man (or Woman) in the sky in whom believers can put their trust or whose existence atheists need to disprove. Like the wizard of Oz, that god is an invention and a fraud, genial perhaps or fearsome, but unreal. God must be qualitatively different to be God, at the very least both a superlative scientist and a consummate artist. But all metaphors and proofs are obviously inadequate. God is 'wholly other', even though we must continue to imagine and describe who God is for us in order to relate and converse. God is also not to be found in the gaps yet to be filled by science, however alluring they may appear.

Not in the gaps

Well before his imprisonment, Bonhoeffer recognized the futility of trying to find God in the ever shrinking gaps in human knowledge.[34] But in prison he began to think about the problem with greater intensity while reading C. F. von Weizsäcker's *The Worldview of Physics* in which the celebrated physicist insisted that every scientist sets 'himself the goal of making the hypothesis 'God' superfluous in his field'.[35] I first heard the phrase 'God of the gaps' in lectures while a student. 'God', I read in one of my text-books on science and religion, 'was found an unnecessary hypothesis in one field after another field of study and experience, until he seemed to have become a silent actor in the play, scarcely needed even to present himself upon the stage'.[36] Invariably, as science progresses, the gaps in our knowledge shrink and God is banished from yet another sphere where he had previously been the sole answer to our questions. But what is not banished is a sense that there is always more to discover. Martin Rees, the

34 See the extended footnotes 5 and 6 in Dietrich Bonhoeffer, *Letters and Papers from Prison*, Dietrich Bonhoeffer Works, edited by John W. de Gruchy, vol. 8, Minneapolis: Fortress Press, pp. 405–6.

35 Carl Friedrich von Weizsäcker, *The Worldview of Physics*, Chicago: University of Chicago Press, 1957, p. 157.

36 C.A. Coulson, *Science and Christian Belief*, Oxford: Oxford University Press, 1955, p. 13.

renowned cosmologist and former president of the Royal Society, speaks of science as 'an unending quest', whose frontiers advance as 'new mysteries come into focus just beyond those frontiers'.[37]

Despite productive attempts to reduce the tension and over-come the sometimes open hostility between science and religion over the past few centuries, the tension remains and perhaps necessarily so.[38] The story is well known. But for the sake of those unfamiliar with it, and in order to locate the current challenges presented to faith by science, let me briefly sketch how the gaps in which Christian apologetics had located God were gradually filled by scientific investigation.

Beginning in the late fifteenth century, science progressively dealt a series of knock-out blows to a faith in God built on the conviction that there are areas of human existence and the cosmos that science is unable to penetrate and uncover.[39] At first, the full extent of the damage done to belief was not obvious because most of the great scientists were believers who sought to reconcile their findings with their faith. You could remain a pious person and continue your work as a sceptical scientist by living in two worlds at the same time, uneasily for some, more comfortably for others, much like the pioneering biblical critics. Typical of the believing scientists was Nicolas Copernicus (1473–1543), a Polish doctor, mathematician and priest, whose calculations led him to conclude that the earth revolved around the sun and was, therefore, not the centrepiece of the universe as had long been thought on the basis of the Bible and the work of the Greek philosopher Ptolemy.

37 Martin Rees, 'Conclusion', in Seeing Further: The Story of Science & the Royal Society, edited by Bill Bryson, London: Harper, 2010, p. 469.

38 The literature on the relationship between science, religion and theology is extensive. An excellent overview is John Russell and Kirk Wegter-McNelly, 'Science', in The Blackwell Companion to Modern Theology, edited by Gareth Jones, Oxford: Blackwell Publishers, 2004, pp. 512–33. Readers outside South Africa may be interested to know that the debate here has also been lively. See Homo transcendentalis? Transcendence in science and religion: interdisciplinary perspectives, edited by Cornel W. du Toit, Pretoria: UNISA, 2010, Volume 14 in the South African Science and Religion Forum series.

39 On the history of science see John Gribben, Science: A History 1543–2001, London: BCA, 2002.

Proving this by mathematical formulae was convincing to the few who understood, but not earth shattering in its impact for the many that did not. Empirical evidence, confirming Copernicus' views, came later as a result of the work of several astronomers, initially the German Thomas Kepler (1571–1630), who discovered the laws of planetary motion, and most notably the Italian Galileo Galilei (1564–1642).

A mathematician and astronomer, Galileo laid the foundations for empirical research, insisting that science was not dependent on what the Bible said about the material universe, nor on deduction from first principles following the Greek philosopher Aristotle, but on the evidence that could be gathered from scientific investigation through the use of the telescope. Galileo was condemned by the Vatican as a heretic and kept under house arrest, refusing to recant on his proven convictions. But the belief that the earth and our place in the universe are special was seriously undermined. Descartes (1596–1650), who we met in the first chapter, played a pivotal role in preparing the next step with his dualistic understanding of the world and human beings, theoretically separating science and theology into two radically different spheres. While Descartes provided ammunition for Christian theologians in their attack on the atheism of the day, his equally famous mathematician and philosopher opponent Blaise Pascal insisted that Descartes' God was that of deism, a God analogous to an absent clockmaker, not the God of the Bible engaged in the life of the world. But the ground had been laid for the next major scientific leap forward taken by Isaac Newton (1642–1727), whose discovery of the law of gravity and hypothesis of the ordered structure of the universe held sway until Albert Einstein's break-through theory of relativity in the early twentieth century.

If the Copernican Revolution relegated the earth from being the centre of the universe to its periphery, the Darwinian Revolution in the nineteenth century relegated humans from being exceptional or fundamentally different from the rest of nature and placed us firmly within the evolving 'animal kingdom'. Charles Darwin's monumental work laid the foundations for much that was to follow. Among these developments was the deciphering of the structure of DNA by Francis Crick and James Watson in the mid-twentieth century. This replaced 'the mysterious ghost of life with something that we can write down in sequences of four letters and store in a computer'.[40]

Few contemporary Christians are likely to feel threatened by the notion that the earth is not the centre of the universe. But Darwin's theory of evolution radically challenged the notion of human exceptionalism and therefore the belief that human beings are created 'in the image of God'. Despite an abundance of 'creationists' among Christians, contemporary theologians generally have little difficulty in integrating the insights of evolution into their anthropology.[41] Teilhard de Chardin's ground-breaking *The Phenomenon of Man* set this process in motion and his work continues to inspire many despite its flaws.[42] Equally important was the work of the biologist Theodosius Dobzhansky, a Russian Orthodox Christian, who insisted that 'nothing in biology makes sense except in the light of evolution', but argued for a more organic rather than molecular understanding of life.[43] Other attempts to take the discussion further include John Haught's *God after Darwin*, which directs our attention not to any divine 'plan' for the universe, but to God's 'vision' for it. Theology, he said, is less interested in human origins than it is in nature's unfolding, 'including humanity's unique history in a still unfinished universe'.[44] More recently, Wentzel van Huyssteen has helped us rethink embodied human uniqueness, traditionally understood as 'being in the image of God', within an evolutionary framework,

40   David Eagleman, *Incognito: The Secret Lives of the Brain*, New York, NY: Pantheon Books, 2011, p. 193.

41   See Russell, 'Science', *Blackwell Companion*, pp. 523–5.

42   Teilhard de Chardin, *The Phenomenon of Man*, New York: Harper & Brothers, 1959. See also Teilhard de Chardin, *The Future of Man*, New York: Harper & Row, 1964.

43   Theodius Dobzhansky, 'Nothing in biology makes sense except in the light of Evolution', *American Biology Teacher* 35 (1973), pp. 125–9.

44   John F. Haught, *God After Darwin: A Theology of Evolution*, Boulder, CO: Westview, 2000, p. 191.

a subject to which I will return in the next chapter.[45] But we should note that attributing everything to genetic development is no longer beyond dispute, if it ever was. There is a hierarchy of complexity that embraces the cosmos of which human beings are a tiny part, and this demands, as van Huyssteen demonstrates, more complex answers than any one discipline can offer.

The development of quantum physics during the past century, with its theories of uncertainty and indeterminacy, of chaos and complexity, have, like evolutionary biology, also radically altered our perception of reality. Gone is the 'dream of a controllable measurement process', and the 'fantasy of deterministic predictability'.[46] Potentially more remarkable still is the outcome of the CERN project in search of the Higgs boson, popularly referred to as the 'god-particle'. Whether this will put the final nail in God's coffin as some assert, is a matter of debate, but it will undoubtedly 'shed light on other mysteries of our universe'.[47]

Christians should approach this ever changing world of science with due wonder, and humility, acknowledging the amazing revolutions that are taking place in our understanding of ourselves, the world in which we live, and the universe(s) beyond. We can also discern fresh possibilities for retrieving Christian faith, but only if we recognize that the terrain keeps on changing. Building theology on the rapidly shifting sands of scientific discovery is not a good idea, but neither is burying one's head as if it will all go away. On the contrary, the dethronement of inadequate theories along with questionable theologies is part of being led deeper into mystery, for each discovery teaches us 'that reality far outstrips human imagination and guesswork'.[48] There are infinite mysteries in the universe awaiting exploration.

There is good reason, then, to heed Philip Clayton's caution that theologians should not, like some latter day Don Quixote,

45 J. Wentzel van Huyssteen, *Alone in the World? Human Uniqueness in Science and Theology*, Grand Rapids, MI: Eerdmans, 2006.
46 See James Gleick, *Chaos: The Amazing Science of the Unpredictable*, New York: Vintage, 1998, p. 6.
47 CERN Director General Rolf Heuer, Press release 17.12, 4 July 2010.
48 Eagleman, *Incognito*, p. 195.

'go on battling the windmills of reductionism – or worse, assume that the windmills have won and retreat from the field'.[49] We are at a different historical point in the long debate between theology and science made inevitable by the increasing awareness of the complexity of an expanding universe and of our own brains. From the perspective of science, if not that of Christian faith, the future of the planet on which we live and of which we are an integral part is by no means certain, nor is the future of humanity and its evolving consciousness. Boundaries will be transgressed as science pursues its historic path, but mystery will undoubtedly deepen at the same time. Scientists, writes Maitland,

> far from pushing us into an apologetic God-of-the-Gaps sheepishness, are in fact opening up for us a vision of God infinitely greater, bigger, cleverer, wilder than our somewhat stunted imaginations have allowed us; a God who is not tamed and constricted by our definitions; a God who challenges us.[50]

How, then, are we to begin to understand this God who is beyond our definitions yet relates to us and the world in which we now live, in a meaningful way?

God beyond modernity

In *Being Human* I described my journey in faith in terms of Christian humanism in an attempt to distance myself from religious fundamentalism as well as from the secularism and scientism that pervades modern culture. 'There is something absent from' their stories, writes Maitland 'which makes them not merely unsatisfactory but actually untrue'.[51] A further reason, as indicated

---

49 Philip Clayton, 'Theology and the Physical Sciences', in *The Modern Theologians: An Introduction to Christian Theology in the Twentieth Century*, *Third Edition*, edited by David F. Ford with Rachel Muers, Oxford: Blackwell Publishers, 2005, p. 344.

50 Maitland, *A Big-Enough God*, p. 50.

51 Maitland, *A Big-Enough God*, p. 72.

in the Prologue, was to help those who wish to affirm their faith in God in a way that is authentically Christian, engaged with contemporary issues, and humanist in character. Yet, in speaking of God within that framework I said little about the ultimate *mystery* into which we are led as human beings on the journey of faith. Let me provide an explanation that will help us go further in our reflections on the God question.[52]

In the Western tradition, humanism gestated during the Renaissance and was largely Christian in ethos until the eighteenth century, when it became increasingly secular and antagonistic to an often reactionary Christianity. Ever since then, secular humanism has been regarded as normative in both scholarly and popular discourse. Although Christian humanism pre-dated secular humanism and stands in critical tension with it, it was imbued with the same emerging spirit of modernity. Christian humanists during the European Renaissance and Protestant Reformation, for example, were at the forefront of critical textual biblical studies, of positively engaging scientific achievements and of promoting reasoned rhetoric in the communication of ideas, not least that of the Christian gospel – and they were wary of religious mystification. In his *Praise of Folly*, Erasmus, the prince of Renaissance Christian humanists, typified the mood when he poured scorn on the religious superstitions of his day kept alive by the wiles of unscrupulous priests, and applauded, as he himself promoted, scholarship as a means of getting at the truth.[53] This led to suspicion of any recourse to mystery, for religious superstition could too easily be smuggled into the life of Church and society under its umbrella. The reality of mystery was not denied, but the notion was prone to religious obfuscation and was problematic for those who promoted a reasoned faith and responsible life in the world.

Modernity, though rooted in the Renaissance, is a shorthand description of the epoch that stretches from the eighteenth-century

---

52 An important contribution to the discussion, but one which I received too late for consideration in my discussion, is Jens Zimmermann, *Humanism & Religion: A Call for the Renewal of Western Culture*, Oxford: Oxford University Press, 2012.

53 See for example Erasmus, *Praise of Folly and Letter to Martin Dorp 1515*, Harmondsworth: Penguin Books, 1971, pp. 129–30.

European Enlightenment through to the second half of the twentieth century. It is characterized by a growing confidence in the power of reason to solve human problems and to shape the world through scientific endeavour. Modernity challenged mystery; it championed clarity, certainty, and scientific progress. It was the heyday of European colonialism and the beginning of capitalist expansion. Theologically it found expression in liberal Protestant thought that prided itself on its reasoned, scientific approach to explaining the Christian faith to 'modern man'. Modernity's defining myth of inevitable progress was destroyed on the battle fields of France during the First World War, as was the confidence and credibility of liberal Protestant theology that, in Germany, had justified the war in the name of God. Barth, who led the charge, anticipated later post-modern developments in his critique of the power of reason to know God, and largely changed the face of twentieth-century theology in the process. An awareness of the awesome mystery of God known only to faith was recovered. This was the theology that attracted Bonhoeffer as a student despite the objections of his liberal teachers who insisted that Barth's 'unscientific theology' would destroy all the gains made in bringing Christianity into the modern era.[54]

How, then, are we to understand the significance of what is called *post*-modernity, roughly the period that followed the devastation of the Second World War through to the new millennium? Post-modernity defies easy definition, but it is characterized by the paradigm shifts in science that have undermined previously held certainties, by global multiculturalism, challenges to entrenched power-relations, traditional understandings of human sexuality, discrimination against 'the other', moral and philosophical relativism and by late capitalism. Post-modernism, as distinct from the post-modern epoch, is the attempt to understand and critically evaluate modernity from within this post-modern framework.

---

54 Martin Rumscheidt, *Revelation and Theology: An Analysis of the Barth–Harnack Correspondence of 1923*, Cambridge: Cambridge University Press, 1972; Michael P. DeJonge, *Bonhoeffer's Theological Formation: Berlin, Barth, & Protestant Theology*, Oxford: Oxford University Press, 2012.

It emphasizes respect for difference, rejects meta-narratives and hierarchies, challenges patriarchy, anthropocentrism and destructive power-relations along with global cultural and economic hegemonies, and is sceptical of dogmatic truth claims.

Post-modernist thought undoubtedly helps us question and rethink modernity; it also prompts us to think afresh about how to speak of God beyond the straight-jacket of modernity with its scepticism about mystery.[55] Theological reflection today cannot return to either the notion of a universal rationality associated with modernity any more than it can to the 'pre-modern notion of tradition as a repository of privileged data and specially protected, exclusive criteria'.[56] But, however much post-modernism may break open theological enquiry and offer new possibilities for thinking about God, it is not without its own problems. These stem from the fact that it remains trapped in some of the myths of modernity. In some respects, it is 'the flip-side of fundamentalism'[57] and when pushed too far it ends in nihilism.[58]

Huston Smith neatly sums up the situation when he writes that whereas 'the Modern Mind assumed that it knew more than its predecessors because the natural and historical sciences were flooding it with new knowledge about nature and history, the Post Modern mind argues (paradoxically) that it knows more than others did because it has discovered how little the human mind *can* know'.[59] Reason has again become aware of its limitations and the fact that there are different rationalities. This brings epistemology, or the theory of knowing, onto centre stage, for how then *can we know* God? It is not simply a theoretical question but one of enormous practical significance. How shall we live in a world given

---

55 Graham Ward, 'Introduction, or, a Guide to Theological Thinking in Cyberspace', in *The Postmodern God*, edited by Graham Ward, Oxford: Blackwell Publishers, 1997, p. xxv.

56 Huyssteen, *Alone in the World?*, p. 308.

57 Eagleton, *Reason, Faith & Revolution*, p. 136.

58 John Milbank, *Theology & Social Theory: Beyond Secular Reason*, Oxford: Blackwell Publishers, 1990, pp. 278–94.

59 Huston Smith, *Beyond the Post modern Mind*, Wheaton, IL: Quest Books, 2003, pp. x–xi.

that the centre (faith in God), which seemed so secure in the past, no longer holds as it once apparently did? Is there what Critchley calls an 'infinite demand' to which we as human beings are responsible, and if so, is this demand transcendent, a divine imperative, as Christians insist, or simply a social contract, a shared commitment to justice and the common good, as in secular humanism?

In his prison correspondence, Bonhoeffer noted that the 'fundamental concepts of humanism . . . in their finest form' pre-dated the Renaissance.[60] This train of thought led him to consider again the importance of the high Middle Ages in providing insight for rethinking Christianity in the 'modern' world. He was not engaging in some romantic flight of the imagination, trying to find an escape route from post-modern reality by returning to a pre-modern era.[61] It was, rather, an attempt to recover a vision of the world and ourselves that was holistic rather than subject to the Cartesian dualism that underpinned modernity and led to the separation of faith and reason, theology and science, transcendence and immanence. For Bonhoeffer, the clue to overcoming this dualism was to be found in the mystery of the Incarnation, for in Christ the reality of God and the reality of the world were disclosed at the same time.[62] This was in continuity with his much earlier critique of the idealist epistemologies of Kant, Hegel and Heidegger, which were so formative in his own thinking, but were incapable of 'rendering the 'encounter with an other' . . . whether God, neighbour or enemy'.[63] The transcendentalism of Idealism was unable to break through the ceiling of rationality, history or experience to the transcendent that held them to account and gave

---

60 Bonhoeffer, *Letters and Papers from Prison*, p. 320.
61 Bonhoeffer, *Letters and Papers from Prison*, p. 478.
62 Bonhoeffer, *Ethics*, pp. 47–75; see also Peter Dabrock, 'Responding to "Wirklichkeit"; Reclaiming Bonhoeffer's Approach to Theological Ethics between Mystery and the Formation of the World', *Mysteries in the Theology of Dietrich Bonhoeffer*, edited by UlrikNissen, Kirsten Busch Nielsen, Christiane Tietz, Göttingen: Vandenhoek & Ruprecht, 2007, pp. 49–80.
63 Wayne Whitson Floyd, Jr., 'Encounter with an Other: Immanuel Kant and G.W.F. Hegel in the Theology of Dietrich Bonhoeffer', in *Bonhoeffer's Intellectual Formation*, edited by Peter Frick, Tübingen: Mohr Siebeck, 2008, p. 119.

them significance.[64] This, as we shall later see, is why, for Bonhoeffer, the mystery of God is best expressed in Trinitarian theology, exemplified for some in the novels Dostoevsky, a Christian humanist, who never lost sight of the divine mystery.[65]

The problem of relating transcendence and immanence, that is, divine and human/worldly reality, is reflected in the resurgence of spirituality in our post-modern but largely secular age which feels trapped in the iron cage of instrumental reason and historical fate. William Schweiker speaks of a 'spiritual longing of the age' in which we live, not for meaning, which is a very 'modern' quest, 'but for an 'outside,' transcendence, to the human project that liberates us from the horror of history'.[66] The notion that we humans are somehow called to control nature and 'make history', either in the name of God or modernity ('spreading civilization') to justify imperial and similar claims, is idolatrous. The post-modern secular humanisms of our time recognize the impotence of older forms of liberal humanism to transcend such triumphalism. But they continue to understand transcendence in a purely lateral way in terms of our fellow human 'other' rather than the 'Other' who encounters us as the 'other'. What fundamentally separates contemporary Christian humanism from such forms of neo-humanism is not its shared commitment to the 'human project' and the claims of the environment in which we live, but the basis on which that commitment is made, namely the transcendent claims that keep it human and challenge the absolutizing of the human under whatever banner. Critchley's desire for faithfulness to an 'infinite demand', I submit, requires that it be infinite, and that opens up the possibility of transcendence.

Moral responsibility and action in the world is dependent on transcendent critique and empowerment from beyond itself. In

---

64   See Dietrich Bonhoeffer, *Act and Being: Transcendental Philosophy and Ontology in Systematic Theology*, edited by Wayne Whitson Floyd Jr., Dietrich Bonhoeffer Works volume 2, Minneapolis: Fortress Press, 1996. See also DeJonge, *Bonhoeffer's Theological Formation*, pp. 15–35.

65   See Bruce K. Ward, *Redeeming the Enlightenment: Christianity and Liberal Values*, Grand Rapids: Eerdmans, 2010, p. 22.

66   William Schweiker, *Dust That Breathes: Christian Faith and the New Humanism*, Chichester: Wiley-Blackwell, 2010, p. 88.

Schweiker's words, human responsibility and flourishing 'arise out of and are empowered by gratitude for the infusing of finite life with the *power to do good*, the moral capacity for goodness'.[67] Such gratitude and responsibility are indicators of the divine presence among us. This leads us directly to the domain of mystery, not as something alien to Christian humanism, but as fundamental. For our understanding of God disclosed in the mystery of the Incarnation as 'truly human' does not remove God from the world, on the contrary, it is in the world that God encounters us as ultimate mystery in 'the other', in the claims of creation, at the centre and on the boundaries of our existence. That is why our knowledge of God is inseparable from our knowledge both of ourselves and 'the other' through whom God encounters us as 'infinite demand', or in Tillich's phrase, 'ultimate concern'.[68]

Ultimate mystery and concern

The French philosopher Gabriel Marcel gave his Gifford Lectures at the University of Aberdeen in Scotland in 1949–50 on 'The Mystery of Being'.[69] He had just lived through the Second World War with its horrific slaughter of millions of human beings, its destruction of cities and devastation of vast tracts of the environment. Modernity had not only failed to halt evil, it had contributed to its rise as ideology, theology, science and technology combined to tear apart nations proud of their culture, religion and civilization. Fascism, Nazism, Soviet Communism, along with military and industrial interests, reduced human beings to material objects that had no value other than their usefulness in labour camps or on the battle field. They had been dehumanized and trashed, their dignity and rights trodden underfoot. Nihilism had triumphed. In

67 Schweiker, *Dust That Breathes*, p. 99.
68 Paul Tillich, *Systematic Theology* I, London: Nisbet & Co, 1955, pp. 14–16.
69 Published in two volumes as *The Mystery of Being*, Chicago: Henry Regency Company 1960.Volume 1 'Reflection and Mystery'; Volume 2 'Faith and Reality'.

protest Marcel spoke of an alternative understanding of what it means to be truly human in terms of 'the *mystery* of being' arising from the creative testimony of Christian faith, of justice and truth, freedom, grace and hope which has its source in the ultimate mystery we call God.

Just a decade after Marcel gave his lectures, as the Cold War was threatening to erupt into another global conflagration, as the Civil Rights Movement was gathering momentum in the United States and the struggle against apartheid was entering a new phase in South Africa, I listened to Tillich lecturing at the University of Chicago on God as that which concerns us ultimately, excluding 'all other concerns from ultimate significance'.[70] To elevate something else to ultimacy is idolatry, whether nation or race, religion or individual self-interest. The revelation of God as ultimate concern expresses itself, Tillich went on to say, in 'symbols and myths which point to the depth of reason and its mystery', and it does so always in 'a concrete situation of concern'.[71] If the revelation of mystery does not happen objectively, 'nothing is revealed', but equally if 'no one receives what happens subjectively, the event fails to reveal anything'.[72] Faith in God's self-disclosure in history in Jesus as the Christ is not the acceptance of a doctrine, but a commitment to God as our ultimate concern and all that this implies.

God as ultimate mystery and concern is not to be found in the gaps of our knowledge, but neither is God one religious concept among others, for then, as Bonhoeffer says, 'there is no reason why there should not be, behind this apparent "ultimate" reality, a still more ultimate reality: the twilight or the death of the gods'.[73] God remains unfathomable mystery even when revealed, for what is revealed is what we need to know about God, not everything there is to know. What we glimpse of God is never enough but always more than sufficient for us. Jesus as the revelation of God is truly God but not the whole of God. This distinction was drawn

---

70 Tillich, *Systematic Theology* I, p. 16.
71 Tillich, *Systematic Theology* I, pp. 122–3.
72 Tillich, *Systematic Theology* I, p. 124.
73 Bonhoeffer, *Ethics*, p. 48.

with precision in the writings of Thomas Aquinas. Rahner, one of his modern interpreters, follows him in speaking of God as 'ultimate mystery' and incomprehensible unless God in some way communicates with us.[74] We can speak about it in responding 'but we can never really know about it'.[75] To speak of God as ultimate mystery and therefore our ultimate concern, is making a faith claim and a moral commitment.

Dawkins, you may recall, indicated that his attack on God was not directed at God as understood by the likes of Tillich and Bonhoeffer. I am not convinced that he has really taken them as seriously as his comment suggests. If so, then, the God in whom I and many others believe is not the 'straw' deity he demolishes. Yet even if *this* God is not to his liking, there is not much I can do about it, and I am aware that defining God in terms of 'ultimate mystery' will probably not satisfy other 'new atheists' either. For this reason it is true to say with Eberhard Jüngel, that in philosophical debate it 'helps little to call on God as mystery'.[76] When we appeal to God as mystery, we always do so too late to convince those who do not believe. This does not alter the fact that faith 'knows God as the ultimate and authentic mystery of the world', or that it 'understands God as that which is most self-evident'.[77] For such reasons, Bonhoeffer was adamant that it was foolish to try to 'decode God's mystery, pulling it down to the commonplace, miracle-less words of wisdom based on human experience and reason'! The task of theology he insisted is 'to comprehend, defend, and exalt the mystery of God, precisely as mystery'.[78]

I will return to Bonhoeffer's attempt to speak of God in a 'world come of age' in a short while, not least because I assume that both Dawkins and Critchley had this in mind in speaking of him. But

74 Karl Rahner, 'Mystery', in *Encyclopedia of Theology: A Concise Sacramentum Mundi*, ed. Karl Rahner, London: Burns & Oates, 1975, p. 1002.

75 Rahner, 'Mystery', p. 1002.

76 Jüngel, *God as the Mystery of the World*, p. 251.

77 Jüngel, *God as the Mystery of the World*, p. 246.

78 Dietrich Bonhoeffer, 'Meditation on Christmas, December 1939', in *Theological Education Underground, 1937–1940*, Dietrich Bonhoeffer Works, vol. 15, edited byVictoria J. Barnett, Minneapolis: Fortress Press, 2012, p. 529.

let us note here that one of the difficulties in speaking of God as 'ultimate mystery', is that it makes God seem so remote and impersonal. Einstein, who was comfortable with God as 'ultimate mystery' refused to believe in God as personal, regarding such a belief as a major reason for the conflict between religion and science. But much has to do with what is meant by God *as person*. Einstein's objection has been discussed at length and clarified even if not entirely resolved.[79] God is not a person in the sense that we humans are individuals, but neither is God impersonal in the sense of being an entity that we control.[80] The 'ultimate mystery' we call God is not an object we study but an active Subject, hence the many personal and relational metaphors used to speak about God. What makes it possible for us to respond to God is precisely that as humans we are oriented towards mystery *as persons*. This implies that in some meaningful sense God too is personal, otherwise a relationship whether in contemplation or action would not be meaningful.[81] Faith in God as ultimate mystery, far from being an abstraction, implies a commitment to God as ultimate concern in living our lives. This leads us deeper into reality, not away from it.

Critchley concludes *The Faith of the Faithless* by reminding us of Søren Kierkegaard's radical understanding of faith not as belief in doctrines or the affirmation of the Creed, nor as glib certainty that participation in formal Christianity might promise, but as a relationship of trust that expresses itself in love of God and the 'other'.[82] All that counts, says Paul in a moment of deep insight, 'is faith working through love' (Gal. 5.6). Faith understood in this way is therefore a commitment that has to be made every day within the realities of the world. It is not a certainty that we possess, but a certainty that comes to possess us, the mystery of grace that makes believing possible in the first place. It is not a way of escape from reality, but a way of engaging reality and, in doing so, dealing with suffering, perhaps the greatest obstacle to faith in God.

---

79 Max Jammer, *Einstein and Religion*, Princeton, NJ: Princeton University Press, 1999, pp. 107–14.
80 Hans Küng, *Does God Exist?*, London: Collins, 1980, pp. 632–3.
81 Rahner, 'Mystery', p. 1003.
82 Critchley, *Faith of the Faithless*, pp. 247–50.

God's strange power

While on sabbatical in Princeton in 1983, we received a letter from Steve in Cape Town in which he told how he had spent the previous night with a group of student activists protesting against the forced removal of black people from an 'illegal' informal settlement called Crossroads. The police had arrived and, with the use of tear gas and whips, forced them to leave in the early hours of the morning. Steve described the scene in vivid terms, but ended his letter with a surprising twist to his tale. He went back to his apartment and finished his paper on Schleiermacher's theology for his graduate seminar class later that day. While Schleiermacher was at one stage in his life a political activist in the struggle against Napoleonic hegemony in Germany in the early nineteenth century, his theology is not normally considered in such terms. Even so, his theology, as Steve told us in his letter, had come alive in a way that took him (and me) by surprise. God may not have been a reality in Prussia for the bourgeoisie 'cultured despisers of religion', who had embraced modernity and to whom a youthful Schleiermacher addressed his famous *Reden* or speeches *On Religion*,[83] but God was a reality for those Christian students engaged in the struggle against apartheid, just as God was a reality for its victims.

Bonhoeffer was fully cognizant of Schleiermacher's contribution to theology and hermeneutics, as well as of those who followed him in the task, notably Wilhelm Dilthey, whose 'philosophy of life' Bonhoeffer read again at some length in prison.[84] It was in this context that he wrestled anew with the same question as had Schleiermacher: how to speak about religion to its enlightened and disenchanted sceptics. But his proposal went in a different direction. Bonhoeffer did not assume some kind of religious sensibility to which the gospel could appeal, but spoke

83   Schleiermacher, *On Religion: Speeches to Its Culture Despisers*.

84   The literature (novels, history, science and theology) read by Bonhoeffer or referred to in passing in his letters and papers, is listed in Bonhoeffer, *Letters and Papers*, pp. 616–25. See also Ralf K. Wüstenberg, *Faith as Life: Dietrich Bonhoeffer and the Non-Religious Interpretation of the Biblical Message*, English, Grand Rapids: Eerdmans, 1998.

of Christian faith in terms of living fully and responsibly in the world.[85] His was not the language of piety but of engagement where the reality of God and the world are united in the crucified and risen Christ. It was there that God encounters us rather than in religious intuition and feeling, however significant. In speaking of God we should neither assume some religious *a priori* nor try to find God in the gaps in our knowledge, but seek God in what we do know.[86] This not only applied to 'the relation between God and scientific knowledge', but also to 'the universal human questions about death, suffering and guilt'. 'God', Bonhoeffer wrote, 'wants to be recognized in the midst of our lives, in life and not only in dying, in health and strength and not only in suffering, in action, and not only in sin'.[87] God was no *deus ex machine* who suddenly arrives to save us in the boundary situations of life when all else fails.[88]

In this way, Bonhoeffer went to the heart of the scientific challenge to faith in God, namely God's agency in the world – whether or not God could intervene in nature in ways that were traditionally understood as miraculous. Apart from traditional biblical theism which teaches that God is distinct from creation but actively engaged in history, several alternative positions have been adopted over the centuries. Chief among them are pantheism, the view favoured by Romanticism, that God is *in all* things; deism, the position of Enlightenment Rationalism that God, having set all things in motion, is no longer directly involved but lets the laws of nature and history run their course;[89] and panentheism, literally meaning that everything exists *in* God, even though God transcends everything.

Some of the leading philosophers of religion of the twentieth century have espoused panentheism, notably Charles Hartshorne, who spoke of the world as God's body of which God is the mind.[90]

---

85   See Wüstenberg, *Faith as Life*, pp. 112–45.
86   Letter to Eberhard Bethge, 29 May 1944, *Letters and Papers*, pp. 405–6.
87   Bonhoeffer, *Letters and Papers from Prison*, p. 406.
88   Bonhoeffer, *Letters and Papers from Prison*, p. 450.
89   See Bonhoeffer, *Letters and Papers*, pp. 475–8.
90   See William L. Reese Hartshorne (ed.), *Philosophers Speak of God*, Chicago: University of Chicago Press, 1963, pp. 499–514; Sallie McFague, *The Body of God: An Ecological Theology*, Minneapolis: Fortress Press, 1993.

This has had considerable influence on some Christian theologies, such as process theology, and those engaged with science. In fact, panentheism is not unrelated to the Hellenistic view noted positively by Paul in his famous sermon in Athens, that 'we live, move and have our being in God'.[91] It may also be related to such New Testament assertions there is only 'one God and Father of all, who is above all, and through all and in all', that all things cohere in God and will in the end be restored in God.[92] In his *Confessions*, Augustine comes close to its meaning:

> Do heaven and earth, then, contain the whole of you, since you fill them? Or, when once you have filled them, is some part of you left over because they are too small to hold you? If this is so, when you have filled heaven and earth, does that part of you which remains flow over into some other place? Or is it that you have no need to be contained in anything, because you contain all things in yourself and fill them by reason of the very fact that you contain them?[93]

Of all the philosophical descriptions of God's relation to the world, panentheism probably fits best with the biblical concept of God as Spirit, not located in any place, but pervading creation.

In the story of Jesus and the Samaritan woman, told in John's Gospel, Jesus rejects all understandings of God that are defined by place (or ethnicity). The time is coming, he tells the woman, when those who rightly worship God will do so 'in spirit and truth' because 'God is Spirit' (John 4.23–4). In the Old Testament, spirit (*ruach*) is not contrasted with the material but refers to the life-giving activity of God who is not bound to creation, but freely and creatively committed to and engaged in it. It is with this understanding of God as creative and redemptive Spirit rather

91 Acts 17.24–8.
92 See 1 Corinthians 15.28; Ephesians 4.6 and 1.20. See also Bonhoeffer's discussion in *Letters and Papers from Prison*, p. 230.
93 *St. Augustine: Confessions*, edited by R.S. Pine-Coffin, London: Penguin Classics, 1961, Bk. 1, ch. 3, p. 22.

than from a philosophical perspective, that the bible approaches the question of God's agency in the world.

But the question of God's agency is undoubtedly problematic, especially when considered in relation to human tragedy and suffering: one of the most perplexing of all mysteries into which we are inevitably led in the course of our lives. There are reasonable responses to the problem that carry some explanatory weight. One is that God has given us freedom to make choices but that we do not always make good ones and that these often result in suffering and even death, both of ourselves and others. Natural disasters are likewise explainable by reference to the nature of the earth and the solar system of which it is part. Steve's death was the result of a combination of both an error of judgment on his part and a storm in the Drakensberg that had swollen the Mooi River and increased the velocity of the rapids where he was tubing.

But even so, the problem of faith in God in the midst of human suffering remains; tempting us, with Job, to 'curse God and die'.[94] If God is God then surely somehow, somewhere amid such tragic events God must be present even if hidden, otherwise, as Desmond Tutu has said, 'God is God's Worst Enemy'.[95] Tutu was reflecting on the fact that Steve and so many others die young, just as they are making a significant contribution to social and human well-being.

We have heard or even ourselves uttered the agonizing cry "But why . . ." In an ultimate sense I really don't know. In the end for me as for most of us it is a mystery and I have to accept that I must have a reverent agnosticism. Why did God create precisely this sort of universe? I would have to be God to know the ultimate answer. But there are things that I have noted. Why would a good God permit such atrocities to happen when they happen?[96]

---

94 Job 2.9

95 In the first Steve de Gruchy Memorial Lecture, held in the Rondebosch United Church, Cape Town, 24 April 2012.

96 Desmond Tutu, 'God is God's Worst Enemy', in *Living on the Edge: Essays in Honour of Steve de Gruchy, Activist Theologian*, edited by James R. Cochrane, Elias Bongmba, Isabel Phiri, and Des van der Water, Pietermaritzburg: Cluster Publications, 2012, p. xii.

Tutu is correct. Perhaps, as John Hick said, there is no 'solution' this side of eternity,[97] for the problem 'remains unjust and inexplicable, haphazard and cruelly excessive', or at the very least, a mystery 'impenetrable to the rationalizing human mind'.[98] Though it may well be that its irrationality and lack of ethical meaning 'contribute to the character of the world as a place in which true human goodness can occur'.[99] But maybe the agnostic Oscar Wilde came closer to the truth when, reflecting in prison on the suffering of Christ, he wrote in his deeply moving essay *De Profundis*, that the experience of suffering is not so much a mystery as it is a revelation.

> One discerns things one never discerned before. One approaches the whole of history from a different standpoint. What one had felt dimly, through instinct, about art, is intellectually and emotionally realised with perfect clearness of vision and absolute intensity of apprehension.[100]

Any genuinely Christian theodicy, that is, any attempt to justify God's permitting of human suffering, must surely begin with the suffering of Jesus on the cross as the revelation of the mystery of who God is. However much pleasure enriches life, Wilde confessed, it is in suffering that we are led into the depths of God's mystery, and through pain that new life is born. Our deepest knowledge comes, as the Psalmist discerned, 'out of the depths' of human experience.[101]

Keith Ward helps us go further when he writes more analytically about God having 'a universe-long intention to bring conscious beings into a community of freely chosen loving relationships', which shapes the laws of nature and the complex possibilities

---

97 John Hick, *Evil & the Love of God*, London: Macmillan Fontana, 1968, p. 398.

98 Hick, *Evil & the Love of God*, p. 371.

99 Hick, *Evil & the Love of God*, pp. 371–2.

100 Oscar Wilde, 'De Profundis', in the *Complete Works of Oscar Wilde*, London: HarperCollins Publishers, 1994.

101 The opening words of Psalm 130 which, in Latin, became the title of Wilde's essay 'De Profundis'.

that emerge within it. So in general 'God will exert the maximum influence for good compatible with the preservation of the relative autonomy of nature and its probabilistic laws, and with the freedom of finite agents'.[102] In short, God 'is continuously, pre-eminently, but not all-powerfully, active in evolution, influencing events through persuasive love but not controlling them unilaterally'.[103] This may not be of much comfort to those who are suffering and are crying out for some answers to their plight from an apparently silent and hidden God. But it does relate well to what Bonhoeffer wrote for his secular co-conspirators in the German Resistance shortly before he was arrested and imprisoned:

> I believe that God can and will let good come out of everything, even the greatest evil. For that to happen, God needs human beings who let everything work out for the best. I believe that in every moment of distress God will give us as much strength to resist as we need . . . I believe that God is no timeless fate but waits for and responds to sincere prayer and responsible actions.[104]

It is not a question of whether God is omnipotent, but the nature of God's power and how it is exercised. In the Creed, God's 'almightiness' is always placed in relation to God's parenting, which provides an analogical clue to the conundrum, for good parents know that their authority is contingent upon their love, not the reverse. Even so, with reference to God, as Tutu says: 'It is one of the abiding mysteries that there can be the oxymoron of a weak omnipotence.'[105] It is a strange power that we discern as we are led into the ultimate mystery we name God.

Much contemporary theological discussion around these issues takes its cue from a passage in Bonhoeffer's prison letters, where he says that if we are honest with ourselves, we have to 'recognize

---

102 Keith Ward, *God, Chance and Necessity*, Oxford: Oneworld, 2001, p. 80.
103 See Russell, 'Science', p. 524.
104 Bonhoeffer, *Letters and Papers*.
105 Desmond Tutu, 'God is God's Worst Enemy', in *Living on the Edge*, p. xiii.

that we have to live in the world – "*etsi Deus non daretur,*" that is, as if God were not present'. This is our situation in a 'world come of age', a world shaped by modern science and secularization. But to say that we should live 'as if' God is absent does not mean that God is not present. The issue concerns the mode of God's presence as the God whose mystery is revealed in the crucified Jesus as self-giving love, not unbridled power that overrides human freedom and responsibility. We continually stand before God, Bonhoeffer says, but before a God who 'would have us know that we must live as those who manage their lives without God'.

> God consents to be pushed out of the world and onto the cross, God is weak and powerless in the world, and in precisely this way, and only so, is at our side and helps us . . . Christ does not help us by virtue of his omnipotence, but rather by virtue of his weakness and suffering! . . . Human religiosity directs people in need to the power of God in the world . . . The Bible directs people toward the powerlessness and the suffering of God; only the suffering God can help.[106]

To speak of God's impotence and pathos is shocking to our normal sensibilities of divinity. But no more so than when Paul told the Corinthian church that Christ crucified is the power of God at work in human life and the world.[107] Such language rudely breaks open the door into the ultimate mystery we name God; it also radically challenges the human will to power which inevitably leads to violence, including the violence of the cross through which the mystery of God's power and wisdom is revealed as unfathomable love.

Infinite beauty and unfathomable love

The unending quest of science and the theological sense of being led into mystery are analogous and converge in some respects,

---

106   Bonhoeffer, *Letters and Papers*, p. 479.
107   1 Corinthians 1.23–5.

but they are not the same. Yet, when Einstein says that the 'most beautiful thing we can experience is the mysterious', and that this is 'the source of all true art and all science', he is referring to that ultimate mystery which transcends art, science and theological enquiry itself. Being led into mystery is, however, more than a never ending intellectual search – it is being drawn into the embrace of a love and beauty that is both disclosed yet always exceeding what we can fathom. Only this ultimate reality is worthy of the name God, and therefore of our worship, that which makes us 'pause to wonder and stand rapt in awe'.[108]

Soon after the changes that led to the first post-apartheid election in 1994, I became interested in theological aesthetics through the writings of Hans Urs von Balthasar, but with a particular focus on the relationship between beauty and justice and the role of art in social transformation.[109] I had already come to the conclusion that apartheid was ugly because it was unjust, and that those images of God that are used to support it were not only false but also repulsive. This was the beginning of a journey that led me to a new appreciation of the importance of beauty for understanding faith in God and life in the world. In the process, I gained inspiration from Dostoevsky and was particularly struck by his observation in *The Idiot,* spoken through Prince Myshkin, the 'holy fool' and figure of Christ, that beauty saves the world.[110] This radically changed my understanding of beauty. For how can we possibly describe as beautiful such a violent deed as the crucifixion? It contradicts all norms of aesthetic sensibility.[111]

A clue to understanding this strange beauty is found in *The Brothers Karamazov* in the confessions of Dimitri Fyodorovich, the profligate eldest son: 'The terrible thing is that beauty is not only fearful but also mysterious. Here the devil is struggling with

108   Albert Einstein, back cover of *Inside the Mind of God.*

109   John W. de Gruchy, *Christianity, Art, and Transformation: Theological Aesthetics and the Struggle for Justice,* Cambridge: Cambridge University Press, 2001; Hans Urs von Balthasar, *Theo-Drama: Theological Dramatic Theory,* Vols. 1–3, San Francisco: Ignatius Press, 1988–92.

110   Fyodor Dostoevsky, *The Idiot,* London: Penguin, 1986, p. 394.

111   Seede Gruchy, *Christianity, Art, and Transformation,* pp. 97–102.

God, and the battlefield is the human heart.'[112] The 'terrible beauty' of the cross, its mystery, is that God is present there, 'descending into hell'. Or, in Dimitri's words, 'in Sodom itself', becoming repulsive in order to transform what is ugly into something beautiful. In such ways, Dostoevsky draws us deeply into a conversation around the thorny issues that evoke doubt and scepticism, and nudges us deeper into the mystery of faith in God. The question shifts from whether we believe that God exists, to what difference this makes if we do. How does faith in God take hold of our lives, and influence the way in which we engage the world and respond to evil, tragedy and suffering? The refrain, as in Zosima's final homilies, is that such faith is real only when active in love.

> . . . do not be afraid of men's sin, love man also in his sin, for this likeness of God's love is the height of love on earth . . . If you love each thing, you will perceive the mystery of God in things. Once you have perceived it, you will begin tirelessly to perceive more and more of it every day. And you will come at last to love the whole world with an entire, universal love.[113]

For Dostoevsky, embracing the 'other', not least the sinner and children, is to embody the 'likeness of God's love', the mystery of God present in all creation and all people, in their pain as well as their joy, in their weakness and their strength. This love, embodied in the life and death of Jesus Christ and expressed in his humble followers, is the 'beauty that saves the world'.

Dostoevsky's relationship to Christianity is complex though his passionate embrace of Russian Orthodoxy is omnipresent even if often hidden beneath the surface.[114] He was also well-informed

---

112 Fyodor Dostoevsky, *The Brothers Karamazov,* trans. by Richard Pevear and Larissa Volokhonsky, London: Vintage Books, 2004, p. 108.

113 Dostoevsky, *The Brothers Karamazov,* p. 319.

114 See *Dostoevsky and the Christian Tradition,* edited by George Pattinson and Diane OenningThimpson, Cambridge Studies in Russian Literature, Cambridge: Cambridge University Press, 2001; Rowan Williams, *Dostoevsky: Language, Faith and Fiction,* London: Continuum, 2008, pp. 5–14.

about the critical intellectual and theological debates and issues of his day – philosophical challenges to faith in God, the historical reliability of the biblical narrative, the superficial aestheticism of Romanticism and the liberal attempt to adapt its message to modern culture. This is evident in *The Brothers Karamazov* as the relationships and conversation develops most notably between the three Karamazov brothers, in the homilies of the elder saintly Zosima and the temptations presented by the sophisticated Grand Inquisitor. In the course of the dialogue, Dostoevsky's own struggles with suffering, doubt and faith are present but not always obvious, for there are many voices engaged in the conversation each with its own identity and independence. So while he refrains from offering an obvious apologetic of easy answers, his novel becomes the prism through which reality is perceived in the light of Christ.[115] In this way, Dostoevsky leads us deeper into the Trinitarian mystery of the God in whom he believed.[116]

In Christian tradition the doctrine of the Trinity is central to the mystery of faith in God; the most complex and profound of all Christian images constructed of God as ultimate mystery. The philosopher Hans-Georg Gadamer writes of it not only as the 'deepest mystery of Christian doctrine', but also as the doctrine that 'has constantly stimulated the course of thought in the West as a challenge and invitation to try to think that which continually transcends the limits of human understanding'.[117] Yet, it is a doctrine so burdened by metaphysical language that is has become incomprehensible to most people. The danger that this might happen gave rise in the early Church to the 'arcane discipline' (*disciplina arcani*), something Bonhoeffer commends in his prison letters as necessary in proclaiming the gospel in a 'world come of age' in order to prevent the profanation of the mystery

115   See AvrilPyman, 'Dostevsky in the prism of the orthodox semiosphere', in *Dostoevsky and the Christian Tradition*, pp. 104–5.

116   David S. Cunningham, '*The Brothers Karamazov* as Trinitarian Theology', in *Dostoevsky and the Christian Tradition*, pp. 134–152.

117   Hans-Georg Gadamer, *The Relevance of the Beautiful and other Essays*, Cambridge: Cambridge University Press, 1986, p. 5.

to which the doctrine points.[118] The creeds, he earlier told his students, were intended for use in worship, not to be 'screamed loudly in a propagandistic manner'.[119]

The main point of the doctrine of the Trinity is not to decipher God-in-God's self, but to describe in so far as words allow, the 'pattern of God's self-expression' in Jesus Christ and as Spirit derived from the gospel narrative. The fact that it seeks to express the inexpressible in words, not only in the original Greek but also in translation, is one reason why it is generally misunderstood.[120] I cannot unravel all the intricacies here, but on a point of clarification, the three 'persons' or *persona* of the Trinity are not three individuals,[121] but the way in which the mystery we call God has become known to faith experienced through the Spirit and in the life, death and resurrection of Jesus. This does not mean that God's plurality compromises God's unity, for there is total harmony of being and action in God. The doctrine rejects any dualism between the material and the spiritual on the basis of the Incarnation; it rejects pantheism and deism by asserting both God's transcendent freedom *from the* world and God's immanent freedom *for* its well-being, and it rejects both individualism and the submersion of identity in the collective by affirming God's sociality and relationality. Yet, in the end, as Bonhoeffer declared, the 'doctrine of the Holy Trinity is nothing but humankind's feeble way of praising the mighty, impetuous love of God in which God glorifies himself and embraces the world in love'.[122] And it is this 'impetuous love' which is the 'secret of God's beauty' that redeems the world. [123]

---

118 Bonhoeffer, *Letters and Papers*, pp. 365, 373.

119 From a sermon preached on Trinity Sunday in London in 1934. Bonhoeffer, *Ecumenical, Academic and Pastoral Work: 1931–1932*, Dietrich Bonhoeffer Works, vol. 11, Minneapolis: Fortress, 2012, pp. 285.

120 Catherine Mowry Lacugna, *God for Us: The Trinity and Christian Life*, San Francisco: Harper Collins, 1991, p. 225.

121 Much confusion has arisen because the original Greek term *hypostasis* was translated as *persona* in Latin, and then directly as *person* in English where it assumed the sense of individual contrary to the original.

122 Bonhoeffer, *London*, p. 363.

123 Karl Barth, *Church Dogmatics* II.1, Edinburgh: T. & T. Clark, 1964, p. 661.

God's beauty is nothing less, then, than God's creative and redemptive, self-giving or kenotic love, which is described in the New Testament as *agapé*, that is another way of speaking of God as triune:

> God is *agapé*. God's *agapé* was revealed to us in this way: God sent his only Son into the world so that we might live through him. No one has ever seen God: if we love (*agapōmen*) one another, God lives in us and his *agapé* is perfected in us . . . we know that we abide in him and he in us, because he has given us the Spirit . . . God is *agapé*, and those who abide in *agapé* abide in God and God abides in them. (1 John 4.8–9, 12–13, 16b)

All other terms used to describe God, such as omnipotent, omniscient, and omnipresent, transcendent and imminent, freedom and power, are qualified and determined by God as *agapé*. Such love is not sentimental but 'holy' because it is qualitatively different from, even if related to other forms of love, whether erotic, filial or genuine self-love. It is not a love we can manipulate for our own ends, but the love which seeks the good of the other without denying the other freedom to spurn or accept it. It is also a love that seeks justice, especially for the oppressed, and at the same time judges those who perpetrate evil, but for the sake of their redemption not their destruction. Nowhere in the biblical prophetic literature is this more poignantly expressed than it is by Hosea, whose favourite word *chesed* captures the faithful, gracious love of Yahweh towards an unfaithful, obstinate Israel, affirming that God's justice is restorative not punitive (Hosea 11:8–9). This is the 'righteousness of God' revealed in Christ, the righteousness of restorative not retributive justice.[124] I will return to this critical dimension of God's love as restorative justice in my final chapter. In concluding this one, led me reflect briefly on the gratuitous hospitality of God's love as the mystery that seeks to embrace us.

---

124 See my discussion in John W. de Gruchy, *Reconciliation: Restoring Justice*, London: SCM, 2002, pp. 44–78.

Those familiar with Eastern Orthodoxy will know that icons alongside Scripture provide the lens through which believers glimpse the glory of the mystery that is revealed in Jesus Christ. Icons are beautiful, but they are not considered primarily as 'works of art'.[125] Their radiance derives from the beauty of the narrative they tell. No icon does this more than Andrei Rublev's Icon of the Holy Trinity. In 'writing' his icon, Rublev built on a typological interpretation of the story of Abraham and Sarah providing hospitality for three mysterious visitors depicted as angels (Gen. 18.1–5; Heb. 13.2). But in the icon these divine visitors become those who offer hospitality to all who contemplate it, and ultimately point to the triune God as inviting us into the community of divine love. This is not an escape from the harsh reality of lived experience. On the contrary, Rublev lived at a time of considerable conflict within Russian society in the fifteenth century. He wrote his icon as a means to foster healing and reconciliation among warring people. This was the same reason why the Volmoed community was founded in 1986 during the struggle against apartheid. So it is appropriate that facing us each day when we enter the chapel at Volmoed for Morning Prayer is a copy of Rublev's icon.[126] Contemplating it we know we are being invited to share the generous hospitality of God's banquet around the table, and at the same time being led deeper into the unfathomable *agapé* and infinite beauty of the triune God.

Some days our response is perfunctory; but there are those occasions when we sense, in David Hart's words, 'an overwhelming givenness in the beautiful', and become aware 'of something fortuitous, adventitious, essentially indescribable; it is known only in the moment of response, from the position of one already addressed and able now only to reply'.[127] No one to my mind has expressed this better than Augustine in describing his conversion.

125 John W. de Gruchy, *Icons as a Means of Grace*, Wellington, RSA: Lux Verbi. BM, 2008.

126 The icon was written by Isobel. See de Gruchy, *Icons*, plate 11.

127 David Bentley Hart, *The Beauty of the Infinite*, Grand Rapids: Eerdmans, 2003, p. 17.

'I have learnt to love you late, Beauty at once so ancient and so new! . . . The beautiful things from this world kept me from you and yet, if they had not been in you, they would have had no being at all.'[128] Being led into mystery is being embraced by love and beauty, even if our response is often reluctant, ungrateful or lukewarm. George Herbert, the sixteenth-century poet, expressed this in incomparable words, echoing Augustine:

Love bade me welcome; yet my soul drew back,
Guilty of dust and sin.
But quick-eyed Love, observing me grow slack
From my first entrance in,
Drew nearer to me, sweetly questioning
If I lacked anything.

"A guest," I answered, "worthy to be here";
Love said, "You shall be he."
"I the unkind, ungrateful? Ah, my dear,
I cannot look on thee."
Love took my hand and smiling did reply,
"Who made the eyes but I?"

"Truth, Lord, but I have marred them; let my shame
Go where it doth deserve"
"And know you not," says Love, "who bore the blame?"
"My dear, then I will serve."
"You must sit down," says Love, "and taste my meat."
So I did sit and eat.[129]

---

128 Augustine, *Confessions*, Bk 10, chap. 27, 321.
129 George Herbert, from his collection of poems entitled *The Temple*, as revised in *The Norton Anthology of Poetry*, pp. 346–7.

4

The Human Enigma

There are times when my own faith seems to me like a stranger: there is a gap between me the believing or praying me and the reflecting me. This cannot be a mere accident. The possibility of this gap between me and myself seems to be implied in what I am, and it is this thing which I must face.
Gabriel Marcel[1]

As the creature has its own existence, rhythm, contrariety, regularity and freedom, so it has its own mystery. And in and with all its declarations, it always and everywhere declares also the mystery in which it is itself concealed.
Karl Barth[2]

Human persons are not accidental mistakes in a pointless perambu-lation of fundamental particles. They are a window into the inner reality, value, and purpose of the cosmos.
Keith Ward[3]

I cannot grasp all that I am.
Augustine[4]

In England in the 1870s, so we are told, 'a famous experiment with a frog caused a great stir in scientific circles. Its brain was removed, yet the frog could still perform some apparently purpose-ful actions. This proved to the wise men of the time that there was no longer any need to hold a spiritual view of human beings, since physiology now explained everything. One of them wrote gleefully

---

1 Gabriel Marcel, *The Mystery of Being (2) Faith and Reality*, Chicago: Henry Regney Company, 1960, pp. 141–2.
2 Karl Barth, *Church Dogmatics* IV/3.1: *The Doctrine of Reconciliation*, Edinburgh: T. & T. Clark, 1961, p. 149.
3 Keith Ward, *More than Matter: Is there more to life than Molecules?*, Grand Rapids: Eerdmans 2010, p. 8.
4 *Augustine: Confessions and Enchiridion*, Book 10/viii/15, The Library of Christian Classics, vol. VII, edited by Albert C. Outler, London: SCM, 1955, p. 210.

that a "frog with no brain has destroyed more theology than all the doctors of the Church with their whole brains could ever build up again"'. The teller of the tale, an Irish Dominican priest and philosopher concludes with the wry comment: 'I consider now that it comes back to whether you want to live like a brainless frog or like a doctor of the Church.'[5] Not much of a choice, we might retort. But advances in neuroscience and molecular biology since then have led to the claim that we have little if any freedom to choose, and that notions such as the human 'soul', or 'being made in the image of God', or personal freedom and responsibility, or even having a mind independent of the brain, are fictions. This is obviously a full frontal, and potentially fatal, attack on theology.[6] If true, it undermines the *theological* basis for human uniqueness, or the Christian hope of life beyond death. In short, the mystery of being human is expunged, the enigma explained. Secular humanism would be our best hope; not any religious, theological or Christian humanism, or divinely sanctioned set of laws and commandments.

As intimated in my Prologue, this challenge to Christian faith was one of the major reasons why I began to write this book in response to questions raised by Steve's death. So let me take stock of where we are. In Chapter 1, I considered ways in which the notion of mystery struck my imagination in an assortment of texts I read or recalled in the months that followed Steve's death. In Chapter 2, I turned to the Bible as the chief source of the Christian understanding of mystery, discussing not only what Scripture says on the subject, but also how, through its witness, we are encountered by the mystery of the living Word disclosed in Jesus Christ. Everything else Christians believe is shaped by this conviction. With this centre in place, in Chapter 3, I considered what it means to believe in God as ultimate mystery and concern and concluded with the image which Christian tradition has constructed of God

5 Donagh O'Shea OP, *Take Nothing for the Journey: Meditations on Time and Place*, Dublin: Dominican Publications 1990, p. 84.
6 Philip Clayton, 'Theology and the Physical Sciences', in *The Modern Theologians: An Introduction to Christian Theology in the Twentieth Century, Third Edition*, edited by David F. Ford with Rachel Muers, Oxford: Blackwell Publishers, 2005, p. 352.

as unfathomable love and infinite beauty. This has now brought
me to consider the mystery of being human and the challenge presented to our self-understanding by neuroscience. Is the human
being simply a phenomenon that can be explained in functional
terms or, as Emmanuel Levinas has insisted, an Enigma that cannot be reduced to any objective description?[7]

My point of departure is the acknowledgment that the contemporary debate between theology and neuroscience is critical for
understanding who we are, how we should live, and what happens
to us in death. For this reason the search for the self is 'one of the
most salient interdisciplinary academic discussions of our time'.[8]
Irrespective of whether we approach the issues from the perspective
of science or theology, we are all in this together as human beings
seeking to know ourselves better and so hopefully make the world a
better place. Without this self-knowledge, it is difficult to know how
we are going to survive as a species, let alone flourish and evolve in
more compassionate and just ways. For that reason the questions
that face us are not just about the *meaning* of life and death; they
are at the same time about the ethical imperatives that shape our living and determine our future on this planet. Such imperatives were
always central to Steve's theological understanding, but increasingly
they became his preoccupation and passion towards the end of his
life in his work on theology and development.[9]

In a concluding chapter to a collection of essays in which the
authors seek to integrate the findings of biology, neuroscience and
theology, Philip Clayton notes that '*much more* of both sets of disciplines can be retained than one might have expected. Much biology
can be right in explaining human behaviors, and much of religious language can be retained for formulating matters of ethics,

7 Emmanuel Levinas, *Basic Philosophical Writings*, Bloomington: Indiana
University Press, 1996.
8 Introduction to *In Search of Self: Interdisciplinary Perspectives on Personhood*, edited by J. Wentzel van Huyssteen and Erik P. Wiebe, Grand Rapids,
Michigan: Eerdmans, 2011, p. 1.
9 See the essays in the 'Steve de Gruchy Memorial Edition' of the *Journal
of Theology for Southern Africa* 142 (2012); and in *Living on the Edge*, edited
by Cochrane et. al.

morality, and ultimate purpose'.[10] His guiding question in bringing his discussion to a conclusion is to discern 'the core phenomena of human experience, as informed by both science and faith'.[11] In reflecting back on my sorties into neuroscience, I can certainly say that I appreciate now far more than I did when I wrote *Being Human* that our humanness is deeply embedded in our skulls and that 'the explosion of new findings about the brain is', in David Hogue's words, 'pressing us for new and deeper understandings of who we are and what it means to be human'.[12] But I remain equally convinced that the mystery of what it means to be human disclosed in Jesus Christ is of fundamental significance in pursuit of self-knowledge, human wholeness and the common good. How to bring these two worlds into conversation is the task ahead.

A fragment of mystery

Augustine was the first great Christian thinker to explore the mystery of being human. In doing so, he confessed that he could not grasp all that he was. In particular, he marvelled in astonishment at the mind which, as we noted in Chapter 1, he described as a spacious storehouse of memories on which the imagination drew. But he went further in acknowledging the mind as 'far too narrow to contain itself' and asked 'where can that part of it be which it does not contain? Is it outside and not in itself? How can it be, then, that the mind cannot grasp itself?'[13] There was something mysterious about being human, an enigma that could not be understood in and of itself.

In *De Profundis*, to which I referred in the previous chapter, Oscar Wilde also pondered the inexplicable nature of being

---

10 Philip Clayton, 'Biology and Purpose: Altruism, Morality, and Human Nature in Evolutionary Perspective', in *Evolution and Ethics: Human Morality in Biological & Religious Perspective*, edited by Philip Clayton and Jeffrey Schloss, Grand Rapids, Michigan: Eerdmans, 2004, p. 323.
11 Clayton, 'Biology and Purpose', p. 324.
12 Hogue, *Remembering the Future*, p. 3.
13 *Augustine: Confessions*, Book 10/viii/15, The Library of Christian Classics, vol. VII, p. 210.

human. Weary of both the hypocrisy of religion and the barrenness of rationalism, he came to the conclusion that while to know oneself is 'the first achievement of knowledge. To recognize that the soul of man is unknowable is the ultimate achievement of Wisdom'. He went on to say:

> The final mystery is oneself. When one has weighed the sun in a balance, and measured the steps of the moon, and mapped out the seven heavens star by star, there still remains oneself. Who can calculate the orbit of his own soul?[14]

Wilde is echoing Augustine, but his bewilderment arose out of his confessed agnosticism or, to use Critchley's term, 'faithlessness', whereas for Augustine it was the outcome of faith seeking to understand itself. It is in this latter spirit that Marilynn Robinson, in her *Absence of Mind,* invites us to imagine and acknowledge 'some small fragment of the mystery we are'.[15] We are not the 'final mystery' as Wilde proposes, but fragments of a greater, more ultimate mystery. For this reason, as theologians have long insisted, our knowledge of God and ourselves is inter-connected. So, says Robinson, we have to recognize 'that the strangeness of reality consistently exceeds the expectations of science' just as the 'assumptions of science, however tried and rational, are very inclined to encourage false expectations'.[16]

Scientists seek to dispel the enigma of being human. They break the genetic code, develop techniques and technologies to understand how the brain works and search for cures to life-threatening diseases. The number and scope of scientific research projects on such matters at any one time around the globe is staggering, each promising to improve the quality of life. But scientific research is not the only resource at our disposal for understanding the enigma of who we are, or the fragments of mystery that is us, and there

---

14   Oscar Wilde, 'De Profundis', in the *Complete Works of Oscar Wilde,* London: HarperCollins Publishers, 1994, p. 1038.

15   Marilynn Robinson, *Absence of Mind,* New Haven, CT: Yale University Press, 2011, p. 135.

16   Robinson, *Absence of Mind,* p. 124.

are limits to what it can achieve. To explore the whole of human reality we also need to step outside the laboratory and enter the world of the artist, dramatist, musician, poet, myth-makers and story teller, prophet and sage, and biblical writers. For them, self-knowledge develops out of lived experience in the journey of life. They see things differently, discerning the mystery beneath the real.

Dorothy's journey to the mysterious Land of Oz is everyone's journey of self-discovery marked by anxiety, disenchantment and disappointment, as well as surprise, discovery and affirmation. To find herself Dorothy had to face her *self*, her *persona* if you like, albeit by a circuitous and fantastical route. But in awakening from her dream she was back where she had started, except that now her childhood innocence had dissipated and she saw things differently. This, as T. S. Eliot observed, is common human experience. The place where we conclude our journey of self-discovery is often the place from which we began, but we end hopefully wiser and more whole.[17] But we do not all start at the same place or for the same reason. Brink's Philida ended her journey of self-discovery at the same place from which she had set out, but it began as a struggle for freedom from slavery and oppression. Her story continues to resonate with that of far too many people today who are the victims of injustice, violence and war. Sometimes we may already be well into our journey, accustomed to its pace and satisfied with its unfolding character, when we are stopped in our tracks by tragedy and thrust into territory not previously explored. We cannot begin our journey again, but we may have to change direction and pace. Disturbing questions that we thought were resolved, confront us with a new intensity that force us to turn in our tracks. Possible answers that have been given over the generations are combed for clues and insight; processed and examined again as if for the first time. We go in search of a guru. Even Christian faith, set aside after school years and adolescent

---

17 T. S. Eliot: *The Four Quartets; Little Gidding*, in *Collected Poems 1909–1962*, London: Faber and Faber, 1963, p. 222.

rebellion, may be reconsidered. Yet, in the end, we may still not be convinced that Eliot, echoing Julian of Norwich, is right in his concluding affirmation to 'Little Gidding':

> all shall be well and
> all manner of things shall be well.[18]

But about this we can be sure: to become truly human we invariably have to revisit the perplexing questions about being human for ourselves; they have to become *our* questions, just as the answers have to be ours as well, even if they resemble those of others, or take us in a different direction. Only when we are hungry and thirsty for self-knowledge and humble enough to know that we actually don't know are we ready to be drawn deeper into the meaning and mystery of life.

Yet all the time the shadow of death crosses our path and encroaches on our space as though we are in the midst of a mystery novel, except that it is we who are the characters embedded in the plot. And, as in a good mystery story, so too in our quest for self-knowledge we are *led* into mystery, sometimes before we consciously undertake the journey. Mystery approaches us, perhaps slowly like gently falling in love, or with sudden fury beside a raging torrent. We are teased, puzzled, grasped or shocked by mystery long before we try to understand its fragments, whether in sacred texts or elsewhere, seeking some meaning and coherence even while being drawn deeper into the mystery. Where are we in this vast universe? How shall I live? What happens when we die? From the moment the first humans became self-conscious, such questions were already evolving in their minds as though planted there.

All this happens in our brains; it cannot be otherwise. Like Augustine I marvel at the capacity of the brain to process the events that shape our lives through memory and imagination, and seek after answers to our questions about who we are and what is

---

18   Eliot, *The Four Quartets*, p. 223.

our destiny. It boggles my mind to think that while I write on my computer, and as it captures my thoughts on the screen and saves them in its memory, so an infinitely more complex but comparable operation is in progress within my skull driven by myriads of molecules, atoms adhering to each other in various formations. The molecular structure of our brains and the way it functions is truly amazing. Consider my wife Isobel's reflections on the molecular structure of our DNA, unique to every creature even if the structure is the same.

And what is this DNA – this deoxyribonucleic acid?
a molecule of protein, a large and complex molecule,
the largest molecule known to exist.
It consists of two long cords of nucleotides,
back-boned by sugars and phosphates;
two long cords – polymers –
tightly twisted into a spiral,
organised in chromosomes,
stored in humans in the cell nucleus.
In the chromosomes, special proteins,
chromatin proteins compact and organise the DNA
and guide interactions between the DNA and other proteins.

The set of chromosomes makes up the genome of the cell,
and the human genome consists of an astonishing number of
base pairs of DNA,
arranged in 46 chromosomes – around three billion!
All the information carried is encoded in a sequence of segments of DNA
called genes –
the organisms genotype being the complete set of information.
Genes are the unit of heredity;
genes determine what the phenotype of an organism will be,
bird or buck or human being;
genes influence the particular characteristics displayed
by each individual creature.
And while we understand,

or rather, while scientists understand,
so much more of the structure of DNA
and its component parts,
the way it replicates,
and the way it passes on information;
and although the human genome has been mapped,
mysteries remain,
many mysteries that perplex the finest minds.
It is still a mystery why more than half of human DNA
consists of non-coding repetitive sequences,
which seem to do nothing.
It is still a mystery why
the genome size differs so much between species.[19]

For me this is all a mystery. But for Francis Crick, who first deciphered the DNA, the mystery was revealed. All our joys, sorrows, memories, ambitions, sense of personal identity and free will, he concluded, 'are in fact no more than the behavior of a vast assembly of nerve cells and their associated molecules'. Or, as Lewis Carroll's Alice might have phrased it: 'You're nothing but a pack of neurons'.[20] For him the human enigma was solved; we had been reduced to our molecules.

Nonetheless, Crick admits in the concluding chapter to his book, that while his 'Astonishing Hypothesis may be proved correct', there could be alternative outcomes, including religious ones. Or a new way of looking at the mind-brain problem may emerge 'that is significantly different from the crude materialistic view many neuroscientists hold today and also from the religious point of view'.[21] Mysteries apparently remain despite our knowledge of molecules, among them our self-consciousness, though that enigma might soon be solved. But can we find a path into the future between reducing everything to molecules and denying

19 Isobel de Gruchy, a section from her unpublished 'poem', 'From Organism to Atom', 8 August 2012.
20 Francis Crick, *The Astonishing Hypothesis: The Scientific Search for the Soul*, London: Touchstone Books, 1995, p. 3.
21 Eagleman, *Incognito*, p. 224.

the truly astonishing role of the brain in determining our lives? Does the meaning of life originate in the brain or is the brain the amazing processor that grapples with information that originates beyond it? Whatever else we may and must conclude, we can certainly say that the brain is undoubtedly at the same time both 'a perplexing masterpiece',[22] and 'the most wondrous thing we have discovered in the universe, and it is us'.[23]

Brain, mind and the meaning of life

An early intimation for me of the challenge presented to theology by contemporary neuroscience was William Sargant's controversial book on conversion and brainwashing entitled *Battle for the Mind*, which was published in 1957. Basing much of his research on Pavlov's famous experiment with dogs, Sargant acknowledged that while 'men are not dogs, they should humbly try to remember how much they resemble dogs in their brain functions, and not boast of themselves as demigods'. Yet, Sargant continued, human beings 'are gifted with religious and social apprehensions' and 'with the power of reason' though all of 'these faculties are physiologically entailed in the brain'.[24]

Sargant reassured his readers that what he wrote was not an attack on religion, but on 'any religious or political mystique that stunts reason, or any form of crude rationalism that stunts religious sense'.[25] He was at pains to reassure preachers to 'rest assured that the less mysteriously "God works his wonders to perform", the easier it should be to provide people with an essential knowledge and love of God'.[26] Sargant was not a believer, but he was from a devout Methodist family, his grandfather and five uncles being ministers and one of his brothers a bishop. This being so, these last sentiments might have given the rest of the

22 Crick, *The Astonishing Hypothesis*, pp. 262–3.
23 Eagleman, *Incognito*, p. 224.
24 William Sargant, *Battle for the Mind: A Physiology of Conversion and Brainwashing*, London–Dublin: Heinemann, 1957, p. 236.
25 Sargant, *Battle for the Mind*, p. 236.
26 Sargant, *Battle for the Mind*, p. 234.

family some reassurance that William was not completely out of his mind. But we look for such reassurance in vain in much neuro-scientific literature today. Eagleman states the position bluntly when he tells us that while the majority of people on the planet believe in a soul of some kind, the majority of neuroscientists insist that it is our 'biological network that produces our hopes, aspirations, dreams desires, humor and passions'.[27] Critics label this 'reductionism', a word that can be understood, as does Crick, not as 'the rigid process of explaining one fixed set of ideas in terms of another fixed set of ideas at a lower level, but a dynamic interactive process that modifies the concepts at both levels as knowledge develops'.[28] This, he rightly says, is the theoretical method of all science. But reductionism also implies that empiri-cal research is the *only* way of knowing the truth, and it is this absolute variety of reductionism that must be challenged.

Paul Thagard is a typical more recent example of such reduc-tionism. His claim in *The Brain and the Meaning of Life* is that the human search for and sense of the meaning of life can all be traced to the functioning of the brain rather than to some other possibly transcendent source. 'The Brain Revolution now in progress', he writes, 'is even more threatening to the human's natural desire to think of ourselves as special, for it implies that our treasured thoughts and feelings are just another biological process'.[29] Notions such as immortality, free will, altruism and moral responsibility associated with the mind or soul should be discarded. There are no grounds for achieving knowledge, morality and all the other ingredients that make love, work and play mean-ingful human activities, outside the brain. Even our capacity to hope, which is essential for our survival, is hardwired into the brain. In short, any dualism that differentiates between body and mind, or posits a separate or discrete soul, is ruled out on the basis of scientific evidence. There is considerable truth in what Thagard is saying. But is his radical reductionism warranted?

27 Eagleman, *Incognito*, p. 203.
28 Crick, *The Astonishing Hypothesis*, p. 8.
29 Paul Thagard, *The Brain and the Meaning of Life*, Princeton, NJ: Princeton University Press, 2010, p. 42.

Thagard tells us that the journey of discovery that led him to his current position began when he turned from religion to philosophy. He is at pains to show how, even though we may miss having God around, neither theology (which is better than magic, he admits) nor philosophy in general, have much if anything of value to contribute to the discussion about the meaning of life. But on his own reckoning he is not a nihilist for, he insists, he is concerned about human well-being, about ethical responsibility, and about making sense of life. For him, it is important that life has meaning. What religion and philosophy have traditionally been about is his concern, but they have simply got it wrong and have lost whatever credibility and value they previously had. Still, he concludes, 'philosophical issues about knowledge, reality, meaning, and morality cannot be ignored by anyone who wishes to think deeply about what to believe and what to do'.[30] Interestingly, the word 'believe' keeps on cropping up. But he counsels us not to turn to the many self-help books widely available that are religious in character and 'appeal to the gullible.' I cannot fault him on that.

Despite his more general scepticism about the genre, Thagard does applaud one self-help volume entitled *The How of Happiness*, because it is based 'on a wealth of recent research on the sources of positive emotions'. Furthermore, it recommends 'a dozen concrete actions that have been shown experimentally to contribute to happiness'. Thagard lists these 12 actions, all of which, he says, fit in well with his own position on how people develop happiness and meaning in their lives, all, that is, except action number 11: 'practicing religion and spirituality'.[31] In other words, even if demonstrated 'experimentally' as he admits all 12 actions can be, religion and spirituality have no relevance whatsoever in the pursuit of his happiness trilogy of 'love, work and play'. Religion is simply bad news. Much of it is, I agree. But does this mean that religion and spirituality must be abandoned if we are to know ourselves?

---

30 Thagard, *The Brain and the Meaning of Life*, p. 229.
31 Thagard, *The Brain and the Meaning of Life*, p. 180.

There are, after all, other neuroscientists who encourage 'religion and spirituality' within their framework, while endorsing the findings of current research.[32] They acknowledge that faith is central to the way our brains function in making sense of the world and in responding to its challenges. The brain takes leaps of faith whether in science or religion, enabling us to believe things we cannot prove. In fact, says Linden, our brains 'evolved to make us believers.'[33] This does not mean that what we believe is empirically true, though investigation and experience may prove that it is. We could also argue that our brains have evolved to respond to God's self-disclosure. But in general, neuroscientists, even those keen to engage spirituality, insist that 'the experience of self, soul, consciousness, spirit, ghost, god, everything that populates the spiritual world, is a *perception of mind* and is created by the social machinery of the brain.'[34] They are reasonably and sometimes assertively confident that they will, in time, demystify the final mystery of being human, namely self-consciousness.

A controversial exception is neurosurgeon Eben Alexander who recounts and assesses his near death experience in his best-selling *Proof of Heaven*, and insists that consciousness or spirit is 'the great and central mystery of the universe.'[35] Alexander's claims are remarkable not least given his scientific background. My wife has also drawn my attention to the similarities between Alexander's account of his experience and that of Julian of Norwich whose 'revelations' also occurred after she was considered to have died.[36] Both scientist and mystic describe their experience

32 See Eric Bergemann, Daniel J. Siegel, Deanie Eichenstein and Ellen Streit, "Neuroscience and Spirituality," *In Search of Self: Interdisciplinary Perspectives on Personhood*, edited by J. Wentzel van Huyssteen and Erik Wiebe, Grand Rapids: Eerdmans, 2011, 83–103.

33 Linden, *The Accidental Mind*, 234.

34 S. A. Graziano, *God, Soul, Mind, Brain: A Neuroscientist's Reflection on the Spirit World* (Teaticket, Mass: Leapfrog Press, 2010), 16.

35 Eben Alexander, *Proof of Heaven: A Neurosurgeon's Journey into the Afterlife*, New York: Simon & Schuster, 2012, 169.

36 Julian of Norwich, *Showings*, New York: Paulist Press, 1978, 179–80.

of 'heaven' as being enfolded by love and, on 'coming back to life,' declared 'all is well.'[37] If these testimonies are in any sense credible and therefore potentially true, they corroborate the conviction that we humans are connected to the ultimate mystery of the universe understood as infinite love and beauty, and not merely a machine 'bound in the hard shell of the skull.'[38] I will say more about heaven in the next chapter, though I will not base my discussion on near death experiences.

Reducing everything about us to molecules is like saying that a motor car is only the sum of the particles that constitute the materials out of which it is made. Undoubtedly this is true at one level, but is that an adequate explanation of what *constitutes* the machine *as* a car in *every* respect? Even from within the Neuroscientific guild, Eagleman insists that while reducing everything to biological materialism is compelling, total 'reductionism isn't the whole story'.[39]

Thagard, as we have seen, is only interested in philosophy when it supports his claims. This echoes the view of the distinguished philosopher of an earlier generation, Antony Flew, who insisted that the issues are 'primarily philosophical' but 'can be resolved satisfactorily only by a philosophy receptive to a scientific outlook, and informed by scientific knowledge'.[40] Past enquirers not informed by such empirical knowledge, no matter how philosophically astute they may have been, are really not helpful. This is because, Flew continued, they 'have had at least half an eye, and sometimes both eyes, on the implications which the various possible views of the status of the mind hold for the question of a future life'.[41] In other words, their views have been predetermined by religious commitments and concerns which have clouded their judgments. This may be so, but it is a huge if not arrogant claim

---

37 Alexander, *Proof of Heaven*, 113.
38 Wendell Berry, *A Timbered Choir*, Berkeley, CA: Counterpoint, 1998, p.117.
39 Eagleman, *Incognito*, p. 209.
40 *Body, Mind and Death*, edited by Antony Flew, New York, NY: Macmillan, 1973, p. 2.
41 Flew, *Body, Mind and Death*, pp. 2–3.

nonetheless, when you consider the history of philosophy, as Flew himself came to recognize in his later years.[42]

Early on in my theological studies I was introduced to the philosophical debate about the 'body, mind and soul' as it developed from ancient Greece and India through to modern times. In the Western tradition, a central figure in the story was Descartes whose dualism we have already encountered. Descartes proposed that the human body functioned like a machine according to natural laws, whereas the mind or soul (a ghostlike immaterial substance) was independent of them even though it controlled the body. On occasion the body could also influence the mind, especially through its passions. Separating body and soul in this way was partly intended to protect the soul from scientific scrutiny, keeping it safely ensconced in the realm of theology, while science was set free to explore material reality without any deference to religious opinions. But the effect of this dualistic and mechanistic understanding of the human person was counterproductive for both science and religion. This can be seen in the field of Western medical practice until fairly recently. If you treat the body as a machine without reference to other aspects of being human, healing can be impeded even if surgery is successful.

Such dualism was thoroughly debunked in the twentieth century by Oxford philosopher Gilbert Ryle who dubbed it the 'absurd dogma of the Ghost in the machine.'[43] For Ryle, Cartesian dualism was based on a category mistake. But his rejection of an immortal soul did not mean that human beings had been reduced to machines; they could be regarded as 'higher mammals' or even as 'man!'[44] Keith Ward, one of his students, who cannot be faulted for not taking seriously either his arguments or the findings of science has, however, found both scientific

42   Anthony Flew, *There is a God: How the World's Most Notorious Atheist Changed His Mind*, New York, NY: Harper/Collins, 2007.
43   Flew, *Body, Mind and Death*, pp. 248–57.
44   Keith Ward, *More than Matter*, pp. 112–25.

materialism and common sense philosophy deeply flawed. As an alternative for understanding the human enigma he proposes a qualified or 'sensible dualism' that, I suggest, carries considerable weight. To quote him:

> Against Ryle, I argue that sensible dualists do not think the mind is a separate hidden world connected arbitrarily to the body. It is the inner aspect of the material person, but it is a realm of partly unverifiable privately accessed data, and its rich, value-filled complex of feelings, thoughts, and intentions (its 'inner life') is a key element of human personhood.

Ward then goes on to say: 'It is logically possible that this inner aspect could, very unusually, exist without the body. But its proper and normal place is precisely as the inner aspect of a material body and brain, situated in a shared social environment.'[45]

The upshot of Ward's argument is that while minds are embedded in the brain and could not have developed otherwise, they *emerge* from matter. This means that they could 'in principle be decoupled from matter', which implies that 'the brain state and the mental state are not strictly identical'.[46] Ward's parting shot fired across Ryle's bows is a trenchant statement of his position: 'There is no ghost, and there is no machine.' What, then remains? '. . . only the reality of mind, and its expression in the dynamic and developing forms of an open and emergent material universe.'[47] That is a striking restatement of Idealism. Although embodied, the mind takes on a dynamic life shaped by memory and imagination. The mind is what the brain does rather than the brain being the mind. The brain actually enables us to transcend the reductionist understanding of ourselves and so explore the mystery of our embodiment as something more than that which biology can explain. For Ward, then, the battle lines are drawn between a

---

45 Ward, *More than Matter*, p. 112.
46 Ward, *More than Matter*, p. 116.
47 Ward, *More than Matter*, p. 197.

purely materialist view of our humanity, and one that both affirms and transcends it.[48]

It is important, then, to distinguish between a fully reductionist materialism which denies the reality of anything other than the material, as do Dawkins and Thagard for example, and what Nancey Murphy refers to as a 'non-reductive physicalism' which does not.[49] For good reason, Murphy claims that the dominant biblical position is materialist in this non-reductionist sense, which is why Christianity, with its doctrine of the Incarnation, is sometimes referred to as the most materialistic of all religions. The mystery of being human is an *embodied* mystery. Although there is a philosophical difference between the Idealism of Ward's qualified, sensible dualism and Murphy's 'non-reductionist physicalism', both are compatible with trajectories in the biblical text that also inform my own position. To these I now turn.

Animals in God's image

The first Christians were Jews and their Scripture was the Old Testament, which provided both the key terms and the framework for understanding the human mystery. The dominant framework, developed through the lens of Paul's reading of the creation narratives in Genesis 1–3, continues to influence Christian anthropology, whether read literally or as myth.[50] Understood as myth, the narratives of creation and the Fall of Adam and Eve, who represent all humanity, offer much that can contribute insight in the contemporary multi-disciplinary discussion.[51] Taken literally they are easily debunked.

Three texts in the creation narratives are foundational. The first is from the older creation story in Genesis 2. There we read that

---

48 Ward, *More than Matter*, p. 11.
49 Nancey Murphy, *Bodies and Souls, or Spirit Bodies?*, Cambridge: Cambridge University Press, 2006, pp. 5–6, 52.
50 See for example Romans 5.12–21.
51 See, inter alia, Dietrich Bonhoeffer, *Creation and Fall: A Theological Exposition of Genesis 1–3*, edited by John W. de Gruchy, Minneapolis: Fortress Press, 1997.

'the Lord God formed man (*adam*) from the dust of the ground (*adamah*), and breathed into his nostrils the breath (*nephesh*) of life; and the man became a living being (*nephesh*)' (v. 7). According to this text, that which gives animals, including ourselves, vitality or life is *nephesh,* translated in the Greek Septuagint as *pneuma,* then as *anima* in the Latin Vulgate, and later as 'breath' in English translation. *Nephesh* is always embodied in 'flesh' (*basar*), but without *nephesh* the flesh has no life. The phrase 'living being' captures well the Hebrew holistic understanding of human beings as bodies animated by spirit. But a more Platonic reading of the text creeps into popular use, as in the King James Bible which has long shaped English-speaking Christianity. There we read 'man became a living *soul*', which is a translation not of the Hebrew *nephesh* but of the Septuagint's use of *psyche.* So whereas in the Hebrew *nephesh* is that which gives the body life and sustains it in life, in KJV English there is a Platonic nuance that influences our reading. Instead of being understood as holistic animated bodies, humans are understood as embodied immortal souls. But the Hebraic view is not that human beings *have* souls, they *are* living souls.[52]

The second text, from the later creation narrative told in Genesis 1, informs us that what distinguishes humans from other animals is not that we are animated bodies – for all life has 'the breath of God' – but being made 'in the image of God' (v. 27), or what is traditionally referred to as the *imago Dei*. There is no need to rehearse here the long and involved discussions that have taken place over the centuries with regard to the meaning of this phrase. Van Huyssteen's admirable overview in his Gifford Lectures is both comprehensive and informs my discussion. In its deepest sense, he says, the *imago Dei* is to be understood 'as embodied human uniqueness' which he links to 'notions of human uniqueness in the sciences', notably the 'evolution of human cognition as a deeply embodied process, functioning interactively in a

---

52 Jürgen Moltmann, *God in Creation: A New Theology of Creation and the Spirit of God*, San Francisco: Harper & Row 1985, p. 256.

real world of challenges and opportunities'.[53] This makes possible
the unique relationship humans have with God and each other,
referring as it does to self-consciousness, reason, imagination,
subjectivity and freedom, and therefore personal identity, but
always in psychosomatic unity.[54] As human beings we live and
exist in social relationships. Recognizing that we are social beings
and not just self-sufficient individuals, is acknowledging that we are
in the image of God. We exist as human beings through others and
in relation to them.

A third crucial text in Genesis is: 'Then the Lord God said, "See,
the man has become like one of us, knowing good and evil"' (3.22).
This provides us with 'the most comprehensive meaning of the biblical notion of the *imago Dei*', because it reflects 'the emergence of
an embodied moral awareness, and a holistic, new way of knowing'.[55] But it is a text located in the narrative of the Fall, which,
in Christian understanding, is an account of the human condition
experienced as sinful, tragic and alienated from God. Humans are
unique not only because they are in a conscious relationship to God
and others, but because they can distinguish between good and evil
and, being free to decide, are prone to make irresponsible, self-
destructive and therefore sinful choices. This clearly distinguishes
us as much from other animals as does our uniqueness as created
in the 'image of God'.

The myth of the Fall is an attempt within ancient Semitic thinking to explain the origin of evil and suffering in the world, the
cause of violence and war, of murder and rape and the dehuman-
ization of others, from the perspective of faith in God. As such,
it is a response to more fundamental questions: are we humans
genuinely free to choose, and if so, why is it that we misuse our
freedom with all the terrible consequences that follow? Are we
morally responsible and accountable for what we do, or are we
determined by our genes, or by God, to act in a particular way?

53   van Huyssteen, *Alone in the World?*, p. 162.
54   See Wolfhart Pannenberg, *Systematic Theology*, Grand Rapids: Eerdmans, 1994, pp. 194–200.
55   Huyssteen, *Alone in the World?*, p. 160.

One influential tradition of interpretation can be traced back to the writings of Irenaeus, the second-century martyr-bishop of Lyon, who was a foremost apologist for Christianity in the struggle against Gnostic dualism. Strongly opposed to the notion that the material world and the body are evil, Irenaeus believed that everything God made was very good, but humans were not created perfect, only potentially so. What we call the Fall was a necessary stage in human development, from the awakening of consciousness and the ending of innocence to full maturity through the education of desire under the influence of the Spirit of Christ.[56] The more dominant tradition of interpretation is that of Augustine, who read the story in terms of his personal experience of sin, his overwhelming sense of guilt and his dramatic conversion, and in the light of the calamitous fall of Rome to the Goths and Huns in 410 CE when he was bishop of Hippo in North Africa. Like the Fall of the Empire, so the Fall of Adam was the result of human arrogance and abuse of freedom, and its consequences were tragic. The Fall was not a necessary stage in human development, but the corruption of what had been created perfect. It was not a stage in growth to maturity, but the defacing of God's image, the corruption of the soul, and the bondage of the will.

These two interpretations of the Fall provide us with diverse, yet in some respects complementary, frameworks within which we can interpret the myth, and seek answers to the questions which gave rise to it. Irenaeus' perspective is undoubtedly more helpful in relating the Fall to contemporary ideas about the growth of human personality, and the evolution of the human race. I shall have reason to return to his thought in the next chapter. Augustine's interpretation is more realistic in its assessment of the human capacity for both good and evil. Almost in a Freudian manner, it challenges us to consider our motives, behaviour, and self will, and it does the same in analysing the corruption, hubris and will to power of nations and rulers. Although unnervingly realistic in its assessment of human nature, Augustine's view is not ultimately

---

56 See the writings of Irenaeus in *The Early Christian Fathers*, edited by Henry Bettenson, Oxford: Oxford University Press, 1969, pp. 67–74.

a pessimistic account, as though all were determined by original sin. Read in the light of Christ as the Second Adam, God's grace enables humans to change, to become free and morally responsible, and transcend the self in knowledge of God.

There is, nonetheless, a resemblance between Augustine's view of human nature corrupted by the Fall and Dawkins' 'selfish gene',[57] or the human ego understood as 'the *selfish self*' which seeks 'only its own needs, its own gratification'.[58] As Susan Thistlethwaite observes, it is 'no leap at all to see that genetic determinism proposes simply to replace the doctrine of sin with the doctrine of genetic compulsion'.[59] Reflecting further on the way in which human beings act violently against each other and themselves, and even more characteristically 'are violent toward one another in the name of good', Thistlethwaite proposes that this 'is where we leave the orangutan, with his desire to assert dominance over females and other males, behind on the evolutionary ladder. The social construction of sin, she adds, 'allows us to see human reason's infinite capacity to delude itself'.[60] Whether Adam blames Eve, or both blame the snake, it is just confabulation.

However we read the creation narratives, there is little doubt that fundamental to biblical anthropology is the conviction that our identity as human beings is *not* based on some inner substance described as a disembodied 'soul', or even our capacity to reason. What characterizes the biblical view of human being is its synthetic nature, what Aubrey Johnson described as 'the awareness of totality', or what we would now refer to as psycho-somatic. This was the '"open sesame" which unlocks the secrets of the Hebrew language

---

57   Richard Dawkins, *The Selfish Gene*, Oxford: Oxford University Press, 2006.

58   Albert Nolan, *Jesus Today: A Spirituality of Radical Freedom*, Maryknoll, NY: Orbis Books, 2006, p. 23.

59   Susan Brooks Thistlethwaite, 'A Gene for Violence? Genetic Determinism and Sin', in *Adam, Eve, and the Genome: The Human Genome Project and Theology*, edited by Susan Brooks Thistlethwaite, Minneapolis: Fortress Press, 2003, p. 149.

60   Thistlethwaite, *Adam, Eve, and the Genome*, p. 157.

and reveals the riches of the Israelite mind'.[61] This is one reason why the Old Testament does not try to define what it means to be human, or engage in speculation about some human 'essence' or where the *imago Dei* resides, but rather describes our humanity in narrative terms in relation to God and the whole of reality of which we are a part and in which we exist.[62] From this perspective, human beings comprise two integrated elements – the physical body and an inner self. This is variously described in the Hebrew text by words we translate as body and mind, soul and spirit, as well as heart and other parts of our anatomy, such as kidneys, which, though undoubtedly physical in character, metaphorically refer to our affective states and will power. Such metaphors demonstrate how closely, in ancient Hebrew thought, the body and the inner self are connected. The *imago Dei*, then, refers to human beings in their psychosomatic wholeness and relationship to the totality of their existence under God, to their uniqueness in the animal kingdom, and to their God-given dignity. This does not mean that other animals are not in their own way unique and also as God's creatures have their own dignity.

Following the Old Testament, there is general consensus among the authors of the New Testament that humans are psychophysical unities who find their identity in relationship to each other and God; that the material world and the human body is created good, not evil; and that being human carries with it moral responsibility within the life of the world. This rules out of contention any radical dualism in which the body is totally separate from the soul and a hindrance to its well-being, and any reductionist materialism that denies the mystery of human uniqueness in relation to God and others. But as Christianity expanded beyond the confines of Judaism into the Hellenistic world, it entered a new cultural context, one where the Greek Septuagint became its version of the Old Testament. This meant that all the key terms used in the New Testament to describe the constituent parts of being human are Greek

---

61   Aubrey R. Johnson, *The Vitality of the Individual in the thought of Ancient Israel*, Cardiff: University of Wales Press, 1949, pp. 7–8.
62   See Moltmann, *God in Creation*, p. 257.

translations of the original Hebrew. The problem was that these terms – *basar* = *soma* (body), *nephesh* = *psyche* (soul), and *ruach* = *pneuma* (spirit) – were not exact equivalents of the Hebrew nor are the English words precisely what is meant either in the Hebrew or the Greek. In addition, authors of the New Testament did not take a clear position on how the terms were actually used within Hellenistic culture, nor were they much interested in consistency of their use.[63]

The scene for this linguistic problem was set centuries before either the production of the Septuagint or the New Testament, when the ancient Greek philosopher Anaxagoras wrote about the mind (*nous*) as a reality distinct from the body (*soma*) in contrast to others who conceived of the soul (*psyche*) as primary. The latter led directly to Plato's advocacy of a body–soul dualism in which the soul was immortal and divine. Plato's student, Aristotle, understood human beings in a more holistic way, describing the soul as the 'form' of the body. According to him, all animals have 'souls', that is the 'form' that gives them their particular identity. But among animals, the human 'soul' and the rationality of the mind are unique to human beings. Although Aristotle's more holistic understanding of being human accorded better with the Old Testament, it was neo-Platonic dualism that became the chief lens through which most Christians read the scriptures until the Middle Ages. This influenced them in interpreting the Greek terms we translate as body, soul, mind and spirit,[64] even though, contrary to Plato, Christian theologians regarded the 'soul' as created, and though immortal, not divine, and always related in some intrinsic way to the body.

An important example of the problem of the translation of Hebrew terms into New Testament Greek can be seen in the way in which the word for the physical body (*basar*) was translated into Greek by two words *soma* and *sarx*, which in English became

---

63   See James D. G. Dunn, *The Theology of the Apostle Paul*, Grand Rapids: Eerdmans, 1998, p. 54; Murphy, *Bodies and Souls*, pp. 6–11; van Huyssteen, *In Search of Self*, p. 2.

64   See Pannenberg, *Systematic Theology*, pp. 181–202 and Moltmann, *God in Creation*, pp. 244–62.

body (*soma*) and flesh (*sarx*).[65] *Sarx* primarily refers to our physicality in terms of weakness, sinful inclinations and mortality and therefore in contrast to God. So to live 'according to the flesh' in Paul's writings means living contrary to God's will. *Soma* also refers to human beings in their external material existence living fully in the world, but as created *for* God. While the flesh cannot inherit God's kingdom, the body can. It would be impossible to speak of the resurrection of the flesh or *sarx*, but it is possible to speak of the resurrection of the body or *soma* as I will argue in the next chapter. When Paul writes about the tension in the life of the believer as that between living according to the flesh and life in the Spirit (Gal. 5.16–26; Rom. 8.1–14), he is contrasting life lived against and life lived for God. It is the new life believers have in Christ. So while both *sarx* and *soma* refer to human beings in their totality, they refer to them differently.

Failure to recognize this distinction between body and flesh inevitably results in a disparaging of the human body and the senses as antitheses and opponents of the Spirit. The 'world, the flesh and the devil' have been lumped together as sinful and evil in a way that suggests our physical bodies (and therefore our sexuality) and the world in which we live are by their very nature sinful rather than God's creation, controlled by evil forces rather than by God's will. Instead of trying to subdue our bodily senses, a consequence of this misunderstanding in much Christian tradition, we should understand them, as Timothy Gorringe helpfully suggests, as 'the means through which we explore materiality' or better, 'the means by which God chooses to explore materiality through us, just as the Spirit prays through us'.[66] This means further, that the Spirit or presence of God in our lives is not confined, biblically speaking, to what we call our souls, but to us as psychosomatic wholes.[67]

---

65   See John A. T. Robinson, *The Body: A Study in Pauline Theology*, London: SCM, 1957, pp. 17–33.

66   Timothy J. Gorringe, *The Education of Desire*, London: SCM, 2001, pp. 10–11.

67   See Moltmann, *God in Creation*, p. 259.

Victor Frankl, writing out of a Jewish background, captures this sense of human wholeness when he says that 'the true meaning of life is to be found in the world rather than within man or his own *psyche*, as though it were a closed system'.[68] For many Christians, this seems to run counter to what they have traditionally been taught and believed. Is not the psyche or soul somehow contained within our bodies awaiting the release of death, and the saving of such souls the primary purpose of Christianity? After all, Jesus taught that it does not profit us to gain the whole world and in the process lose our souls (Matt. 15.26). But what is this 'soul' we are in danger of losing, the soul with which we love God, along with our hearts and minds, and how is it distinguished from them if it is?

The complexity of soul

Biblically and theologically speaking, body and soul belong together, comprising the human person, as reaffirmed by the Catholic Church at Vatican II.[69] Or, as Bonhoeffer put it in *Creation and Fall*: 'A human being does not "have" a body – or "have" a soul; instead, a human being "is" body and soul.'[70] So would it not be better to ditch 'soul' and simply refer to the human *person*, implying both our physicality and our uniqueness within the animal world? Until recently, I assumed this to be the case and therefore hesitated to use the word 'soul', preferring simply to speak of person or human being. But I have come to see the value of the term as representing something more complex and significant than is normally understood by the word. After all, it is employed

---

68   Victor Frankl, *Man's Search for Meaning*, New York, NY: Washington Square Press, 1963, p. 175.

69   See *Gaudium et Spes*, in *The Documents of Vatican II*, edited by Walter M. Abbott, S.J., London–Dublin: Geoffrey Chapman, 1966, part 1, chap. 1, pp. 210–12. This is thoroughly and well discussed by Cardinal Joseph Ratzinger (later Pope Benedict XVI) in the *Commentary on the Documents of Vatican II*, edited by Herbert Vorgrimler, New York: Herder & Herder, 1969, pp. 127–31.

70   Bonhoeffer, *Creation and Fall*, p. 7.

when we speak about the uniqueness of other things, such as the 'soul of African music'.

When I think of Steve, I cannot conceive of him apart from his body, but I know that Steve as soul is far more. It has to do with everything he was and is, including the music he wrote and played and to which we can still listen. For Steve to 'lose his soul' would mean he was no longer Steve, no longer the person we knew, the person he had become, the person to whom we continue to relate. As Schweiker observes, 'soul' captures 'something that seems lacking in contemporary forms of thought'.[71] Bonhoeffer sensed this when in prison he drafted the outline for the book he was writing on Christianity and spoke of the lack of the 'power of the soul' within a technologically organized 'world come of age'. By this he meant those inner resources of intellect and psyche that were critical to being human.[72] Can we not speak, then, about the soul of being human, as that which makes us distinct, and so convey better the mystery and complexity, the dynamic and dignity of being human and becoming more so in a dehumanizing world? I think we can and must, and that it is also helpful to do so in responding to the questions raised by Steve's death. But we must be ever mindful of the critique of notions of a 'disembodied soul' presented by both neuroscience and the biblical tradition.

Neuroscience presents a radical challenge to traditional views about the soul as a discrete element *in* the body, whether identified with rationality or self-consciousness or as an immortal and divine entity. We certainly 'cast no light on the consciousness of a human' by thinking that there is some kind of 'inner homunculus' or little human being within our bodies that we describe as an independently existing soul.[73] That is not only scientifically

---

71　William Schweiker, *Dust That Breathes: Christian Faith and the New Humanism*, Chichester: Wiley-Blackwell, 2010, p. 71.

72　Dietrich Bonhoeffer, *Letters and Papers from Prison*, Dietrich Bonhoeffer Works, edited by John W. de Gruchy, vol. 8, Minneapolis: Fortress Press, 2010, p. 500.

73　Roger Scruton, 'Neuronononsense and the Soul', *In Search of Self: Interdisciplinary Perspectives on Personhood*, edited by J. Wentzel van Huyssteen and Erik P. Wiebe, Grand Rapids, MI: Eerdmans, 2011, p. 339.

implausible, it is also biblically and theologically unacceptable, and fails to reflect the complexity of what I suggest soul should designate. If we are going to use the word soul at all, we need to understand it not as a ghost-like being, or an inner essence, but as embodied *human uniqueness at its most complex and dynamic.*

Having said this, we have not dealt with the most challenging aspect of neuroscience on the subject. There is a growing conviction among many scholars that neurobiology will soon tell us how the brain produces moral judgments, social inclinations, aesthetic experiences, religious ecstasies, and emotional attachments – all without reference to anything that could conceivably deserve the name of 'soul'.[74] Everything that was previously attributed to the soul, that is, as something other than the body, would then be acknowledged as the outcome of complex organization within the brain.[75] As Roger Scruton tells us, 'recent advances in mapping brain functions through Magnetic Resonance Imaging have given rise to the view that we are getting constantly closer to explaining consciousness, to locating it as a physical process'. If this happens, it is claimed, the 'final mystery' of the human condition is removed.[76] This is a far more serious challenge than the rejection of the soul as a discrete entity independent of the body, something which the Bible also rejects. So how are we to respond to it?

Let me begin by considering how we might understand human uniqueness today following van Huyssteen's interdisciplinary examination of the issues in a way which he refers to as 'transversal rationality'. The outcome is not only a multi-faceted understanding of human uniqueness, but also one in which it is understood as a dynamic process. This is deeply embedded in our remote prehistoric past, but at the same time is expanding into the future; it has to do with humans becoming more truly human *through engagement with others and the world.* I suggest that if we are to develop a contemporary understanding of the person as body *and* soul, it has to be along these lines. Neither the *imago Dei* nor the soul, traditionally the metaphors for human uniqueness, can be understood

---

74 Scruton, 'Neuronal nonsense and the Soul', *In Search of Self*, p. 340.
75 Murphy, *Bodies and Souls*, p. 57.
76 Scruton, 'Neuronal nonsense and the Soul', *In Search of Self*, p. 338.

as static metaphysical realities, simply because the human person is always in a process of becoming, whether through physical growth and decay, or through intentional and therefore self-conscious development towards personal and spiritual maturity that we identify as the growth of the soul.

In this regard, it is helpful to think with John Polkinghorne of the soul as that which provides continuity within our lives, given the fact that my physical body is today not what it was when I was eight months old, or even yesterday. To address this, Polkinghorne recasts the Thomist view that 'the soul is the form of the body' in speaking of 'the almost infinitely complex, dynamic, information-bearing pattern in which the matter of our bodies at any one time is organized'.[77] Whether we adopt a fully Thomist position or not, what is important as we prepare for the next chapter on the resurrection, is this understanding of the soul as providing continuity, as the dynamic information-bearing pattern of who we are in ourselves and in relation to others. But this does not mean that soul is something inherently immortal *in itself*, akin to an imperishable divine spark. I will say more about this in the next chapter so let me pass from the subject here.

How, then, is the soul understood in this complex sense related to self-consciousness? Consciousness has to do with the self-reflective power of the brain at work; in other words it is inseparable from the body. This sense of a separate conscious self is usually regarded in neuroscience as an illusion produced by the brain. But because we understand how consciousness arises and works, we do not necessarily understand what consciousness is *all* about. I suggest it is more correct to say, with Scruton (and Ward in the background), that consciousness is not a 'feature of the *brain*' but 'of the person whose brain it is'.[78] The human person (body and soul), in other words, cannot be equated simply with self-consciousness nor reduced to only biological explanation.

77   John Polkinghorne, 'Eschatological Credibility: Emergent and Teological Processes', in *Resurrection: Theological and Scientific Assessments*, edited by Robert John Russell, Ted Peters and Michael Welker, Grand Rapids, MI: Eerdmans, 2002, p. 51.
78   Scruton, 'Neuronsense and the Soul', pp. 340–1.

To use Scruton's analogy, in seeking to understand, we are not analysing the paints and pigments or the canvas on which they are imprinted, but the image that is created by the artist. Part of the problem is that the causal theories of science, when it comes to human consciousness, find no room for and apparently cannot take into account first-person knowledge that makes inter-personal relations possible. In such theories, the 'I' and the 'Thou' have no place, and it is precisely this that repulses us when 'human love, desire, longing, grief and resentment' are explained simply in terms of hardwiring or neurochemicals.[79]

Unlike other animals our self-consciousness means that we are able to reflect on experiences such as suffering or wellbeing beyond the actual stimulus that we experience. We have the capacity to engage in critical moral reasoning, the ability to know the difference between good and evil and, as I will shortly argue, the freedom to make choices accordingly. But even more, through our self-consciousness we are inseparably connected with the self-consciousness of other humans and the world we inhabit. Our internalized representation of 'the other' to which self-consciousness refers, as Clayton says,

> gives to the human animal an inner complexity that corresponds to the unique complexity of our central nervous system, *without being identical to it*. It is this complex brain and nervous system that causes our inner complexity – even though . . . the world of subjective awareness is neither equivalent to, nor reducible to, the physical structures of the brain.[80]

To speak of 'our inner complexity' is a way, then, of speaking about the soul always in relation to the body and importantly, to the 'other'. Schweiker speaks to this when he not only reminds us that the origins of the notion of soul are to be found 'in a native sense of inwardness, the stream of desires, impressions, hopes, loves, lusts, confusions, and aspirations that flow in and through

---

79 Scruton, 'Neurononsense and the Soul', p. 343.
80 Clayton, 'Biology and Purpose', *Evolution and Ethics*, p. 327.

our lives', but also says that being a soul means being 'capable of directing those energies towards some integration of one's being in relation to others'. And, moreover, that this has to do 'with respect to some norm or measure of goodness no matter how incomplete the project might finally be'.[81]

Schweiker thus speaks of the soul as 'a kind of *sacred space* that defines both the inviolable dignity of human beings but also the vulnerability, limits, and struggle of human existence, a "space" that can be violated and profaned by external forces but also by oneself'.[82] On this understanding, 'soul' has to do with more than value-free psychological dynamics; it is an *ethical construction*, providing the basis for upholding human dignity and rights. The key is the notion of conscience, often associated with the 'heart' in the Bible, along with the notion of 'formation', as Bonhoeffer develops it in his *Ethics*.[83] The fact that many humans seem to lack any sense of conscience so that their formation has been stunted, does not mean that the soul cannot be understood 'as the labour of conscience integrating the dynamics of life while also desig-nating the right to have rights'.[84] For the 'soul' as 'sacred space' gives humans dignity and the right to be respected *as human beings* irrespective of who they are or their failures. Our forma-tion as 'souls' is, moreover, contingent on our respecting the 'sacred space' of others.

By soul, then, I do not mean a discrete, immortal entity, but the complexity and continuity of the person-in-relationship, the soul as a work in progress rather than a static entity, an ongoing con-struction in which disparate parts or multiplicities are integrated around an emerging, evolving new self-consciousness in relation to God and the rest of the natural order. Such an understanding of soul is not an individualistic ego-centric notion, nor one removed from the world and primarily interested in escaping from it into some kind of afterlife. In Christian terms, the soul has to do with the renewal of the 'image of God' in us in Christ, which enables us

---

81   Schweiker, *Dust That Breathes*, p. 73.
82   Schweiker, *Dust That Breathes*, p. 72.
83   Bonhoeffer, *Ethics*, pp. 76–102.
84   Schweiker, *Dust That Breathes*, p. 80.

to become morally responsible human beings. It is an understanding of being human that resists profaning the 'other' by respect for the integrity of life and the sacredness of being human. This correlates with what a young Bonhoeffer already noted in his doctoral dissertation, that a 'person exists always and only in ethical responsibility', in the flux of life and within the concrete situation where he or she is confronted by the overwhelming claim of the other.[85] The exercising of such responsibility implies that humans are, at least to some degree, free to act in this way in solidarity with others. But is this the case, given what we know about genetics and the working of the brain?

Freedom, responsibility and sociality

Our bodies have a complex history imprinted in our genome records which we cannot change. Much of our behaviour is driven by instincts that arise in our brains, and our actions can largely be understood and explained in this way. Even 'our higher-order drives', Clayton reminds us, 'including our drives for novelty and creativity – bear the marks of our genetic origins and evolution'.[86] Our sense of moral responsibility, for example, can be explained by our comparatively large neocortex that makes us aware of our self-in-relationship, and, unlike other animals, aware that we can hurt others by our actions or lack of them. Like other animals our behaviour is determined to a large degree by instincts. At the same time, and this is the critical point, we are much more involved in and responsible for constructing the world in which we live and the formation of persons we become. We are not fully conditioned or determined by our genetic make-up or sociological conditions, but responsible human beings living in relation to others in specific historical contexts. We are active agents in our evolution, hopefully becoming nurtured in conscience and more truly human

85 Dietrich Bonhoeffer, *Santorum Communio: A Theological Study of the Sociology of the Church*, edited by Clifford J. Green, Minneapolis: Fortress Press, 1998, pp. 48–9.
86 Clayton, 'Biology and Purpose', p. 325.

in the process in order to choose between good and evil and select options in relative openness to the world. In short, our uniqueness within the animal kingdom has to do with a relative freedom to act in morally responsible ways.

If we were only programmed to be ego-centred, or hard-wired to act in certain ways, we would not be free to be morally responsible, only a-moral. But neuroscience also indicates that we can at the very least decide *not* to perform certain deeds, and that such action 'counts as free'.[87] Solms speaks of our 'freedom *not* to act in an automatic and preprogrammed fashion' as is the way with other mammals. Though I think it is appropriate to point out that Solms' own remarkable pursuit of social justice and transformation in the wine farming community of Franschhoek, on the very same farm that provided the location for Brinks story of the slave-girl, Philida, suggests that this should be phrased in more positive terms.[88] But even stated negatively as Solms does, humans are clearly not just at the mercy of compulsive instincts; we have the capacity to think rationally and the freedom to make choices.[89]

The mystery of being human, however, is not that we so often choose to act selfishly or in self-destructive ways, or even that we are free to choose *not* to act in certain ways, all of which can be explained by neuroscience, but that we so often choose, at considerable personal cost, to act altruistically and compassionately towards others. Such freedom Clayton calls 'agential', by which he means the 'freedom for which *the agent's own choice* is the sufficient cause for at least some of her actions'. This is an emerging capacity and can be regarded as 'both a product of evolution *and* a sign of the image of God in humanity'.[90] As Clayton says:

> As the product of evolution, freedom indicates a greater richness and potential in the evolutionary process than is often acknowledged. As a sign of the *imago Dei*, purposive freedom

87 Clayton, 'Biology and Purpose', p. 332.
88 www.solms-delta.co.za.
89 Solms, 'Neurological Foundations', p. 53.
90 Clayton, 'Biology and Purpose', pp. 332–3.

suggests the possibility of divine purposes that underlie the flow of history as a whole. If the one phenomenon of human freedom in fact reflects both dimensions, then it is possible to link these two sources – what biological evolution can produce and what God may purpose – in a close and mutually reinforcing way.[91]

If this is true, as I believe it is, then we have the basis for altruism or love. For love, understood as *agapé*, is choosing to act in the interest of the other even though this may go contrary to biological drives and social acculturation. This goes to the heart of what Christian tradition has called 'sanctification', because by exercising choice when it goes against the grain of my selfish genes, my cultural predispositions and self-interests, I *could* be living 'the life of a saint'.[92] And in so far as *agapé* is the nature of God, to choose to live accordingly is to participate in the life of God, it is to live 'in the image of God'. It is precisely for this reason that we can affirm the mystery of the Incarnation as the embodiment of self-giving *agapé* and confess Jesus Christ as 'truly human and truly God'.

I detect deep connections between the work of the Spirit, the activity of the brain, and the struggle for justice that need to be further explored in taking us into a more humane and just future. What that future might be is the theme of the next chapter, when we consider what Jesus meant by the coming of God's reign on earth as in heaven, the eschatological promise of a 'new earth and new heaven'. There, too, we must consider what Christians believe about life before and beyond death. But at least for now it is clear to me that our world needs both theological reflection and scientific investigation working in tandem, it also needs saints, compassionate scientists and social activists, with a little help from theologians, to better embody and express the mystery of our humanity in the world today. But this also requires

---

91 Clayton, 'Biology and Purpose', p. 333.
92 Clayton, 'Biology and Purpose', p. 333.

the recognition that human beings cannot be understood, nor be engaged responsibly in the world, as isolated individuals.

Human sociality is deeply ingrained in our biological and psychological nature. We cannot and do not exist in isolation from other humans; we are locked into the sociality of humanity from the beginning of our lives. Our brains are not just our own; they bear the DNA imprint of humanity as a whole just as our development as persons occurs in relationship with others. Likewise we are bound together with the natural order, with all creatures and plants, with the ocean, the earth and the cosmos. This is our home. Unless we recognize and cherish this connectivity we can neither grow fully as humans, nor contribute to the well-being of that which makes life possible. Thus human sociality precedes individuality. This does not mean that the individual has no personal identity, any more than it means the priority of the social over the personal. It means, rather, that the discovery of genuine personal identity and nurturing of the soul, is only possible in community, that is, through 'the other'. Genuine community, as Bonhoeffer insisted, is not the absorption of the individual into the mass but a community of wills 'built upon the separateness and difference of persons'.[93] In an oft-quoted passage, he writes:

> God does not desire a history of individual human beings, but the history of the human community. However, God does not want a community that absorbs the individual into itself, but a community of human beings.[94]

All this is affirmed in the biblical creation narratives, the truth of which is amply demonstrated both in the estranged history of humanity and its constant search for Utopia or Paradise. Jesus' proclamation of the mystery of the kingdom or reign of God speaks directly to this human longing for reconciliation and restoration, for without this our humanity remains unfulfilled.

---

93 Bonhoeffer, *Sanctorum Communio*, p. 86.
94 Bonhoeffer, *Sanctorum Communio*, p. 80.

The new humanity

Whatever else the gospels tell us about Jesus, his redemptive solidarity with the human race in its joys and hopes, as well as its suffering, brokenness and despair, is fundamental to the gospel narrative. So, too, is his desire to create an inclusive community that respects difference while transcending its divisions, and responsibly recognizes its connection with the rest of creation, honouring its integrity and caring for its well-being. All of this is the mystery disclosed in Jesus as God's reign of *agapé* within the life of the world. Where God's *agapé* is present in the creation of a community in which forgiveness, reconciliation, love of enemies and the struggle for justice is evident, there the mystery of God's kingdom is revealed and historically embodied. For this reason, we must go beyond the notion that the mystery of being human has to do with us solely or even primarily as individuals. If our understanding of the image of God is triune, so that within God there is both difference of *personae* and yet perfect unity and communion, then to become truly human in God's image revealed in Christ means acknowledging human solidarity and establishing true community. It is only within this framework that we can begin to understand what the New Testament refers to as the *ekklesia*: that is, the community that comes into being as a sign and witness to the mystery of God's kingdom in the world.

The word *ekklesia* is translated into English as 'church', but like the words 'God' and 'soul' it has increasingly become misused, abused and virtually unusable. After all, when it is used, to what does it refer? To one of the thousands of denominations that exist, to an article in the creed, to the Roman Catholic Church and that alone, to the local congregation or some ideal religious community of saintly people, or even a building . . .? If we take our bearings from the New Testament, the *ekklesia* is not primarily an institution nor is it a conglomerate of pious individuals; it is an integral part of the mystery that has been disclosed in Christ. And like the mystery of God or of being human, it is not empirically verifiable. This is how Bonhoeffer understood the nature and purpose of the Church, when he wrote in his dissertation: '*The reality of the church is a reality of revelation, a reality that essentially must be* either believed or denied.'[95] The mystery that has been revealed to faith is nothing other or less than the birth of a new humanity. That is, the rebirth of humanity 'in Christ' as the 'Second Adam', the creation of a community of *agapé* that transcends the claims of ethnicity, nationality, gender and race, that lead to division and violence.

The problem with this understanding of *ekklesia* or church, as Bonhoeffer well knew, is that it not only appears idealistic, but is too often contradicted by the facts on the ground, a significant number of exceptions notwithstanding. The truth is that while the *mystery of the Church as sign of the new humanity* is not empirically verifiable, its historical existence as an institution is clearly open to critical examination and often justifiably damning criticism. But the empirical church as a sociological reality cannot hide behind the claim to be a mystery only known to faith any more, that is, than post-apartheid South Africa can claim to be a model of democracy, because it has a great Constitution. At the same time, this does not nullify that to which the Constitution points and day by day, inch by inch, is being struggled for and sometimes achieved. Bridging the often stark gap between reality as we experience it and the vision and hope of what we should be as a society, is what the struggle for transformation is about whether in Church or society.

Analogously, this gap between ideal and reality is often referred to as the 'invisible' and the 'visible' church, or the church existing at the same time as a community of sinners and a community of saints.[96] There is always a struggle within the church to be truly the church of Jesus Christ, a struggle for the soul of the church as 'sacred space' which embodies the mystery of the reign of God as the 'body of Christ' (*soma Christi*). The church is at the same

---

95 Dietrich Bonhoeffer, *Sanctorum Communio: A Theological Study of the Sociology of the Church*, Dietrich Bonhoeffer Works I, edited by Clifford Green, Minneapolis: Fortress, 2009, p. 127. Emphasis in original text.
96 See Hans Küng, *The Church*, London: Burns and Oates, 1968, pp. 3–42.

time historically and contextually embedded, and yet *believed* to be empowered by the Spirit to be a witness to the good news of God's inclusive reconciling love for the world. The Church is a fallible, experimental community seeking to anticipate God's ultimate purpose for humanity. Sadly, it is an experiment that fails as much as it succeeds, but where it does succeed, it bears witness to the mystery of God's reign and becomes a sign of hope for the future – not of the church or Christianity – but of humanity and the earth. That is what I mean when I say 'I *believe* in the church.'

Those of us who participated in the struggle against apartheid in South Africa experienced the church in ways which both contradicted and affirmed its calling to be the sign and embodiment of the new humanity. The Church was both involved in supporting apartheid and in fighting against it, a vivid expression of the ambiguity that has marked the church globally throughout the history of Christianity. Despite this, many of us experienced something of the new humanity as we found solidarity across denominations, racial and class groupings, in the struggle for liberation. This was Steve's experience of the Church from his days as a young person in his home congregation in Rondebosch, during his student years as a Christian activist and conscientious objector and later as a young ordained minister in Athlone and then as director of the Moffat Mission in Kuruman. Like many of his contemporaries, he had serious criticisms of the Church's failures, but in spite of that he was committed to its well-being and therefore to its development as a moral community providing an alternative vision of the world, and an alternative space in the world, in its witness to the love and justice of God.

Steve's vision of the Church was ecumenical, not only in its embrace of Christian diversity, but also in relation to people of other faiths and secular social activists, a reality he experienced in the struggle, as he also did in prison. In a detailed diary which he kept while in prison after his arrest during the Release Mandela Protest March in August 1985, he told how a 'depth of friendship and community' had grown up among those in the cell with him, irrespective of race or denomination, religion or lack of it.[97] But his awareness of the Church as an inclusive community in its witness to the 'new humanity' is most striking in his essay, in 1997, entitled 'Human being in Christ: resources for an inclusive anthropology'.[98] It is a remarkable account of what it means to be human both 'in Adam' and 'in Christ', and largely on that basis, a critique of homophobia within the life and practice of the Church. The argument resonates with the general development of this chapter, ending as it also does with a section entitled 'Being human means being in community'. There Steve reminds us that the church does not exist for its own sake, but for the sake of others, and that it cannot be this if it treats the victims of prejudice or politics as aliens within its own life. The Church is not meant to mirror humanity 'in Adam' in all its divisions and brokenness, but humanity 'in Christ', and therefore it is called to be an inclusive community of reconciliation, healing and wholeness. This is what it means to be the 'body of Christ' in the life of the world; this is the mystery of an emerging, inclusive new humanity that is the work of the Spirit.

My exploration of the mystery of being human has taken us on a long and, at times, circuitous journey. In the course of the journey I have indicated the extent to which I have learnt from the insights of neuropsychology in understanding the human self, though I have refused to adopt a reductionist position. The human being is unique within the animal world of which we are so integral a part. That uniqueness, traditionally described in biblical terms as being in the 'image of God', refers to the mystery of our being, fragments, if you like, of a much larger, cosmic mystery we call God. Central to that understanding of being human is the notion of soul, a complex embodied reality, which gives continuity to our identity as persons in relation to others, a 'sacred space' which gives us dignity and in turn provides a basis for moral

---

97 Steve de Gruchy, 'The diary of a few days in Pollsmoor Prison: 28 August–2 September, 1985', unpublished.
98 Published in *Aliens in the Household of God: Homosexuality and Christian Faith in South Africa*, edited by Paul Germond and Steve de Gruchy, Cape Town: David Philip, 1997, pp. 233–69.

responsibility, human rights and respect. And we have finally come to the recognition that the mystery of being human cannot be reduced to us as individuals; it has to do with us in relationship to one another. For Christians, this refers especially to being part of a community called to embody the new humanity in Christ that anticipates the coming of a new creation. What that means is the subject of my final chapter.

5

The Hope Within Us

Only when one loves life and the earth so much that with it every-
thing seems to be lost and at its end may one believe in the resurrec-
tion of the dead and a new world.
Dietrich Bonhoeffer[1]
For in hope we were saved. Now hope that is seen is not hope, for
who hopes for what is seen?
Paul[2]
The laughter of the universe is God's delight. It is the universal
Easter laughter.
Jürgen Moltmann[3]
God has given us a new birth into a living hope
through the resurrection of Jesus from the dead.
1 Peter 1.3

Steve's death evoked some surprising yet enriching developments.
One of these was the renewal of friendship with people who had
gone on different paths to Isobel's and my own over the years, but
who knew Steve at some stage in his life and wanted to be in touch
with us again. One friend, whom we had not seen for some years,
was among the first to visit us after the event, and both Isobel and
I deeply appreciated his empathy and support. In his youth, he had
been a convinced Christian, but for a variety of reasons had long
since set his faith aside, though not his moral values and ethical commitments. Changing circumstances had edged him back to thinking about the tradition in which he had been nurtured, and Steve's

---

1 Dietrich Bonhoeffer, *Letters and Papers from Prison*, Dietrich Bonhoeffer
Works, edited by John W. de Gruchy, vol. 8, Minneapolis: Fortress Press, 2010,
p. 213.
2 Romans 8.24.
3 Jürgen Moltmann, *The Coming of God: Christian Eschatology*,
Minneapolis: Fortress, 1996, p. 339.

death contributed to the process. His previous antipathy towards the church had subsided though some remained, and he was eager to revisit the faith that had shaped his earlier years. However, as he put it to me in a letter, did he have to believe in the resurrection of Jesus in order to become a 'card carrying member'?

The reader will recall from the Prologue, that I began writing this book in an attempt to answer a question asked me by an old friend in a letter following Steve's death. He asked whether I still believed in the resurrection, whether of Christ or more generally of the dead. What I have written thus far has been, in large part, an attempt to lay the foundation for my answer which will emerge as this chapter unfolds. But now, in addition to that initial question, I also have in mind this more recent one: is faith in the resurrection necessary in order to be a Christian? The answer, as my friend suspected, must be in the affirmative if we are to take seriously the testimony of the New Testament and the convictions of Christians through the centuries. I would be misleading him if I were to say anything else. But my response begs two other questions which set the agenda for this chapter, questions which I know Steve would push me to answer as honestly as I can.

The first question is this: how are we to *understand* the resurrection, whether of Christ or the dead? The second is: what does it mean to *believe* in the resurrection? After all, there are those regular church goers who agnostically mumble their way through the Creed with its confident assertions of faith in the resurrection and 'the life everlasting', uncertain about whether they are true, and if so, what they might mean for them today. There are also many whose dogmatic certainty on such matters makes me wonder if they comprehend the challenges posed by science and philosophy to such assertions, and have thought much about the issues. And there are those who, like my friend, appreciates his relationship to the Christian community, lives by Christian moral values, and yet has too many doubts to believe honestly in the resurrection.

Believing in the resurrection is giving our assent to the reality of the risen Christ in our lives and in the world. But it is more than an article of doctrine to which the mind dutifully, unthinkingly or confidently consents; it is faith and love active in hope even, and perhaps most often, when you are bombarded by doubt and despair. That is the mystery of Christian hope. It is relatively easy to utter the great Easter acclamations or sing the majestic Easter hymns; it is much more difficult to live and act in ways that demonstrate their truth amidst the challenges and tragedies of daily existence and the struggle for justice in the world. Just as faith and love were central to my discussion in previous chapters, it is now the turn of hope, the mystery we acclaim when we say 'Christ is risen.'

But is not this hope, Steve would push me to answer, the ultimate confabulation? Is it any different from that which 'springs eternal in the human breast', as Alexander Pope described it in his *Essay on Man*?[4] That is, is it substantially different from that sense of optimism produced by the brain to help us negotiate adverse circumstances? Let me immediately answer that you don't have to be an optimist to be a Christian, nor is acute depression unknown in the lives of Christian saints, let alone the rest of us. Optimism to my mind is infinitely better than pessimism and certainly cynicism, but Christian hope is qualitatively different, a 'hope against hope' as Paul describes it (Romans 4:18). Like optimism, Christian hope is processed through the brain, but unlike optimism, which is dependent on the likelihood of something happening for our good, such hope is contingent on God's promise even when the good appears unlikely; it is hoping against the odds because you believe in the faithfulness, love and justice of God revealed in the resurrection of Jesus. Hope, in other words, is based on trust in that which is not yet seen but which has already been promised. The whole biblical story of redemption whether understood in terms of the penultimate struggle for justice, or the ultimate restoration of all things, is premised on this conviction.[5] There were often times during the apartheid years when there was little reason for optimism in South Africa; what kept people engaged in the struggle was hope, because they believed that in the end truth and justice would win the day even if utopia would not be achieved.

---

4 Alexander Pope, *An Essay on Man: Epistle 1*, first published in 1733.
5 Anthony C. Thiselton, *Life After Death: A New Approach to the Last Things*, Grand Rapids: Eerdmans, 2012.

Nonetheless, the grounds for Christian hope have been challenged from the beginning, and they have grown stronger in the light of the advances of science, whether neuropsychology in the way I have already indicated, or physics and cosmology. This is so because Christian hope is ultimately about the promised coming of a 'new heaven and earth' already anticipated in the resurrection of Christ from the dead. But if scientific predictions about the future of the universe and planet earth, as a fragment within it, are anywhere near correct, and 'the law of entropy has the last laugh', then Christian hope is understandably suspect.[6] Can this prophetic vision of a transformed heaven and earth be anything other than the ultimate utopian dream, even more Quixotic than those that have inspired generations of social visionaries from Isaiah to Karl Marx? So belief in the resurrection of the dead and the restoration of all things is the ultimate test case for those theologians who seek to engage science constructively and for scientists who are open to that possibility.[7] For this reason, Murphy cautions that however fruitful the science–theology dialogue might be in other areas, when we turn to eschatology with its promise of a transformed cosmic future, we reach a point where silence may be necessary.[8] Be that as it may, let me try to give an account of the hope that is within me.[9]

Life after death?

Julian Barnes' autobiography, *Nothing to Be Frightened Of*, deals with death as a natural phenomenon not to be feared.[10] With

---

6 Ted Peters, *God as Trinity: Relationality and Temporality in Divine Life*, Louisville, KY: Westminster/John Knox Press, 1993, pp. 175–6.

7 John Russell, 'Bodily Resurrection, Eschatology and Scientific Cosmology', *in Resurrection: Theological and Scientific Assessments*, edited by Robert John Russell, Ted Peters, and Michael Welker, Grand Rapids, MI: Eerdmans, 2002, p. 4.

8 Nancey Murphy, *Bodies and Souls, or Spirit Bodies?*, Cambridge: Cambridge University Press, 2006, p. 145.

9 See 1 Peter 3.15.

10 Julian Barnes, *Nothing to Be Frightened Of*, London: Jonathan Cape, 2008.

consummate wit, he takes on all sacred cows, leaving us to face death without any rose-tinted glasses. As an author of note, he reflects on the fact that 'for each (writer) of us there will come the breaking of the single remaining thread of this strange, unwitnessed, yet deeply intimate relationship between writer and reader. At some point there will be a last reader for me too. And then that reader will die too'.[11] For those of us who read books and try to write them, nothing could make the point of our mortality more starkly. There will be a last reader of this book, not too soon I hope, but inevitably the book will eventually crumble into dust even if in the meantime it gathers dust on library shelves. But, says, Barnes, there is nothing to be frightened of about dying.

Barnes, like Socrates and many other courageous stoics through the centuries, might not be frightened by death, but the rest of us mortals tend to avoid the subject, as did the characters around the restaurant table in Robertson's *The Cunning Man*. Like our animal cousins, most of us avoid situations where life is threatened precisely because we are fearful of death. Some of us even find it difficult to watch people engaged in extreme sports, and sometimes we embarrassingly make ageing and death a subject of jest. There are undoubtedly some things that are worth dying for, and martyrdom for the right reasons may be celebrated. But however we approach death, it is no illusion, we cannot wish it away, its success rate is total, and while people die differently and for some death comes as a friend, it remains the last enemy, as Paul aptly described it.[12] Jesus' cry of dereliction from the cross stands in stark contrast to Socrates calmly drinking the poisoned cup. For me, no one expressed my experience of Steve's death more bluntly than Carl Jung:

Death is indeed a fearful piece of brutality; there is no sense pretending otherwise. It is brutal not only as a physical event, but far more so psychically: a human being is torn away from us, and what remains is the icy stillness of death. There no

---

11 Barnes, *Nothing to Be Frightened Of*, pp. 225–6.
12 1 Corinthians 15.26.

longer exists any hope of a relationship, for all the bridges have been smashed at one blow.[13]

It is not surprising then, that ever since human beings became self-conscious and thought about death, they developed belief in some kind of after-life to counter their fears. Sceptics regard such notions as confabulations without any empirical evidence to substantiate them. Common sense informed by science understandably dismisses out of hand any attempt to 'prove' life after death on the basis of stories of near death experiences. This includes, perhaps even more vociferously, those told by scientists themselves.[14] Yet the claims and convictions persist, just as from time immemorial all cultures have developed myths about an after-life in order to make the final passage from the one to the other more hopeful. There are, after all, as Wordsworth tells us, intimations of immortality on every hand:

In the primal sympathy
Which having been must ever be,
In the soothing thoughts that spring
Out of human suffering,
In the faith that looks through death,
In years that bring the philosophic mind . . .[15]

But if there is life after death it is undoubtedly a mystery for us earthbound creatures of the dust even if there are myths and revelations to console us. And even if their consolation carries weight, when all is said and done there will be surprises at the end of the mystery story. Only then, but certainly then, will our carefully constructed theologies and philosophies, our religious traditions and institutions, be weighed in the balances of final verification. In the meantime we don't really *know* what awaits us if there is more to death than death itself, and have no way of finding out. But let

---

13 C. G. Jung, *Memories, Dreams and Reflections*, New York, NY: Vintage, 1965, p. 314.
14 See Alexander, *Proof of Heaven*, 140–146.
15 Wordsworth, 'Intimations of Immortality', *Norton*, p. 732.

me try to set out what I *believe* and therefore imagine in seeking answers to the questions facing me. I begin with several options.

During the first few years of my academic career, I lectured on the Indian religious traditions to undergraduate students. In the course of my lectures, I traced the development of the Indian experience from the ancient Indus Valley Civilization through to the profound teaching of the Upanishads, with its recurring refrain 'That you are!'

> With the old age of the body, That (*Brahman*) does not age; with the death of the body, That (*Atman*) does not die . . . It is the Self – free from sin, free from old age, free from death, free from grief, free from hunger, free from thirst . . .[16]

'That' is the true Self, the imperishable Self, the immortal soul, divine and radically distinct from the perishable body – and therefore different from the understanding of soul I developed in the previous chapter. Coupled with this Vedic understanding of the immortal soul is the less consoling view that after death the soul is re-incarnated in another body, so the whole cycle of life, suffering and eventual death begins again. The ultimate aim is to break this fateful cycle of causation in order that the immortal soul will finally be liberated from suffering and absorbed in the life-giving Universal Spirit. Millions live by these convictions. But they are not mine. Certainly I cannot conceive of Steve as an impersonal, disconnected soul for the simple reason that such a ghostly being could not possibly be the Steve we all knew. I can take no comfort in such a concept whatsoever. Nor, I believe, would Steve.

Buddhism does not speak of an immortal soul, but of the phenomenon of the person as being in a state of constant flux which, to my mind, makes more sense. The goal in this life is to break the chain of causation that leads from desire to attachment and suffering and enter the bliss of Nirvana which is literally the 'blowing out' of desire. This can already be achieved through following the eight-fold path. As stated by the Buddha with reference to

---

16 Chhandogya Upanishad vii.i.5 in Swami Nikhilanada ed., *The Upanishads*, New York: Harper, 1964, p. 348.

someone who achieves such bliss, 'It would be absurd to say of such a monk, with his heart set free, that he believes that the perfected being survives after death – or indeed that he does not survive . . . Because the monk is free his state transcends all expression, predication, communication, and knowledge'.[17] Death is the end of life as we know it, a release from the conditions that cause suffering, but we can say no more than that Nirvana is unconditioned bliss. This positive agnosticism has its attractions for many people well beyond traditional Buddhism.

What, then, is the Christian understanding? It may come as a surprise to some readers that many theologians would insist that there is 'no life after death' as this is commonly understood. Christian belief in the resurrection of the dead, Moltmann tells us, 'excludes any idea of "life after death," of which many religions speak, whether in the idea of the immortality of the soul or in the transmigration of souls. Resurrection life is not a further life after death, whether in the soul or the spirit, in children or reputation; it means the annihilation of death in the victory of the new, eternal life. (I Cor. 15.55)'.[18] So N. T. Wright insists that resurrection is not about 'life after death', but about 'life *after* life after death'.[19] It also has to do with life *before* death as we shall see.

Approaching the subject from a slightly different angle, Nicholas Lash suggests 'that it is misleading to speak of "resurrection" as another state of affairs, or event, subsequent to death, or of "risen life" as a prolongation, in however new a form, of temporal existence'.[20] He therefore says that the question we should ask is not what happens *after death*, but 'what happens in death'? To understand this we have to remember that death is actually a process that begins virtually after birth:

17 *Digha Nikaya*, 2.64 *The Buddhist Tradition in India, China and Japan*, ed. William Theodore de Bary, New York: Vintage, 1972, p. 21.

18 Jürgen Moltmann, *The Crucified God*, London: SCM, 1974, p. 170.

19 N. T. Wright, *The Resurrection of the Son of God*, Minneapolis: Fortress Press, 2003, p. 31.

20 See Nicholas Lash, *Theology on Dover Beach*, London: Darton Longman & Todd, 1979, p. 174.

Dying is not just something that takes place during our last few weeks or hours. Just as our physical bodies, from the moment they leave the womb, are set on a journey that leads inexorably and ever more obviously, to senility and decay, so also it is true of the whole of our temporal existence that the process of living is *also* the process of dying. They are not *two* processes that succeed one another.[21]

The process of dying in the midst of life is not simply a matter of the molecules that comprise our bodies changing so that we are continually being re-made, even though our DNA remains the same. It is equally true that we are constantly going through the process of moving on in life: leaving certain things behind, outgrowing our clothes, graduating from school, changing jobs, moving house, saying goodbye to family and friends after holidays, retiring, making and ending relationships. The last time I saw Steve was the evening before he and his family left Volmoed to return home after the Christmas holidays in 2009. I often picture that occasion as I pass by the place where we said our farewells. George Eliot expresses its pathos well:

The sad good-byes had all been said before that last evening; and after all the packing was done and all the arrangements were made, Amos felt the oppression of that blank interval in which one has nothing left to think of but the dreary future — the separation from the loved and familiar, and the chilling entrance on the new and strange. In every parting there is an image of death.[22]

There is no going back, no return to what once was.

We die a thousand deaths;
our world evolves by change, decay – and death;

---

21 Lash, *Theology on Dover Beach*, p. 175.
22 George Eliot, *Scenes from a Clerical Life*, Oxford: Clarendon Press, 1985, bk. 1, chap. 10, p. 70.

seeds die, are buried, give birth to newness;
our bodies die daily, cell by cell, but birth anew.
our minds die to old ideas, old ways – accept the new.
But the heart – the heart holds on, clinging, fighting,
clutching, encasing in our embrace all that has gone. . .[23]

But do we take with us all we have experienced in life, especially the network of relations that constitute who we are?

In African traditional culture, the 'living dead' or ancestors continue to interact with the lives of those who remain. Musa Dube, an African feminist theologian, speaks of their 'essential role in maintaining ethical relationships and responsibility in society'.[24] They are actively interested in the well-being of the living, and often act as intermediaries on their behalf with God. The 'living dead' are so fundamental to African culture that it is difficult for African Christians to ignore them even if they sense that they should if they are to be true Christians. But how to relate respect for ancestors to Christian faith is a matter of considerable debate.[25] At least one major African theologian, Kwame Bediako, has developed a Christology in which Jesus himself is understood as our ancestor within the framework of Akan culture in Ghana.[26]

The biblical belief in the resurrection of the dead as part of eschatological hope in the coming of a 'new heaven and a new earth' may be traced back to post-exilic passages in the book of Isaiah and that of Daniel.[27] Opinions on what this means have varied

23 Isobel de Gruchy, "Dying," *In the Slow Lane*, self-published, 2008, 31.

24 Musa W. Dube, 'Postcolonial Feminist Perspectives on African Religions', in *The Wiley-Blackwell Companion To African Religions*, edited by Elias Kifon Bongmba. Oxford: Blackwell Publishers, 2012, pp. 134–5.

25 See Klaus Nürnberger, *The Living Dead and the Living God: Christ and the Ancestors in a Changing Africa*, Pietermaritzburg: Cluster Publications, 2007. See also the Foreword by Buti Thagale, the Catholic Archbishop of Johannesburg.

26 Kwame Bediako, *Jesus in African Culture: A Ghanaian Perspective*, Accra: Asempa Publishers, 1990.

27 Isaiah 26.19; Daniel 12.2. See James D. G. Dunn, *Jesus and the Spirit*, London: SCM, 1975, pp. 117–22.

from the crudely literal to the more spiritual. The controversy in post-exilic Judaism between the Sadducees and the Pharisees on the resurrection of the dead is evident in the New Testament. In his debate with the Sadducees, Jesus identifies with the Pharisees, saying that God is 'God of the living not the dead', with reference to the patriarchs of old, Abraham, Isaac and Jacob.[28] For Jesus, these ancestors in faith were not just memorable figures of the past; they were part of the 'living dead' that remain connected with us in some meaningful way. They are that 'great cloud of witnesses' described in the letter to the Hebrews (12.1), the reality of whom Christians celebrate on 'All Souls Day'.

There is, then, a history to beliefs about life after death not unrelated to the history of God and of the soul, and this history has taken different twists and turns within Judaism and Islam as well as Christian tradition as it has developed over the centuries. Debates about purgatory, soul-sleep, heaven and hell, as well as resurrection and immortality, are all indicative of an unceasing attempt to gain clarity on the issues, though theological insight and popular religious sentiment do not always tally, and speculation is rife. But let me attempt to say something that makes sense to me about heaven (and hell) before getting to the subject of resurrection.

As it is in heaven

God, so the Bible and the Creed assert, is the maker of heaven and earth and also the judge 'of the living and the dead'; but nowhere is God the designated maker of hell. We can be thankful that the God revealed in Jesus is our judge; I can think of some whose judgment I would not trust in time or eternity. But we can't blame God for creating hell. That is something we human beings create for ourselves and others. The Valley of Hinnom outside ancient Jerusalem was called Gehenna, the place of death, because of the crimes against humanity frequently committed there. The prophet Jeremiah

---

28 The story is recorded in each of the synoptic gospels, suggesting its importance in the early church. Mark 12.18–27; Matthew 22.23–33; Luke 20.27–38.

refers to it as the place of God's judgment as it often was experienced in the course of the history of Jerusalem. Ultimately hell may be nothingness, the ending of all relationships and the absence of God. But hell on earth is real. Hell is death camps, bombed cities, torture chambers, the unending cycle of violence and terror, of war, pillage and rape. Hell is where love, beauty and justice are trashed; where God suffers silently in solidarity with countless victims who can no longer believe that he cares. But Jesus and the prophets tell us that those who perpetrate such crimes against humanity will themselves suffer the consequences. Trapped in a web of their own making they cannot extricate themselves, as Dante's *Inferno* graphically depicts and C. S. Lewis describes in *The Great Divorce*.[29]

God's unfathomable love does not exclude God's judgment of evil even though his judgments are unsearchable.[30] Let the mystery revealed in Christ is that God's judgments are not retributive, driven by vengeance or by the canons of human legal systems. God's justice is restorative justice. To say anything else is to allow that, in the end, the power of evil will trump God's power of love, even if only to some small degree. The notion of eternal punishment is a denial of God's will and purpose declared in the death and resurrection of Jesus.

John Baillie, a Scottish theologian of the first half of the twentieth century, long ago dispelled from my mind any lingering notion of hell as a place of perpetual punishment after death.[31] The notion that God created hell as a place of punishment and torment in which God keeps people incarcerated for eternity is blasphemy, whatever some Christians might think. I am fully aware of those Bible texts, including sayings attributed to Jesus,[32] which speak of 'everlasting punishment', and of the theologies that have been based on them in the history of Christian tradition. Hell for unbelievers and heaven for believers is undoubtedly the dominant position. But there are biblical

29 C. S. Lewis, *The Great Divorce*, New York, NY: Macmillan, 1962.
30 Romans 11.33.
31 John Baillie, *And the Life Everlasting*, Oxford: Oxford University Press, 1956, pp. 241–4.
32 Schleiermacher observes that these texts 'if more closely scrutinized' are 'found insufficient to support any such conclusion'. *The Christian Faith*, p. 720.

texts that suggest otherwise, and there is also a long counter-tradition beginning already in the second century, one which finds expression in Julian of Norwich in the fourteenth, and then more widely after the Reformation among Anabaptists and later Pietists, who found it inconceivable to believe in an everlasting hell for those who did not believe in Christ. In more recent times, Barth's doctrine of universal salvation based on God's election of all humanity in Christ, has also become influential. This does not cheapen grace or make faith unnecessary but locates salvation in the mystery of God's grace.[33] There is certainly no space for hell in the 'new heaven and new earth'.

An edition of *Time* magazine had, as its cover story, an article on 'Rethinking Heaven'.[34] In so far as one can trust such articles it indicated that '85% of all Americans, according to Gallup . . . are apparently confident . . . that life does not end at the grave',[35] and that you go to heaven when you die, at least if you believe rightly and do good. But, as the article indicates, traditional views about heaven, while still held by many religious people, are being challenged by some prominent Christian scholars who insist that such views are unbiblical even though the images derive from the Bible.

What, then, do we mean when we speak of heaven? Is that not also a human construction to give us comfort and keep hope alive that all will be well in the end? The portrayals of heaven, as in the Revelation or Apocalypse of John or Dante's *Paradiso*, have long fed the popular religious imagination. The embodiment of its symbols and metaphors in hymns, liturgies and discourse often leave us hoping we will not end up there in perpetual boredom, like an eagerly anticipated banquet without much of a menu or any of the spices of life. But we misread the text if we draw that conclusion. The book of Revelation was never intended to be taken literally, let alone as a forecast of the future in which we can discern the last days of planet earth; it is its own genre,

---

33 See the extensive discussion in Moltmann, *The Coming of God*, pp. 235–49.

34 *Time*, vol. 179, no. 15, 2012, pp. 40–6.

35 *Time*, p. 42.

more poetry than prose.[36] The notion of 'paradise', conflated as by Dante with 'heaven', does seem a more promising prospect with its Persian images of hanging gardens and cooling streams in the midst of arid deserts. But however we imagine 'heavenly bliss', it is as difficult to expunge the word from our vocabulary as it is 'hell' or 'soul'. The question is whether the metaphor has any transcendental significance, and if so, what. Is heaven a place to which we go beyond the clouds when we die analogous to where computer data is stored? If not, what does it signify?

The word 'heaven' can be traced to *ouranos*, the name given in Greek mythology to the god Uranus and to the furthest planet in the solar system. Biblical cosmology, like all ancient views of the universe, conceived of heaven as the realm above the earth, so that one spoke about ascending into or descending from heaven. Our knowledge of the cosmos today may be very different from that of ancient and biblical times, and our horizons of the universe may be continually expanding, but there are constants in our daily discourse. To speak of heaven or the heavens remains a way of describing the cosmos of which our planet is a tiny part. Christians still speak metaphorically about Jesus as having come down from heaven, descended into the realm of the dead (*Sheol or Hades*), and ascended into heaven. It is a short step from that understanding of heaven as above us, to thinking of it as a synonym for the divine. In fact, in the Old Testament, heaven (*Shaddai*) becomes an alternative reference for God.

The notion of heaven has, from ancient times, been used as a symbol to sanction the status quo. The connection of Uranus and 'the heavens' is a reminder that the 'natural' order of things above and the political–moral order on earth below have more often than not co-existed within one frame of meaning. The magnificent European Baroque churches, which embody the image of heaven with God on a throne and descending orders of angels, are a potent illustration of the way in which the monarchies and aristocracies of Europe were regarded and given legitimacy. Likewise

---

36 The poetry of the Apocalypse is captured well in Kathleen Norris, *The Cloister Walk*, New York, NY: Riverhead Books, 1997, pp. 210–20.

the promise of rewards in heaven has been used as a tool for sub-
jugating oppressed and poor people by the rich and powerful, as
it has also functioned to send soldiers into battle or encourage
martyrdom through acts of terror. Marx recognized this when
he insisted that the criticism of heaven, that is, of the illusions of
religion, is the first step in the criticism of the earth and its injus-
tices, and therefore in the struggle to overcome oppression.[37] The
complex genealogy and abuse of heaven should make us wary in
using the metaphor without some circumspection.

But we do not need Marx to remind us of this. In Jesus' own
teaching, in continuity with prophetic insights from the Old Testament, heaven takes on a different counter-cultural sense to that of
legitimating oppressive hierarchies or unjust social orders. When
Jesus, according to Matthew's gospel, speaks about the 'kingdom
of heaven', he is substituting 'heaven' for 'God' both to avoid
uttering the sacred Name, or using it to sanction misguided messianic ambitions. But he is certainly not speaking about some heavenly kingdom remote from this world, separate from the earth or
from human responsibility. When John's Gospel quotes Jesus in
his defence before Pilate as saying that his 'kingdom is not *of* this
world' (AV) the Aramaic Jesus spoke actually means 'my kingdom is not *from* this world'. (John 18.36). In other words, God's
authority and power is exercised in this world but it does not
derive from us (we have not voted God into power), nor is it the
same kind of sovereignty that we associate with lords and mon-
archs. The misreading of Jesus' words as recorded in John 18.36
lies behind the English philosopher John Locke's argument in his
Treatise on Toleration (late seventeenth century), a key Enlightenment document in the spirit of Descartes. True Christianity,
Locke insisted, is 'otherworldly', having to do with the salvation
of the soul and acquiring eternal life in heaven.[38] Locke's position
is still maintained by many Christians and secularists, though for

---

37 Karl Marx, 'Toward the Critique of Hegel's Philosophy of Right', in
Marx & Engels: Basic Writings on Politics and Philosophy, ed. Lewis S. Feuer,
New York, NY: Doubleday, 1959, p. 263.
38 John Locke, *A Letter Concerning Toleration*, Amherst: Prometheus
Books, 1990, p. 25.

opposite reasons. But this is a far cry from what Jesus meant when he spoke about the kingdom of heaven.

Consider the story told in Matthew's Gospel in which Jesus sends out his disciples to proclaim the good news that the 'kingdom of heaven has come near' (10.7). He then describes the significance of heaven in terms of the transformation of the earthly condition of those who are experiencing the sharp end of life. The mystery of the kingdom is revealed, he tells us, when the sick are cured, the dead raised, the lepers cleansed, and the demon-possessed made whole. The kingdom of heaven, Jesus says elsewhere, belongs to the 'poor' (Luke 6.20) and those who are persecuted in the struggle for God's justice (Matt. 5.10). In his ministry, the revelation of the mystery of heaven keeps on breaking into daily experience with life-renewing and hope-restoring power. Heaven embraces us like the father who runs to meet his long lost child and take him home so that the celebration of restored life can begin.

Heaven in the Bible, Wright remarks, 'is regularly not a future destiny, but the other, hidden dimension of our ordinary life, God's dimension, if you like'.[39] Heaven makes a difference to life, so Christopher Morse tells us, because it has to do with 'nothing less than what are proclaimed to be the current conditions under which our life is really being lived'.[40]

In other words, 'heaven' is not a place you go to when you die if you have faith or are good; it is the realm of God's eternal and just reign redemptively breaking into our time and space. The 'kingdom of heaven' is not a distant star or planet beyond the clouds, but the transforming presence of God at work in our midst. God's reign on earth as in heaven is both near at hand and coming. It is present as love and justice; it is anticipated when the transformation of life will be complete in all its fullness in the 'new earth and new heaven'.

In his conversation with Nicodemus, Jesus tells the enquiring Pharisee that 'no one can see the kingdom of God without being

---

39 N. T. Wright, *Surprised by Hope*, London: SPCK, 2011, p. 26.

40 Christopher Morse, *The Difference Heaven Makes: Rehearing the Gospel as Good News*, London: T&T Clark, 2010, p. 24.

born from above' (John 3.3). Jesus, according to John, is not talking about a place to which Nicodemus might or might not go
when he dies, but rather that unless he is 'born again' or 'born
from above' (both translations are possible) he can neither discern
nor become part of God's reign here and now. Nicodemus had
to become childlike in his perception; his eyes had to be freshly
opened by the Spirit in order to participate.[41] This understanding
of the 'kingdom of heaven' is reinforced later in the same passage
when John tells us that God's love for the world is so great that
he gave us his only Son in order that we might have 'eternal life'
through trusting him (John 3.16). 'Eternal life' (*zōēn aiōn*) is a
favourite phrase in John's Gospel.[42] But it does not refer primarily
to life as we know it as never ending; it refers to a new quality of
life, life in a new dimension – the life of God that we can experience already now, the life of the new age (aeon) inaugurated in
the death and resurrection of Jesus. Eternal life, John's Gospel
tells us in recording Jesus' high priestly prayer, is to know and
share God's love as revealed in his Son (17.3, 26). 'We know that
we have passed from death to life because we love one another.'
(1 John 3.14).

The Swedish movie *As it is in heaven* tells the story of Daniel,
a brilliant musical conductor who, burnt out by overwork and
ill-health, seeks refuge in his isolated childhood village despite its
memories of abuse.[43] Seeking anonymity, he succumbs to local
persuasion and becomes the director of the parish choir, whose
combined talent leaves everything to be desired. But under Daniel's
leadership the choir becomes an alternative community of acceptance and grace in a village plagued by dark secrets. Daniel's
attractive presence brings the shoddy aspects of village life into
the light. In the process, he becomes the victim of the priest's
guilt-ridden envy and of the violence of a wife-beating motor
mechanic who was, it transpires, his boyhood bully. Dismissed

---

41 See Mark 10.15.

42 See Raymond Brown, *The Gospel According to John I–XII*, Garden City,
NY: Doubleday, 1966, pp. 505–8.

43 Directed by Kay Pollak and first screened in 2007.

as choir leader by the priest, Daniel is plunged into despair, only to be redeemed by the love of a woman of ill repute among the self-righteous and sustained by the continuing support of the choir. Against his wishes, this unlikely choir enters a prestigious international choir festival in Vienna. Just before it is about to perform before a packed auditorium for the final judging, Daniel suddenly dies of a heart attack all alone in the bathroom below the auditorium. Leaderless, and to the amazement of the best choirs and judges in Europe, the choir's wordless harmony transforms the event into a festival of glorious sound which embraces all. Below in the bathroom, Daniel hears the distant sound of his own creation, as he dies alone, sad but at peace. The movie substantiates Baillie's comment that

> the only knowledge we can have of eternal life is that it comes to us through our present foretasting of its joys. All that we can know of the other life *there* is what we know of it *here*. For even here there is *another* life that may be lived, a life wholly other than that which commonly bears the name and yet one which may be lived out in this very place where I now am . . . this other life is the life everlasting.[44]

In love with the earth

Volmoed is situated in the Hemel en Aarde Valley. Moravian missionaries from Genadendal, the first mission station planted in southern Africa in the eighteenth century and a day's journey by horse from Volmoed, named the valley, because its beauty suggested that here heaven and earth are connected. Just as there is a difference between body and soul, so there is a difference between heaven and earth, but there is no dualism in either case, as though the earth was in some sense evil and heaven alone good. Heaven and earth may be distinct realities but they are intertwined; the one invisible the other visible, the one eternal the other time-bound,

---

44 Baillie, *And the Life Everlasting*, p. 251.

co-existing and interpenetrating like body and soul. To fix our eyes on heaven, then, does not mean taking them off earth, but seeing earth differently and living accordingly. To 'lay up treasure in heaven' as Jesus advises us to do is about how we live our lives on earth. So, Bonhoeffer tells us in his prison letters, in order to believe in the resurrection, we first have to learn to love life and the earth.[45]

Being in love with the earth had long been Bonhoeffer's passion. In a lecture he gave in Barcelona in 1929, he said:

> Those who would abandon the earth, who would flee the crisis of the present, will lose all the power still sustaining them by means of eternal, mysterious powers. The earth remains our mother just as God remains our father, and only those who remain true to the mother are placed by her into her father's arms.

Bonhoeffer concluded his lecture by saying that only those who engage the world in its struggles 'yearn beyond this, and have but one wish: may our world pass away and your kingdom come'.[46] Years later in prison, shortly before Christmas in 1943, when he was feeling intensely his separation from his fiancée, Bonhoeffer tells his friend Bethge that 'we are so to love God in our *life* and in the good things God gives us and to lay hold of such trust in God that, when the time comes and is here – but truly only then! – we also go to God with love, trust, and joy'. He then adds: 'But – to say it clearly – that a person in the arms of his wife should long for the hereafter is, to put it mildly, tasteless and in any case is not God's will.'[47] God wants us to enjoy earthly happiness; to think otherwise is pious arrogance. But this does not mean that we should not be aware that earthly things are temporal. We die daily even while we live and enjoy life.

---

45 Bonhoeffer, *Letters and Papers*, p. 213.

46 Dietrich Bonhoeffer, *Barcelona, Berlin, America 1928–1931*, Dietrich Bonhoeffer Works, edited by Clifford J. Green, vol. 10, Minneapolis: Fortress Press, 2008, p. 378. In this last sentence, Bonhoeffer is loosely quoting from the second-century Christian document, the *Didache* 10.6.

47 Bonhoeffer, *Letters and Papers*, p. 228.

So, Bonhoeffer says, we should also 'accustom our hearts to eternity, for the time will come when we will honestly say "I wish that I were home . . ."'[48] Bonhoeffer returns to this theme in writing to Bethge a few months later, but with fresh insight on the relationship between earthly love and love of God:

> there is a danger, in any passionate erotic love, that through it you may lose what I'd like to call the polyphony of life. What I mean is that God, the Eternal, wants to be loved with our whole heart, not to the detriment of earthly love or to diminish it, but as a sort of *cantus firmus* to which the other voices of life resound in counterpoint. One of these contrapuntal themes, which keep their *full independence* but are still related to the *cantus firmus*, is earthly love.[49]

In this connection, Bonhoeffer reminds Bethge about the biblical Song of Songs: 'a hotter, more sensual and glowing love . . .' is difficult to imagine! This contradicts 'all those who think being Christian is about tempering one's passions (where is there any such tempering in the Old Testament?). Where the *cantus firmus* is clear and distinct, a counterpoint can develop as mightily as it wants'.[50]

On reading the Old Testament in prison, Bonhoeffer was struck by the fact that its faith was not understood in terms like those of the redemption myths of surrounding cultures, but as 'redemption *within history*, that is, *this side* of the bounds of death, whereas everywhere else the aim of all the other myths of redemption is precisely to overcome death's boundary'.[51] So, too, he insists, Christianity should not focus like the pagan redemptive myths on life beyond death, on redemption from sorrow, hardship, anxiety and longing for a better life somewhere else, because 'the Christian hope of resurrection refers people to their life on earth in a wholly new way . . .'

---

48 Bonhoeffer, *Letters and Papers*, p. 228. Quoting a fifteenth-century German hymn.
49 Bonhoeffer, *Letters and Papers*, p. 394. Emphasis in the original.
50 Bonhoeffer, *Letters and Papers*, p. 394.
51 Bonhoeffer, *Letters and Papers*, p. 447.

Unlike believers in the redemption myths, Christians do not have an ultimate escape route out of their earthly tasks and difficulties into eternity. Like Christ . . . they have to drink the cup of earthly life to the last drop, and only when they do this is the Crucified and Risen One with them, and they are crucified and resurrected with Christ . . . Redemption myths arise from the human experience of boundaries. But Christ takes hold of human beings in the midst of their lives.[52]

We are not on earth in order to get to some distant heaven some day. We are on earth in order to live life to the full as God's gift. To believe in eternal life is not something ethereal; it is an affirmation of the mystery of our humanity. We are more than just dust, and we dare not regard or treat others as if they were only dust. Or, to put it the other way round as Küng does:

Precisely because we affirm life here, we do not permit ourselves to be deprived of hope of an eternal life; in fact, we defend ourselves against the powers of death, where the negativities in this life threaten to gain the upper hand: resignation, despair, cynicism.[53]

Such negativities undermine our ability to act responsibly in the world, and to work for the good of future generations. That is why Moltmann's seminal *Theology of Hope*[54] inspired some of us in South Africa, as it did many in other parts of the world. Christian hope is our humanity protesting against the dehumanizing powers of death. At the time I read *Theology of Hope*, in the late 1960s, I was on the staff of the South African Council of Churches, which, in close co-operation with the Christian Institute, was spearheading the church struggle against apartheid.[55]

---

52 Bonhoeffer, *Letters and Papers*, pp. 447–8.

53 See Hans Küng, *Eternal Life: Life After Death as a Medical, Philosophical, and Theological Problem*, Garden City, NY: Image, Doubleday, 1985, p. 197.

54 Jürgen Moltmann, *Theology of Hope*, London: SCM, 1967.

55 John W. de Gruchy with Steve de Gruchy, *The Church Struggle in South Africa: 25th Anniversary Edition*, London: SCM, 2004, pp. 101–44.

The situation was becoming more ominous by the day, and the churches were divided, both internally and in relation to each other. The lines of division were not just those of delineated by race, political association, or denomination, but also by a different understanding of the gospel of salvation. The problem was eschatology. Was the gospel solely about personal salvation from sin to secure a place in a heaven beyond this world; or was the gospel about struggling against the oppression and injustice of apartheid so that God's will as it is in heaven should become a reality on earth, even if still not fully realized in the politics of our time and space?

Moltmann helped us to see that those 'who hope in Christ can no longer put up with reality as it is, but begin to suffer under it, to contradict it'.[56] Hope is true realism, he declared, because it 'takes seriously the possibilities with which all reality is fraught'.[57] Hope has to do with affirming our humanity and discerning new possibilities for the future within the realities of life here and now. 'This hope', Moltmann added, 'makes the Church a constant disturbance in human society . . .'[58] From this perspective, Paul's words that we are 'saved by hope' took on a radically fresh meaning without which we would have collapsed into self-defeating despair. There was a fundamental connection, continuity if you like, between our penultimate hopes now, and our ultimate hope in God's new creation, even if the two could not be conflated.[59] When all looked decidedly bleak, we clung to the hope we discerned in the gospel. This was later expressed in the celebrated Kairos Document published in 1986 during the horrendous states of emergency that claimed so many lives, especially of young people.

As the crisis deepens day by day, what both the oppressor and the oppressed can legitimately demand of the Churches is a message of hope. Most of the oppressed people in South Africa

56 Moltmann, *Theology of Hope*, p. 21.
57 Moltmann, *Theology of Hope*, p. 25.
58 Moltmann, *Theology of Hope*, p. 22.
59 See Dietrich Bonhoeffer, *Ethics*, Dietrich Bonhoeffer Works, vol. 6, Minneapolis: Fortress, 2005, pp. 146–70.

today and especially the youth do have hope. They are acting courageously and fearlessly because they have a sure hope that liberation will come.[60]

Eschatology, instead of being focused on life after death and the salvation of the soul, had become for us as it is in the Bible, a message of hope in God's faithful redemptive action in history. It was not sociological or political analysis that gave us hope, but the conviction that God's promise of liberation, justice and peace could become a penultimate reality now in anticipation of its ultimate fulfilment, when all things would be brought to completion. The faithful promise of God's justice, God's kingdom on 'earth as in heaven', was the foundation of our hope, not evolutionary optimism.

And it remains so today, as South Africa goes through yet another period of political uncertainty marked by corruption and the failure to deliver on what has been promised. Hence the emergence of a new Kairos initiative among concerned Christians, a new 'hoping against hope' in the future of the country.[61] 'Christian hope', writes South African theologian Ernst Conradie 'is a protest statement, a form of resistance and defiance, instigated by an unacceptable present'.[62] Hope engages what is negative in society and human life in order to negate it, and it participates in those actions and attitudes that anticipate a transformed world. But it is not a falsely utopian ideology that is imperialist in character; it is an antidote to the despair that leads to resignation and the inability to seek the common good.

In his last years Steve was deeply involved in relating Christian hope and environmental issues.[63] One of his colleagues in

---

60 *The Kairos Document*, Johannesburg: Institute for Contextual Theology, 1986, p. 26.

61 *Kairos South Africa* a document addressed to the governing ANC, December 2012.

62 Ernst Conradie, 'In Search of a vision of hope for this new century', *Journal of Religion and Society* 1 (1991), p. 1.

63 I acknowledge here the influence on Steve of Larry Rasmussen, one of his teachers at Union Theological Seminary, New York, during 1987–8.

doing so was Conradie, whose work on theology and ecology has contributed significantly to Christian responses to the challenges facing us in South Africa today. In an essay on 'Resurrection, Finitude, and Ecology', Conradie helpfully brings together creation and eschatology, the struggle for the environment and the hope we have in God's promise of a new creation.[64] The hope that is within us humans is profoundly related to the hope of creation as a whole.[65] The biblical truth is that creation matters to the Creator, not just human beings, and our redemption is inseparable from that of nature and the cosmos.[66] The biblical vision of the end is not the disappearance of the earth, which we are told could well happen, but a 'new earth' which is in some sense in continuity with the earth as we now know it, though also radically new. So what is of ultimate importance for life now 'provides our best insights into what lasts, and so what comes last'.[67] In sum, what happens to you or me, or anyone else after death, is not the central, framing question of the Bible.[68] There are, Bonhoeffer says, 'more important things than this question'.

What matters is not the beyond, but this world, how it is created and preserved, is given laws, reconciled and renewed. What is beyond this world is meant, in the gospel, to be there *for* this world – not in the anthropocentric sense of liberal, mystical, pietistic, ethical theology, but in the biblical sense of

---

Rasmussen's most recent book, *Earth-Honoring Faith: Religious Ethics in a New Key*, New York: Oxford University Press, 2012, arrived too late for my consideration, but it gives a superb account of the issues.

64 Ernst Conradie, 'Resurrection, Finitude, and Ecology', in *Resurrection*, edited by Russell et al., pp. 277–96.

65 See Romans 8.18–25.

66 John Polkinghorne, 'Eschatological Credibility: Emergent and Teological Processes', in *Resurrection*, edited by Russell et al., pp. 48–9.

67 Murphy, 'The Resurrection Body and Personal Identity: Possibilities and Limits of Eschatological Knowledge', in *Resurrection* edited by Russell et al., p. 206.

68 See Wright, *Surprised by Hope*, p. 197.

the creation and the incarnation, crucifixion and resurrection of Jesus Christ.[69]

The Easter mystery story

When Paul arrived in Athens on his second missionary journey, he went to the market-place, where he debated with some Epicurean and Stoic philosophers about Jesus.[70] This led to a disturbance among the assembled crowd, so Paul was taken up to the Areopagus to defend himself before the city elders. The Areopagus is a large rocky outcrop lying beneath the Acropolis where, in ancient times, the High Court of Appeal traditionally met and people gathered to discuss the issues of the day and listen to new ideas. Paul told his hearers that on his way to the Areopagus he had noticed various altars dedicated to the gods worshipped by the Athenians, among them one dedicated to 'an unknown God'. This was the God of all the nations, he declared, who had had created the heavens and the earth, could not be confined to temples or shrines, but was also 'not far from each of us' for in him 'we live, move and have our being'. Paul's audience would have recognized that he was quoting their own philosophers. He also quoted one of their poets: 'For we too are his offspring', thereby affirming that human beings are related to God. All seemed to be going well until Paul proclaimed that the 'unknown God' about whom he was speaking had raised Jesus from the dead and appointed him to be the judge of all people. In response, some scoffed; others said they would discuss it with him again, while a handful became believers.

Faith in the risen Christ was, from the beginning, the cornerstone of Christian faith. Everything else in the New Testament is predicated on the belief that the Jesus who was crucified by human hands, who 'died and was buried', *God* raised from the dead.[71] This was no reanimation or resuscitation of the pre-Easter Jesus as is often assumed even by Christians. Jesus did not rise

---

69 Bonhoeffer, *Letters and Papers*, p. 373.
70 See Acts 17.16–33.
71 See Acts 2.24; 3.15; 4.10.

from the dead as though there was some superhuman power in him enabling him to do so, as when Clarke Kent transmutes into Superman. But the question remains: did the resurrection of Jesus actually occur in our historical time and space, even if it was an event that transcended both? Or is the narrative of Easter Day simply another version of the pagan myth of the dying and rising son of God or the Superman myth of more recent times? Everything rests on how we answer these questions.

There are two considerations we have to take into account in seeking an answer. The first has to do with the philosophical assumptions with which we approach the subject. If our understanding of the world is such that the resurrection is, in principle, impossible, then nothing further can or need be said. Dead humans do not rise from the dead. But if we do believe in the ultimate mystery we call God, and if we acknowledge that the world is not a closed Newtonian system which, in principle, excludes the possibility of something happening that has not previously occurred, such as the improbable evolution of life in the first place, then the resurrection as an event becomes feasible. It is at least a possibility even if not necessarily a probability. As such it cannot be explained as a natural extension of the evolutionary process, but only as the first act in the beginning of a new creation. This still does not, nor can it prove the resurrection of Jesus as an *historical* event, something that can neither be proved nor falsified in that way. It remains an article of faith. But is there good reason to believe that it happened in our time and space or, in C. S. Lewis' terms, did the myth become fact as Christian faith has traditionally claimed?

The second consideration has to do, then, with the historical reliability of the resurrection narratives in the New Testament and therefore the integrity of those who claimed to witness the risen Christ, as well as the reliability of their reports in the gospels. The reader will know, or at least can assume, that these issues have been explored at great length over the centuries, not least since the Enlightenment and the rise of modern science. Apart from those who deny the resurrection on the basis of historical criticism, there are two main positions taken by biblical scholars and theologians. The first is a more subjective approach which insists that belief in the resurrection of Jesus as described in the gospel arose out of the experience of the first disciples. So, for example, the Catholic theologian Edward Schillebeeckx argues that the witness of the disciples to the risen Christ emerged as a result of their conversion to him as Lord after their failure to be faithful to him at the time of his death, rather than to their discovery of an empty tomb.[72] In a slightly different way, Borg argues that it is not possible to know whether Jesus was literally raised from the dead through the use of historical criticism, and it does not matter whether the tomb was empty; what was fundamental in the life of the first Christians and of all Christians since then, was the experience of the risen Christ in the Spirit.

The second approach, taken for example by Pannenberg[73] and Wright,[74] argues that the historical method does provide us with enough evidence – even if not conclusive proof – to believe that the bodily resurrection of Jesus did take place as an historical event. The tomb was empty. In his debate with Wright in their jointly authored book *The Meaning of Jesus*, Borg pinpoints the basic issue between them as follows. Wright's belief in the resurrection of Jesus, Borg says, is based on the fact of the empty tomb and the appearances of Jesus to the first witnesses. This generated the claim that Jesus had been raised from the dead, was alive and is Lord. By way of contrast, Borg claims that the 'experiences of the risen Christ as a continuing presence generated the claim that "Jesus lives and is Lord" and that the statement "God raised Jesus from the dead" and the story of the empty tomb may well have been generated by those experiences'.[75] In other words, it was based on subjective experience rather than objective fact.

Wright's counter argument, developed in far greater detail in *The Resurrection of the Son of God*, is that unless the gospel narratives

72 Edward Schillebeeckx, *Jesus: an Experiment in Christology*, London: Collins, 1979, pp. 380–5.

73 Wolfhart Pannenberg, *Systematic Theology*, Grand Rapids: Eerdmans, 1994, pp. 343–63.

74 Wright, *The Resurrection of the Son of God*, pp. 685–718.

75 J. Marcus Borg & N. T. Wright, *The Meaning of Jesus: Two Visions*, San Francisco: HarperCollins, 2000, p. 137.

are part of a carefully constructed conspiracy to delude, something that is contrary to all the textual and historical evidence, the disciples did witness something unique and earth-shattering on Easter day. Whatever the discrepancies in the various gospel narratives regarding the details of the resurrection, they only serve to reinforce the historical veracity and the authenticity of the witness that lies behind them. After exhaustive consideration, Wright concludes that the 'proposal that Jesus was bodily raised from the dead possesses unrivalled power to explain the historical data at the heart of early Christianity'.[76] The tomb was empty and Jesus encountered them in such a way that they came to recognize him even though he was no longer confined to their time and space. He was in a different dimension.

It is true that Paul does not refer to the empty tomb, though he does accept the credibility of the witnesses of the resurrection. However, the claim that the tomb was empty was clearly important for the four gospel writers otherwise they would not have all insisted that it was. As James Dunn points out, 'it is questionable whether *without an empty tomb* either the disciples would have interpreted their 'resurrection appearance' experience in terms of resurrection', or that many would have believed that God had raised Jesus prior to the general resurrection of the dead. Moreover, says, Dunn, 'we find absolutely no trace of any interest in the place of Jesus' burial within earliest Christianity – a surprising fact if Jesus' tomb remained undisturbed or if his body been removed and buried elsewhere, but not if the tomb was found to be empty'.[77] Just as Jesus had told the Sadducees that God 'is the God of the living not the dead', so the messenger in Luke's account asks the women at the tomb: 'Why do you look for the living among the dead? He is not here, but has risen.'[78]

The question that emerges from this all-too-brief account is this: did the first disciples witness something unique, earth-shattering and life changing which they then shared with others in initial dumbfounded amazement? Or did they experience the Spirit of

---

76 Wright, *The Resurrection of the Son of God*, p. 718.
77 Dunn, *Jesus and the Spirit*, p. 120.
78 Luke 24.5.

Jesus among them soon after his death in a way that convinced them that he was alive and present among them, and that they were both forgiven and empowered to proclaim the good news to others and to give an account of their hope? Whether Wright is correct in asserting that the second alternative, along with other revisionist proposals, lacks *all* explanatory power, as he argues in *Surprised by Hope*, is a moot point.[79] But for me, his position has *greater* explanatory power, and his exhaustive research into the records shows that the historical tradition stands up well to critical scrutiny.

Like all historical events *precisely* what happened on Easter day is impossible to tell through archival recollection, but the testimony of its witnesses can be accepted on good grounds even though it has been shaped by the poetic and theological imagination of the four New Testament evangelists. And these, especially the accounts of Jesus' appearance to Mary Magdalene and the other women at the tomb, to the two travellers on the road to Emmaus, and to doubting Thomas in the 'upper room', strongly assert the continuity between the historical Jesus as the crucified one, and the risen Christ. In other words, their assertion that 'God raised Jesus from the dead', is, as C. K. Barrett says, 'not unrelated to history, for the affirmation began to be made at a particular point in time, which can be dated by historical means, and it was motivated by occurrences which can be described in historical terms'.[80] The Easter mystery does not occur in a realm beyond the clouds, but like all good mystery stories it is located in the real world of politics and violence, economics and greed, religious practices and idolatry, and of women taking care of the dead and fishermen casting their nets.

Let me stress again that historical evidence and analysis cannot prove the resurrection of Jesus; but it gives it plausibility, and therefore makes it reasonable to believe. If we could prove the resurrection beyond any shadow of doubt, there would be no need

---

79 Wright, *Surprised by Hope*, p. 71.
80 C. K. Barrett, *The First Epistle to the Corinthians*, London: Adam and Charles Black, 1976, p. 341.

to *believe* in the risen Christ; it would then be a historical fact awaiting interpretation but not proof. Even if there were witnesses of the empty tomb, there were no witnesses of what actually happened in the tomb between Good Friday and Easter, for the tomb was securely sealed. We have no idea at all what transpired, if something dramatic did. There were no cameras to record the event and the gospels are reverently silent. As Wink says: 'We can only speculate and our speculations will seem reductionist unless we concede from the outset that the mystery that now confronts us is beyond solution'.[81] For that reason, I am attracted to comments made by E. P. Sanders:

> Much about the historical Jesus will remain a mystery. Nothing is more mysterious than the stories of his resurrection, which attempt to portray an experience that the authors could not themselves comprehend . . . we know that after his death his followers experienced what they described as the "resurrection": the appearance of a living but transformed person who actually died. They believed this, they lived it, and they died for it. In the process they created a movement, a movement that in many ways went far beyond Jesus' message.[82]

Easter then, is a mystery story. We cannot fully grasp what happened until the last page is written, and we may well be surprised by the ending. But that something dramatic did happen on Easter Day that transformed the lives of people and awakened hope for a better world then as it continues to do so now, is to my mind and that of many others, beyond doubt. In other words, the resurrection ushers in a new era in world history. This is true even if you do not believe in it, simply because the emergence of Christianity based on this conviction changed the course of history. But its significance, at least from the perspective of faith, goes beyond what obviously happened in history from then on. For Christians,

---

81 Walter Wink, *The Human Being: Jesus* and the *Enigma of the Son of the Man*, Minneapolis: Fortress, 2002, p. 141.
82 E. P. Sanders, *The Historical Figure of Jesus*, London: Penguin, 1993, p. 280.

it actually symbolizes the beginning of the end of history as we know it; the beginning of hope for a new creation.[83]

In his book *The Alternative Future*, Roger Garaudy, a French Marxist converted to Christianity in dialogue with Moltmann and others during the 1960s, makes the connection between faith in the risen Christ and commitment to the social transformation of the world. The resurrection, he writes 'is not a cellular, physiological phenomenon, a return to mortal life through natural reanimation', but 'a creative act'; it is 'an affirmation of the impossible through which history opens the future to all possibilities'.[84] This is what Christian hope is really about. Not the modernist myth of inevitable progress, nor the revolutionary dream that is pursued on the basis that the end justifies the means, but the hoping against hope that inspires and generates concrete acts of justice and compassion in the faith that God will create a 'new heaven and earth'.[85] It is only 'through Christ's resurrection that a new and cleansing wind can blow through our present world', Bonhoeffer wrote in prison. 'If a few people really believed this and were guided by it in their earthly actions, a great deal would change. To live in the light of the resurrection – that is what Easter means'.[86] But how does this relate to the Jewish, Muslim and specifically Christian belief in the general resurrection of the dead? In what sense is this, too, an integral part of the meaning of the Easter mystery?

Resurrection of the body

There has long been a debate about whether or not Paul distorted the teaching of Jesus, and therefore whether or not he must be held responsible for the direction in which Christianity developed

---

83 Moltmann, *The Crucified God*, p. 169.

84 Roger Garaudy, *The Alternative Future: A Vision of Christian Marxism*, London: Penguin, 1976, pp. 96–7.

85 See Trevor Hart Bauckham, *Hope Against Hope: Christian Eschatology at the Turn of the Millennium*, Grand Rapids: Eerdmans, 1999.

86 Bonhoeffer, *Letters and Papers*, p. 333.

over the centuries.[87] How much Paul knew about the historical Jesus is debatable; his knowledge of Jesus was shaped by his experience of the risen Christ.[88] This does not mean that the 'Jesus of history' was unimportant for Paul; after all the suffering and death of Jesus was fundamental to his understanding of who Jesus was, and he does on occasion refer to Jesus' teaching. He also took seriously the historical witnesses of the resurrection to whom he refers in some detail. But the Jesus who encountered Paul on the road to Damascus was the risen Lord who appeared to him through the Spirit as blinding light. This opened his eyes to the messianic significance of Jesus whose followers he was hell-bent on destroying. After a period of reflection, the focal point of his theological endeavour was to understand and communicate the meaning of the mystery revealed in the risen Christ for the whole world and the cosmos.

Paul's subsequent treatment of the resurrection, especially in his first letter to the Corinthians (Chapter 15), has profoundly shaped Christian belief. For that reason alone it requires our attention. But there are two additional reasons that retain significance for us. The first is that Paul thought through the significance of the resurrection for Christian faith *in the light of the delayed return of Christ*, which remains the case today, for God's reign of justice and peace still has not come as promised. The second is that Paul was the first to consider the meaning of the resurrection for Christian faith beyond the boundaries Judaism. It was one thing to believe in the resurrection from within a tradition that assumed its reality; it was quite different to do so within the Hellenistic world, which in some respects mirrors our own.

Like Jesus, Paul's views on the resurrection were derived from Judaism so in that respect there is continuity between them. But the resurrection of Jesus himself as the 'first fruits' (v. 20) of the resurrection of the dead obviously introduced something that was decisive for

---

87 See V. George Shillington, *Jesus and Paul Before Christianity: Their World and Work in Retrospect*, Eugene, OR: Cascade Books, 2011, pp. 13–19.

88 Pannenberg, *Systematic Theology*, 349–52.

understanding its present and future significance. Paul's primary task was to interpret what this meant to Hellenistic converts for whom the whole notion was foreign and unthinkable. This was notably true in Corinth where the Christian congregation, to which Paul wrote, was more in tune with the doctrine of the immortality of the soul, and had an antipathy to the body and the material world.

The questions which the Corinthians put to Paul were not, however, primarily intellectual concerns; they were pastoral in character. People, then as now, wanted to know what happened to their loved ones when they died. The primary issue was not whether there was life after death but how this related to the resurrection of Christ, as well as to what was for them an alien Jewish idea, that there would be a general resurrection of the dead when Christ returned to judge the earth and establish his reign in all its fullness.[89] This was not only alien to their thinking, but was deemed unnecessary as they were already risen 'in Christ' through the Spirit, whose activity was clearly in evidence in their charismatic worship.[90] In addition, the promised Second Coming which they had been told to expect had already been too-long delayed. This meant that the general resurrection of the dead and the final judgment had been put on hold. So the question was not simply how much longer they had to wait for Jesus' return and the beginning of God's reign on earth, but what was the fate of those who had already died, and of those who were still to die before the Second Coming occurred?[91] Do they immediately go to heaven, or are they 'asleep' somewhere waiting for the general resurrection of the dead sometime in the future?

Personally, I find discussions that take place around such questions generally unhelpful and mostly unnecessary, even if the need for answers is understandable and, when provided, help some people. Reverent silence is generally more appropriate than

---

89 On this, see inter alia, C. K. Barrett, *The First Epistle to the Corinthians*, pp. 347–8.

90 See Lampe, 'Paul's Concept of a Spiritual Body', in *Resurrection*, p. 104.

91 See the J. J. F. Durand, 'Theology and Resurrection – Metaphors and Paradigms', *Journal of Theology for Southern Africa* 82 (1993), pp. 14–20.

speculation. In any case, it is difficult for us to put ourselves in that first century context, when recent Christian converts were still hammering out their beliefs at the intersection of diverse cultures. And although some of the key philosophical and religious issues may remain the same, our view of the world, not least of time and space, has been radically changed since the rise of modern science. Yet, is it not the case that sceptics of every age do not believe in life after death and that many Christians, like the Corinthians, are more likely to believe in an immortal soul, however understood, than the 'bodily' resurrection of the dead? As Ted Jennings puts it, contemporary Christianity is imbued with 'modernity's penchant for an anti-body, anti-nature gnosticism'.[92]

In addition, many Christians today, as in previous generations, are interested to know when Christ will return. There are those who actually believe that he will come soon to gather up his followers in some kind of Rapture, leaving the rest behind to sort out the mess on earth for a millennium, that is, until they return to rule the earth. The implications of such views, not least in tacitly encouraging environmental irresponsibility and even in supporting war in the Middle East as a means to hastening the Second Coming, are appalling. Yet the end of world history is no longer unthinkable for post-modern people, nor is it only fundamentalists who believe in the Second Coming, for many 'mainline' Christians declare at the Eucharist that this is one of the mysteries of faith. So Paul, out of pastoral concern, faces the issues raised in Corinth head on for us as for them.

Now if Christ is proclaimed as raised from the dead, how can some of you say that there is no resurrection of the dead? If there is no resurrection of the dead, then Christ has not been raised; and if Christ has not been raised, then our proclamation has been in vain and your faith has been in vain.[93]

92 Ted W. Jennings Jr, 'Theological Anthropology and the Human Genome Project', in *Adam, Eve, and the Genome*, p. 102.
93 1 Corinthians 15.12–14.

If Christ was not raised from the dead, then our faith is in vain, and while we may still live optimistically, we have no grounds for that living 'hope against hope' that saves us from the futility and despair of death.[94] And those who are living their lives, and often suffering because of their witness to the hope that is within them are, Paul goes on to say, to be pitied above all others, because it is all such a waste of time and energy to live and die for something that is patently false. For the issue at stake is not simply the resurrection of Jesus as a solitary individual or our own personal immortality, but whether or not a new age has been ushered in that gives us hope, not only for life after death, but for the world in which we live.[95] If Christ was not raised, Paul is saying, there is no reason for hope, only despair, even if we face that nihilistic possibility nobly and stoically.

Granted that this was so, the next question raised by the Corinthians was when would this general resurrection of the dead happen? Paul wisely does not, nor could he, provide a date. He simply affirms the conviction that the end will come, and when it does death will finally be destroyed, the kingdoms of the world will become the kingdom of God, and God will be 'all in all'.[96] In the meantime, Paul's counsel to the Corinthians is that they should live already now as those who have been raised to the newness of life, and not fret about times and seasons.

Assuming that his readers were still with him (an assumption I am also making) Paul then turns to a third issue that confronts Gnosticism head on. 'With what kind of body are the dead raised?'[97] In response, Paul speaks of the future resurrected body as 'spiritual' in contrast to the present or 'natural body', and he uses the analogy of seed and plant to point to the contrast, and continuity between them.[98] The contrast is obvious: the natural body dies and returns to dust; the spiritual body is raised to eternal life. Let us recall here our earlier discussion of the body

---

94 See Romans 8.18–15; 1 Corinthians 15.12–18; 1 Peter 1.3.
95 See Wright, *The Resurrection of the Son of God*, pp. 331–2.
96 1 Corinthians 15.24–8.
97 1 Corinthians 15.35.
98 Thiselton, *Life after Death*.

understood as both *sarx* and *soma*. Although Paul uses *soma* virtually throughout his discussion, he does distinguish between the 'natural' and the 'Spiritual' body and then, most significantly, he introduces *sarx* into his argument when he writes about what he really means: 'This is what I mean', he says, 'what is made of flesh (*sarx*) and blood cannot share in God's kingdom, and what is mortal cannot possess immortality' (v. 50).

What is critical here in understanding Paul's 'resurrection body' is that it is inseparable from the resurrection of Jesus. Believers, he is saying, are raised to new life not separately as individuals, but 'in Christ'.[99] What is equally crucial is that this 'resurrection body' while not 'flesh and blood' has personal continuity, as was the case of Jesus' own resurrection. Just like an acorn and an oak tree have the same DNA, so the same *person* 'will live on in a different mode of existence, partaking in the life-giving Spirit of the resurrected Christ'.[100] There is a continuity of identity. Our true self is fully restored by the creative Spirit who raised Jesus from the dead. This connects with what we considered when discussing the 'soul' as the embodied self-in-relationship and eternal life as a gift of the Spirit that precedes death. By using the term 'body', Paul is stressing the continuity of the person, but the adjective 'spiritual' indicates that the person is transformed by the Spirit already before death. Here we are a building under construction, but not yet complete. Resurrection 'in Christ' through the Spirit completes our identity as persons-in-relationship. This understanding of the resurrection of the body may stretch credulity to the boundaries, but at least its promise, for me, is of something much more in tune with Steve's own life, his commitment to the earth, his relationship with others, and his own humanity motivated by hope in a world of injustice, poverty and exploitation.

Modern genetics provides certain *analogies* that are useful in thinking about the continuity of identity to which Paul is referring. Any cell, no matter how minute or insignificant in our bodies, 'contains all the information required to assemble an entire

---

99 See Robinson, *The Body*, pp. 49–55.
100 Durand, 'Theology and Resurrection', p. 18.

individual human being'.[101] Admitting that it sounds 'positively bizarre', on this basis Jennings refers to the practice in late antiquity of collecting the relics of saints and martyrs as making more sense than might at first seem likely. It also makes sense, for example, of the concern in post-apartheid South Africa of many a family's need to recover the body-parts, no matter how fragmentary, of the victims of the former regime, so that they can be properly laid to rest. Genetically-speaking, simply to recover a part is to recover the whole. By way of an analogy, we can also say, that 'the DNA of any person contains . . . the DNA history of not only humanity as a whole but of life in general'.[102]

Analogies must not be pushed to absurd lengths, but when Paul talks about the resurrection of the body in terms of the continuity of identity, we can at least see the sense of what he is saying. The argument that the resurrection of the body is an impossibility when everything has been reduced to dust, or blown up into fragments, does not logically follow, implausible as it may sound and seem to modern ears shaped by scientific reductionism. But if we believe in God as the ultimate mystery of the universe who is nonetheless creatively active in giving and sustaining new life, then we begin to see possibilities of convergence. So, John Polkinghorne, a physicist and a theologian, writes:

In natural terms, the pattern that is me, whatever form it actually takes, will be dissolved at my death, as my body decays and my relationships are reduced simply to the fading retention of memories by others. Yet it seems an entirely coherent belief that the everlastingly faithful God will hold that pattern perfectly preserved in the divine memory, and then embody it in the ultimate divine eschatological act of resurrection at the last day, as the new creation enters into the unfolding fullness of time.[103]

---

101 Jennings, 'Theological Anthropology', p. 103.
102 Jennings, 'Theological Anthropology', p. 105.
103 Polkinghorne, 'Eschatological Credibility', p. 52.

If this is so, then 'God's remembering, recognizing, and relating to me', is, as Murphy says, 'essential to my postresurrection identity'.[104] But she adds that the continuity of personal identity is only meaningful if it includes '*self-recognition, continuity of moral character,* and *personal relations,* both with others and with God'.[105] The connecting point for Paul is 'being in Christ'. In Christ, Paul insists, we have already been raised to new life.[106] And it is 'in Christ' that we are reunited with others in a way that fulfils our own identity, for we are only truly ourselves when we are finally made whole in a corporate sense, as selves-in-relationship. The resurrection body is more than the individual. That is why, to repeat, when Paul writes about being 'in Christ' he has the 'risen body of Christ' primarily in mind, the *ekklesia* or church.[107] But there is also, I believe, a universal inclusion implied: the completion of Christian hope in the restoration of all things.

Restoration of all things

Christian hope, whether expressed in terms of penultimate personal well-being or social transformation, or the ultimate restoration of all things, must be expressed in ways that are appropriate, and provide a reasoned account before the jury of the world and academy, as well as within the community of faith. The language of hope will vary as the context demands, but the message remains. In the darkest times of personal tragedy or political violence, we affirm that God's purpose for the well-being of creation will not finally be thwarted. That is the reason why those who constructed the canon of the New Testament placed the Apocalypse at the end as the revelation of God's cosmic will, weaving the suffering of the present time into the tapestry of the ultimate victory of the risen Christ. It depicts the suffering of a persecuted church bearing witness to this hope within the all-powerful Roman Empire as

---

104 Murphy, 'The Resurrection Body', p. 213.
105 Murphy, 'The Resurrection Body', p. 208.
106 See Colossians 3.1 et al.
107 John Robinson, *The Body*, London: SCM, 1957, pp. 49–83.

type of all imperial power, but locates it in the perennial cosmic struggle between good and evil, God and Satan, heaven and hell. Its terrifying images wrench us from our comfort zones and open our eyes to reality, to the way things are in a world beset by natural disaster, famine, disease and war. Evil is so pervasive that only the poetry of the seer can imagine its defeat. But that is what his Apocalypse does. In disclosing the mystery of the end, it

> Pushes us against all our boundaries and suggests that the end of our control – our ideologies, our plans, our competence, our expertise, our professionalism, our power – is the beginning of God's reign. It asks us to believe that only the good remains, at the end, and directs us toward carefully tending it here and now.[108]

That is the nature of Christian hope. It is the anticipation that good will come out of evil, and that in the end evil will be defeated. Creation is redeemed.

Irenaeus, you will recall, thought of the Fall as a necessary stage in human development. But he also believed with Paul that just as all die 'in Adam', so all shall made alive 'in Christ'.[109] This led him to say that in becoming a human being like us, Christ 'recapitulated [or summed up] in himself the long line of the human race'.[110] Bonhoeffer refers to this in his letters from prison in a passage to which I have frequently returned since the death of Steve.

> In recent weeks this line has been running through my head over and over: "Calm your hearts, dear friends; whatever plagues you, whatever fails you, I will restore it all." What does that mean, "I will restore it all"? Nothing is lost; in Christ all things are taken up, preserved, albeit in transfigured

---

108 Kathleen Norris, *The Cloister Walk*, New York, NY: Riverhead Books, 1996, p. 220.

109 Romans 5.14–21.

110 Irenaeus, Adversus Haeresis, III. xviii, in Bettenson, *Documents*, p. 42.

form, transparent, clear, liberated from the torment of self-serving demands. Christ brings all this back, indeed, as God intended, without being distorted by sin. The doctrine originating in Ephesians 1:10 of the restoration of all things, – *re-capitulatio* (Irenaeus), is a magnificent and consummately consoling thought.[111]

In more than one passage in his prison letters and notes, Bonhoeffer reflects on the rapid passing of time and the fragmentary character of life. Acutely aware of the destruction that was daily taking place in Berlin and throughout Europe, he acknowledged that his generation, unlike that of his parents, could 'no longer expect a life that unfolds fully, both professionally and personally, so that it becomes a balanced and fulfilled whole'. At the same time, he felt that 'that which is fragmentary may point to a higher fulfilment, which can no longer be achieved by human effort'. That was the only way he could think about the death of so many of his former students in the war.[112] It is also the only way I can now think as I approach the end of these explorations into the mystery of faith prompted by Steve's own death. In the end, Christian hope is the anticipation that the fragments of life, the fragments that we are as human beings, will be brought to completion as we are finally led into in the ultimate mystery that embraces us.

In the Prologue, I mentioned my sense of Steve peering over my shoulder to see how my argument would develop. He knew me well enough to know that I would try to avoid sentimental 'other-worldly' piety in responding to the questions I set out to answer, trading perhaps on my sense of grief and the sympathy of others. But how, I ask myself, would he have answered them himself? I actually don't know, but as he wrote his doctoral dissertation on the theology of Reinhold Niebuhr, it is possible that he would

111 Bonhoeffer, *Letters and Papers*, p. 230.
112 Bonhoeffer, *Letters and Papers*, p. 301.

have turned to Niebuhr as a guide.[113] In his *Nature and Destiny of Man*, Niebuhr cautions restraint in trying to be too explicit about what we can know about eternal life. But restraint, he insists, does not mean uncertainty about the validity of Christian hope. It is the recognition that the 'consummation of life and history' is not dependent on any inherent human capacity we may have, but on a 'source beyond ourselves'.[114] Christian faith acknowledges that this source is the cosmic mystery we name God disclosed to us in the life, death and resurrection of Christ as unfathomable love and infinite beauty.

113 Stephen Mark de Gruchy, *Not Liberation but Justice: An Analysis of Reinhold Niebuhr's Understanding of Human Destiny in the Light of the Doctrine of the Atonement*, University of the Western Cape, 1992.
114 Niebuhr, *Faith and History*, p. 298.

Epilogue

Dying We Live

This is the end – for me the beginning of life.
Dietrich Bonhoeffer[1]
As unknown, and yet well known;
as dying, and, behold, we live;
as chastened, and not killed, as sorrowful,
yet always rejoicing.
Paul[2]
Death is part of life.
My death is part of who and what I am.
To forget this is to live in some kind of a dream world . . .
When we embrace our uniqueness, we embrace,
among other things, our death.
For you and me today,
embracing death is part of the great adventure
of learning to love ourselves as we are:
one, undivided, and unique
Albert Nolan[3]

One of my favourite memories of Steve goes back to the time when he was Director of the Moffat Mission in Kuruman. He loved the Mission; its history, its large old stone church, the house in which David Livingstone lived while sojourning there and the tree under which Livingstone proposed to Mary Moffat. He loved the austere Kalahari landscape moderated by the flow of water through the Mission gardens from the Kuruman Eye some kilometres away and the old school room which he had turned into a

---

1 The last reported words of Dietrich Bonhoeffer a few days before his execution by the Gestapo in Flossenbürg. Eberhard Bethge, *Dietrich Bonhoeffer: A Biography*, Minneapolis: Fortress Press, 2000, p. 927.
2 2 Corinthians 6.9–10 (AV).
3 Albert Nolan, *Jesus Today: A Spirituality of Radical Freedom*, (Maryknoll, NY: Orbis Books, 2006) 155–156.

museum housing the original press on which Moffat printed the first Setswana Bible he had previously translated. All these images come back to mind as I write, but what prompted them was my recalling the day Steve led a procession of visitors to the Mission graveyard set apart in a secluded grove. Dressed in his clerical robes and singing appropriate songs, he led the group into the sacred precincts where missionaries and their families from the early nineteenth century were buried, as is also Joseph Wing, one of Steve's mentors, who had encouraged him to go to Kuruman.[4] Steve loved to talk about all those whose names were etched on the old tombstones and share their stories with those gathered around him. But the most poignant moment came when he pointed to the graves of missionary children, most of whom died in infancy, and spoke of the hardship and suffering of their parents. How grief stricken they must have been; how difficult it was for them to let go of their children in that remote part of Africa. It seems so out of kilter and unnatural for parents to bury their sons and daughters. Isobel and I heard this sentiment expressed many times following Steve's own death, not in infancy to be sure, but even as an adult at the height of his powers it all seemed so wrong. Yet, it happens all the time. The week Steve died four other young men we knew were all tragically killed, one of whom had been born the same week in the same hospital as Steve, and baptized in the same church on the same day.

Dying prematurely

Vitezslav Gardvský was 55, when he died in disgrace following the Russian suppression of the Czech uprising in 1968. He was a philosopher and an atheist, but also one of those remarkable Marxists

---

4 *Spirit Undaunted: The Life and Legacy of Joseph Wing*, ed. Steve de Gruchy and Desmond van der Water, Pietermaritzburg: Cluster, 2005, pp. 1–126. See also Steve de Gruchy, 'The Alleged Political Conservatism of Robert Moffat', in *The London Missionary Society in South Africa*, edited by John W. de Gruchy, Cape Town: David Philip, 1999, pp. 17–36.

who had engaged in dialogue with Christian theologians in Europe during that decade of disenchantment with Soviet Communism. One of his publications, translated into English as *God is not yet dead*,[5] bears testimony to the extent to which Christian faith challenged his thinking and influenced his life. I only became aware of Gardavský in the course of writing this book, when I came across an article on him written by an English clergyman, who described him as a martyr.[6] In the article are these striking words taken from *God is not yet Dead*:

> In the very moment of victory we are exposed to an even more terrible threat – that we might die earlier than we really do die, before death has become a natural necessity. The horror lies in just such a *premature* death, a death after which we go on living for many years.[7]

These words took me back to another book which deeply moved me when I first read it in 1962. Entitled *Dying we Live*, it contains the final messages written by some of those Germans, Bonhoeffer included, who resisted Hitler and paid the price, the majority of them Christian, but not all.[8] All died prematurely, as did the many others who we rightly celebrate as martyrs in the struggle for justice.

Steve did not die a martyr's death at the hand of any unjust regime. He died prematurely, though not before he had lived fully. I think this is what many of the more than a thousand people, a large number from overseas and distant parts of South Africa, recognised who attended his funeral service in the Anglican Cathedral in Pietermaritzburg on Saturday 27th February, 2010. It was

---

5   Vitezslav Gardavský, *God is not yet dead*, London: Penguin, 1973.
6   See James Bentley, 'Vitezslav Gardavský, Atheist and Martyr', *The Expository Times* 91 (1980), pp. 276–7.
7   Bentley, Gardavský, p. 277.
8   *Dying we Live*, edited by Hellmut Gollwitzer, Käthe Kuhne, and Reinhold Schneider, (London: Collins, Fontana, 1958). Foreword by Trevor Huddleston.

a very hot and humid afternoon and the service lasted several hours. I recall entering the large round building and seeing Steve's coffin in front of the altar. On top was a photograph which captured his warm and embracing personality. I went up to the photograph and kissed him, wiping away the tears from my eyes. I feared this was the end. Nothing could bring Steve back to us. All we now had were memories.

The service, conducted by two of Steve's closest friends, Paul Germond and Wilma Jacobsen, both Anglican priests with whom he had a long association, was a celebration of his life. His wife, Marian, and his daughters Thea and Kate each spoke, and David his son, played a solo on his saxophone. Isobel read a poem she had written for the occasion, and I read a letter that I wrote to Steve recalling our relationship. There were many tributes from representatives of the various sectors of Steve's life. Family friends, colleagues and students spoke about what Steve had meant to them over the years. A choir sang from his daughters' school where Steve was chair of the Board of Governors. It was a sad but joyous occasion in which children and young people were so much a part. In his homily Paul spoke of Steve's passion for life, justice and human well-being, and of its connection with his faith in Jesus Christ. Then, finally, the words of committal were pronounced: "ashes to ashes, dust to dust . . . in sure and certain hope of the resurrection to eternal life; through our Lord Jesus Christ, who died, was buried, and rose again for us."

Letting go and hanging in

Mary Oliver tells us that if we are to live in this world we must learn to "love what is mortal" and "when the time comes to let it go."[9] Mourning and grieving, two of the themes with which I began these reflections in the Prologue, are part of this learning

---

9 Mary Oliver, "In Blackwater Woods," published in Mary Oliver, *Wild Geese: selected poems*, (Tarset, Northumberland: Bloodaxe Books, 2004), 19–20.

process. But it is a hard, long and often tearful road we have to travel, all of us. The problem is that while we need to let go, the questions don't easily let go of us: at least that has been my experience and I am surely not alone in this. But there is more to letting go than simply letting go. What do we let go, and how?

> It's so hard to let go
> of what used to be
> it's so hard to accept that
> things will never be the same
> all these sudden crossings
> when life attacks and hurts
> all these dreadful bridges
> when death dims the light

We hold on to memories, and rightly so; we treasure photographs and much else that link us to Steve; and we celebrate anniversaries of which he was always so much a part and, in another way, is still a part. There is so much that we can hold on to that gives us joy albeit tinged with a great sadness. But in the end, as Steve said to a student shortly before his death, we have to learn to 'hang in there', at the same time as we have to let go 'of what used to be', and learn how to be embraced by the mystery into which we have been led.

> so rest in his chair tonight
> with arms that will hold you tight
> with cushions that soften the blow
> of loss and pain and soul.[10]

Of the detective mysteries on TV that Isobel and I used to watch 'Inspector Morse' was number one. Morse, or John Thaw in real life, died of cancer at the age of 60. The story of his struggle with

---

10   A song composed by Robert Steiner, Minister of the Rondebosch United Church, Cape Town, 2011.

the disease is told by his wife Sheila Hancock in her biography of her late husband. Entitled *The Two of Us*, it is a frank, candid and moving story. The last few chapters are an account of her trying to come to terms with her husband's absence. In the process of sharing in his final months of suffering, she tells us that she lost whatever faith she had in the God of the Bible, but at the same time discovered a new spiritual strength among the Quakers.

But as I read her story I wondered whether she had received any help from the church in understanding that God differently. After all, the God of the Quakers has its source in the Bible if the testimony of George Fox and John Woolman, its two pre-eminent saints, is anything to go by.

Much of what I have attempted to say in this book has been about understanding God in a way that is, I believe, profoundly biblical but not the stereotypical 'LordGod' that many people assume is the 'God of the Bible' without more reflection. There are conflicting images of God in the Bible, but the God disclosed in Jesus is the God who suffers with us, and it is only this God who can really help us whether in life or death. This is the God Hans Küng had in mind when he asked whether it ought not to be possible, 'out of a belief in God . . . to die a wholly different human death, a death with truly human dignity, in fact a *death with Christian dignity*?'[11] None of this exempts Christians from the pain and sorrow that surrounds death. But there is a Christian way of approaching death that most modern-day Christians have not been taught or helped to understand as many were in generations past.[12]

Around the same time as reading Sheila Hancock's book, I read another in which the 'God of the Bible' was very differently understood. Entitled *Wording a Radiance*, it contains Dan Hardy's 'parting conversations on God and the Church', which he shared with those close to him as he negotiated the final months

---

11   Küng, *Eternal Life*, p. 172.

12   Allen Verhey, *The Christian Art of Dying: Learning from Jesus*, Grand Rapids, MI: Eerdmans, 2011.

of his struggle with cancer in 2007. Dan's razor-sharp intellect, Christian commitment, and generous humanity were never more apparent than in this final testimony of his faith in and love for God. In one of his conversations, he offered these moving words:

> I've been content ever since the onset of this cancer to be drawn into death, but I don't take this negatively at all: it is also being drawn into life and the two are closely tied in together . . . I don't know how? being drawn into death is also being drawn into life . . . Perhaps I am being a sort of sign of attraction, going ahead of you into the mystery, an attraction not into anything clear and unambiguous but into the light that is the mystery of death and life, and therein God.[13]

I recall how our close friend, Ron Butler, during the final months of his life cut short by cancer, pasted Paul's words on his computer: 'for me to live is Christ, and to die is gain'.[14] It is this testimony that finds expression in the final stanza of Bonhoeffer's prison poem "Stations on the Road to Freedom."

> Come now, highest of feasts on the way to freedom eternal,
> Death, lay down your ponderous chains and earthen enclosures
> walls that deceive our souls and fetter our mortal bodies,
> that we might at last behold what here we are hindered
> from seeing.
> Freedom, long have we sought you through discipline,
> action and suffering.
> Dying, now we discern in the countenance of God your own
> face.[15]

13 Daniel W. Hardy, *Wording a Radiance: Parting Conversations on God and the Church*, London: SCM, 2010, p. ix.
14 Philippians 1.21 (AV).
15 The final stanza of "Stations on the Road to Freedom." *Letters and Papers*, 514.

Between two worlds

The week of the second anniversary of Steve's death was particularly difficult for us. We were aware now that the distance between Steve being physically with us and our time was becoming more extensive. Our lives had been rudely divided into the years before February 2010 and the years that have followed. He has not grown older as we have grown older. In our memory, he is fixed in the time of his death in his 48th year. As the family gathered in our various home places to remember him and celebrate his life, we thought of those things that had happened to us over the past two years that we would have liked to tell him about if he had to come back on a visit. Books we had read, experiences we had shared, in fact everything we would have normally talked about with him.

One of the surprising things that happened to me over the previous few months was that I had some vivid dreams in which Steve invariably played a central role. I had seldom dreamt much before, so I was somewhat taken aback. The most remarkable dream occurred at the end of the week in which we celebrated the second anniversary of Steve's death. It was, as I have said, an emotionally draining and difficult week, though with the support of our community, many friends, and the wider family we were able to negotiate its passage. I hesitate to make the dream public because is very personal. I also know how the chemistry of the brain functions. So I know that my dream can be explained in terms of the emotional state that week, that it was perfectly natural, but not scientific evidence for an after-life.

I dreamt that our old house in Rosebank, Cape Town, where we lived for 30 years, and where Steve spent his teenage years, was in the final stages of being thoroughly renovated, almost rebuilt. While this process was taking place, we had gone to live elsewhere and had not seen the progress until the night of my dream. As I walked towards the house, Steve joined me. We had not seen each other for some time. We embraced. He told me he was eager to see what we had done to the old house he knew so well. Rebuilding old houses in which he lived was one of his passions. As we entered the grounds, we were astounded by what we saw. The garden had been totally remade and in the back yard was an amazing orchard. 'That is wonderful', exclaimed Steve, 'I did not know you were going to plant all those olive trees.' 'Neither did I', was my response. As we walked through the house, the renovations still in process, we discovered that the walls were all painted in beautiful colours, each blending with the others. There were many new features in the rooms, windows in unexpected places letting in more light . . . I awoke. Steve had left me. I had a sense of peace.

Sigmund Freud's view that dreams are the unconscious expression of repressed wishes is undoubtedly true to some extent. But need we understand all dreams so negatively, as retrospectively focused on past events rather than prospectively, as offering hope and purpose?[16] Reflecting on a dream he had relating to his father and the death of his mother, Carl Jung acknowledged that the allusions in dreams cannot be credited as providing proof for life after death. At best they provide 'meager hints'.[17] But they can, he added, 'serve as suitable bases for mythic amplifications; they give the probing intellect the raw material which is indispensible for its vitality'.[18] Like the myths, they need not be mere confabulations that our brains concoct; they can in fact lead us deeper into the mystery which is beneath the real. This is the poetic imagination at work, which at the same time as we celebrated the second anniversary of Steve's death, found expression in another of Isobel's poems, and correlated well with my dream:

Sometimes the curtain between two worlds is so thin
that I can see you clearly, hear you,
feel you are about to step out,
coffee cup in hand, keffiyeh around your neck,

---

16   Hans Küng, *Freud and the Problem of God*, New Haven: Yale University Press, 1979.

17   Carl G. Jung, *Memories, Dreams and Reflections*, New York, NY: Vintage, 1965, p. 316.

18   Jung, *Memories, Dreams and Reflections*, p. 316.

cocky greeting on your lips:
the last two years of no account:
sometimes, sometimes – but fleetingly.

Mostly the curtain between two worlds is dense
as black velvet, impenetrable as a firewall,
silent as a telephone that will not ring
with an expected call.
Mostly we, on our side, are moving on,
aging, changing, going forward:
stopping often to gaze at the curtain:
Realizing in reluctant sadness that
we are leaving you behind,
you, who are unaging, unchanging,
caught forever in a snapshot moment.

We need your presence, your insight,
your cheer, but it is muffled now, and fading.
We must walk on, we cannot stop.
We must leave you behind,
till one day, one day it will be us
who push the curtain aside
to step into that other world.[19]

The more I reflect on my being led into the mystery of life and death following Steve's death, the more I am convinced that there are dimensions to our existence and that of the universe that sense experience fails to discern and our minds cannot understand. I do not know what may lie beyond the curtain when we 'step into that other world' nor do I fully grasp the complexity of Christian hope in the resurrection which seeks to express that hope.

---

19   Inspired by words of a poem by D. Gwenallt Jones, 'The curtain between two worlds will be so thin', from *In Sensuous Glory: The Poetic Vision of D. Gwenallt Jones*, edited by Donald Allchin, D. Densil Morgan and Patrick Thomas, Norwich: Canterbury Press, 2000.

On some matters I prefer to remain reverently silent. Yet those working on the boundaries of cosmology often point to mysteries that stretch well beyond our knowledge and to dimensions of existence that transcend our capacity to grasp. This, it seems to me, gives added substance to the things for which we hope in Christian faith – the hospitality of an infinite love and beauty in which all things cohere and are made new.

The paschal candle still burns

On Thursday mornings I still hasten to the Volmoed chapel to prepare for the community Eucharist that begins at 10 am. Apart from community members, the dozen or so visitors who regularly attend will begin to arrive five or ten minutes before the service starts. I have time to prepare the communion table, set out the bread and wine and light the candles, including that on the tall Paschal Candle stand, which I finished making the day Steve died. It always brings him vividly to mind. I sit in silence for a while, anticipating the ringing of the community bell and the voices of those who are coming to the service as they mount the steps from the crypt. As I do so, my eyes invariably take in the Icon of the Holy Trinity placed on its stand before the altar. It is a reassuring sign that we are being invited to share in the hospitality of God which renews our hope. Step by step, the liturgy leads us into the mystery of God's self-giving love, as we read the gospel, share the peace, and confess together the 'mysteries of faith'. We remember the night on which Jesus was betrayed – how he met with his disciples to share a meal as he so frequently did, and told them that as often as they gathered in the same way to break bread together and to drink the fruit of the vine, he would not only be remembered by them but would be present in their midst. He also told them that when they did this, they would anticipate the arrival of God's reign when all things would be restored and made new. In doing this, we are also aware that we do not celebrate this mystery alone, but in company with all those who have died and are now also present with us 'in Christ'. And then we are sent into the world as 'stewards of God's mysteries' (1 Cor. 4.1) to share God's self-giving love and therefore God's justice and peace for the world.

Soon after Steve died, my sister Rozelle generously sent a gift to Volmoed suggesting that we erect a memorial in his memory. Eventually we decided to build an African-style gazebo on a wooden platform overlooking the Onrus River that runs through Volmoed. To reach 'Steve's Place', as it is called, you walk along a narrow path below a rocky cliff as if being led into a place of mystery. There are seats built into the wooden structure where you can sit, either alone in prayerful silence or in conversation with others. On significant occasions, we go there with friends to share a simple meal of home-baked bread and wine from the region in which we live. As we do, there is, even if only fleetingly, a sense of the mystery which enfolds us all in life and death. Most days, lived as it were in 'ordinary time', that sense is less acute, but no less real, and sometimes

Days pass when I forget the mystery
Problems insoluble and problems offering
their own ignored solutions
jostle for my attention, they crowd its antechamber
along with a host of diversions, my courtiers, wearing
their colored clothes; cap and bells.
And then
once more the quiet mystery
is present to me, the throng's clamor
recedes: the mystery
that there is anything, anything at all,
let alone cosmos, joy, memory, everything,
rather than void: and that, O Lord,
Creator, Hallowed One, You still
hour by hour sustain it.[20]

---

20 Denise Levertov, *The Stream and the Sapphire*, New York: A New Directions Book, 1997, p. 33.

Index of Biblical Texts

Index of Names

Palmer, Richard 73, 74
Pangritz, Andreas 17
Pannenberg, Wolfhart 78, 80, 153, 157, 200, 205
Peters, Ted 162, 177
Plato 157
Polkinghorne, John 162, 197, 210
Pollak, Kay 190
Pope, Alexander 176
Pavlov, I.P. 144

Rahner, Karl 4, 20, 56, 119, 120
Ratzinger, Joseph (Benedict XVI) 159
Rees, Martin 95, 106, 107
Reimarus, Hermann 69, 70, 73, 74, 81
Reinhart, Adele 82
Ricoeur, Paul 1, 44
Robinson, Marilynne 60, 139
Robinson, John A.T. 158, 209, 211
Rothenberg, David 101
Rublev, Andrei 133
Rumscheidt, Martin 113
Russell, John 107, 109, 126, 162, 177, 197
Ryle, Gilbert 149, 150

Sanders, E.P. 203
Sargant, William 144
Sacks, Oliver 29
Savonarola 51
Schillebeeckx, Edward 200
Schleiermacher, Friedrich 73, 98, 121, 185
Schweiker, William 54, 116, 117, 160, 164
Schweitzer, Albert 82
Scruton, Roger 161, 162, 163
Shay, Suellen 2
Shelley, Percy Bysshe 40
Shillington, V. George 205

Smith, Huston 114
Socrates 178
Solms, Mark 13, 14, 166
Steiner, George 30, 56, 62
Steiner, Robert 218
Strauss, D. Friedrich 51, 52, 56, 67, 69, 70, 73, 76, 78, 80, 82
Strauss, Lévi 30
Suggit, John 89

Thagale, Buti 183
Thagard, Paul 145, 146, 148, 151
Thaw, John 219
Thistlethwaite, Susan 155
Thiselton, Anthony C. 176, 208
Thorwaldsen, Bertel 53
Tillich, Paul 23, 98, 117, 118, 119
Tolkien, J.R.R. 77, 78
Tolland, John 69
Tolstoy, Leo 24
Turner, William 46
Tutu, Desmond 124, 125, 126

Underhill, Evelyn 16
Updike, John 40, 41, 58, 60, 76

van Huyssteen, J. Wentzel 13, 109, 110, 114, 137, 147, 153, 157, 161
Verhey, Allen 220
Vermes, Geza 83
Volf, Miroslav 105
von Balthasar, Hans Urs 128
von Wedemeyer, Maria 19
von Weizsäcker, C.F. 106

Ward, Bruce, K. 116
Ward, Graham 28, 114
Ward, Keith 125, 126, 135, 149, 150, 151, 163
Watson, James 109
Wegter-McNelly, Kirk 107

Wiebe, Erik P. 13, 137, 147, 161
Wiesel, Elie 101, 102
Wilde, Oscar 125, 138, 139
Wilson, A.N. 51, 77, 97
Williams, Rowan 4, 25, 129
Wink, Walter 79, 83, 203
Wing, Joseph 79, 83, 203, 216
Wittgenstein, Ludwig 74, 75
Wright, N.T. 83, 181, 189, 197, 200, 201, 202, 208

Wolterstorff, Nicholas 10
Wordsworth, William 16, 48, 49, 179
Wüstenberg, Ralf K. 121, 122

Yoder, John Howard 83

Zipes, Jack 43

Index of Subjects & Places

materialism
Christian 150
non-reductive 150
reductive 150
meaning (see death, life)
Memorial service 3
memories 8, 31
memory 9, 26, 141
writing 15
Methodism 50
Middle Ages 44, 46, 115, 157
Middle East 207
Middlemarch (Eliot) 50
Millennium trilogy (Larsson) 38, 39
mind
(see body, brain, consciousness, soul)
modernity 46, 111–114
failure of 117
Moffat Mission Church, Kuruman 171, 216
Mooi River 1, 2, 4, 22, 124
moral reasoning 163
moral responsibility 116, 117, 145, 164, 165, 166
More than Matter (Ward) 160
mourning 1, 6, 9
murder mysteries 34, 35
music 25, 28, 29
Muslims 59, 103, 105
scholars 12, 44, 217
musterion (NT Gk)
and hope 89
and love 90
and "secret" 86, 87
cosmic 89, 90
disclosed in Christ 89, 90
in Septuagint 86
meaning of word 86
of God's reign/kingdom 87, 88, 91, 94
of the Incarnation 90
Paul's teaching 88, 89, 90

mysteries of faith 45, 207, 224
mystery 4, 19, 20, 22, 39, 117, 129, 213
and novelists 49
and reality 25, 44
and science 46, 107, 110
and secrets 37
echoes of 21
experiencing 85, 86
in the ordinary 60
journey into 15, 39
language of 6,
locked-room 35–37
meaning of 20
"of iniquity" 39, 88
of life and death 3, 7, 14, 15, 19, 38, 141
of the other 117
stories 36–38, 141
(see God, *musterion*)
mystery cults 86
mysticism 16, 21, 46
myth/mythos 51, 56, 67, 75, 80, 81
and mystery 76
and truth 76
eschatological 80
of God incarnate 78, 80
of inevitable progress 113
myths 14, 25
about an after-life 179
Christian 76, 77, 78
creation 63, 151–154
Fall 151, 153–155, 212
Greek 187
Homeric 41
pagan 77, 78, 193, 199
redemption myths 193, 194

nature 46, 81, 108, 114, 116
as divine 46
disenchantment with 46
laws of 124, 125, 126
(see biology, evolution, human)